What Everyone Knows About Britain

What Everyone Knows About Britain*

*Except the British

Michael Peel

monoray

First published in Great Britain in 2024 by Monoray,
an imprint of Octopus Publishing Group Ltd
Carmelite House
50 Victoria Embankment
London EC4Y 0DZ
www.octopusbooks.co.uk

An Hachette UK Company
www.hachette.co.uk

Hardback ISBN: 978-1-80096-176-0
Paperback ISBN: 978-1-80096-207-1

A CIP catalogue record for this book is available from the British Library.

Printed and bound in the UK.

1 3 5 7 9 10 8 6 4 2

This monoray book was crafted and published by Jake Lingwood, Leanne Bryan,
Caroline Taggart, Mel Four, David Eldridge, Jouve and Peter Hunt.

This FSC˙label means that materials used for the product have been responsibly sourced.

To my family and the many other people
who have helped me along the way.

Contents

Introduction

Return

The golden lion and unicorn emblem is almost faded from the UK passport I slot into the e-gate at Heathrow Airport to come home. The words 'European Union' have all but disappeared from the maroon cover, too. Frequent handling at immigration counters around the world has achieved the erasure sought by those who campaigned to leave the European bloc. The only problem is that Britain's own national symbol has vanished in the process.

The battered booklet has, like the UK, been through a lot since it was issued a month before the 2016 Brexit referendum. Now, in September 2023, I am returning after the best part of 13 years away from Britain, via journalistic postings in Abu Dhabi, Bangkok, Brussels and Tokyo. As the border barriers open for me, I feel a thrill familiar from arriving in places for the first time. I am about to rediscover my own country.

The Piccadilly Line Tube is older and grimier than the spruce Tokyo metro that has been taking me to and from work lately. The train might retort that it fits its user: I am even less to look at than usual after an overnight flight from Asia. I cling to my two large suitcases to prevent them careering into the rush-hour passengers who grow in number at every suburban stop.

At least I don't have too far to go. My destination is the UK National Archives, a short hop across West London and an appropriate first stop.

It is a repository of official accounts of Britain's past actions around the world, including in quite a few former colonies where I've spent time.

I soon make my first bad logistical choice. I switch from the underground to a bus that then crawls for the next 15 minutes through the morning congestion. My homecoming parade is apparently to be a traffic jam just off the A4 near Brentford. I relish the bathos, if not the delay.

An automated announcement tells us the bus will be stopping before its advertised terminus – but it doesn't say when or where. I ask the driver, who says he is awaiting instructions and doesn't know either. The woman behind me is complaining on her phone that she set out early for her appointment but is still going to be late. My pangs for Japan's silken public transport network grow stronger still.

I decide to bail out and continue on foot. I am already behind schedule, given the towers of archive files I can picture with growing anxiety. I barrel down the street with my cases, sweating in the building temperatures of the latest day in the September heatwave. I feel the pitying gaze of a convoy of schoolboys as they pass me on their way to a games lesson. I am dishevelled, encumbered and slightly absurd. In short, I feel ready to be part of life in the UK again.

My return home on a packed Thai Airways flight after a spell working overseas was hardly Odysseus returning to Ithaca. But I did feel I was coming back to a different nation from the one I had last inhabited in January 2011. From overseas, Britain seemed a troubled and anxious place, in a way that cut across society – though of course not everyone was affected equally.

The impression that all was not well had communicated itself to people in the places I'd spent time in. Some asked me about Britain's welfare with concern, some with bafflement – and some with a sense of poetic justice, given my nation's history in the world. Truisms about the country's enduring stability and strength were being reassessed. It was as if Lord Nelson's statue, a famous monument to historic UK power, were wobbling atop his column in London's Trafalgar Square.

For many foreign commentators, Liz Truss's chaotic seven-week premiership in 2022 distilled the sense that Britain was in a bad way. Puzzlement, pity and schadenfreude could all be detected in observations like *Bild* of Germany's that 'The Brexit British currently have a nasty money problem.'[1] The Colombian outlet *El Colombiano*[2] perhaps captured best the evaporation of illusions about how Britain is today. The UK was experiencing an 'interesting hard landing exercise in reality', it said.

Realisation was scaling the walls of the most complacent citadels of the UK establishment, too. Even conservative British media outlets began to cite unflattering cross-cultural comparisons that would once have been anathema. A March 2023 column[3] in the *Daily Telegraph* wailed, 'Britain is in a godawful mess – if we were French, we'd have a revolution.' If the paper saw the chutzpah in running such a piece after 13 years of staunch support for the governing Conservatives, it did not let on.

What Everyone Knows About Britain is about this change in perspective on the country and the reasons for it. I wanted to explore how some in the UK are only now catching up with problems outsiders have understood about it for a while. The nation seems to be struggling not just with its place in the world, but with how it runs itself.

The roots of this book about the UK lie in long absences from it. After I moved to be the *Financial Times* correspondent in Nigeria in 2002, I spent much of the next two decades outside my home country. I have had the privilege of reporting from countries across Africa, the Middle East, Asia and Europe. I have seen sights on my travels, if not quite the burning attack ships off the shoulder of Orion cited in *Blade Runner*'s climactic speech. I have covered revolutions, war, a military coup and the rupture of the UK's near half-century relationship with its continental neighbours. I have felt ashamed in places once occupied by Britain – and guilty about advantages my homeland enjoys today that link back to the abuses it committed. These experiences have gradually – and fundamentally – changed the way I look at my own country.

I return with a welter of modest suggested improvements to domestic life in the UK. I think I will find it impossible to enter a house with my shoes on again. I lament almost daily the lack of the tradition of satisfying, good-value lunches that are the fulcrum of working days from France to Thailand. Belgium's quality of healthcare and Japan's systems for preventive disease screening give even more serious pause (as does the palpably superior spray-based toilet hygiene of the Middle East and much of Asia).

The diversity of countries in which I have lived has been educational in deeper ways. I have reported from the woodsmoke rural poverty of Myanmar and the glass-and-steel riches of the Gulf states. I have covered dictatorships and democracies – and many political systems in between.

Cultural differences count, but there are patterns in how governments exercise power and how groups within societies assert themselves. Many of these observations are highly relevant to the UK as the internal struggle for its future unfolds. In dozens of countries across the world, I have seen political powerplays that stoke poverty, conflict and dangerous national delusions. I see examples of some of them in Britain, too.

Which, perhaps, brings us to the 'B-word'. Brexit is probably the single biggest change to Britain's place in the world since I last lived there – and it has been transformative. But while its effects are unavoidable and relevant, this book isn't about Brexit, or at least not about whether it should be urgently reversed. *What Everyone Knows About Britain* is not the place to look for I-told-you-so lectures on how the UK should rejoin the EU. Britain's evolving relationship with the bloc is hugely important, but it is just one priority among many that the country faces.

What I have found most distressing about Brexit is the way it has caused British people to turn against each other. I see far more common ground in the country than the shrillest voices on either side might suggest. It feels as if many people still recognise we have a responsibility to each other, through both legal structures and the unwritten bonds of society.

I have been away from the UK for a long time, but over the years I have found myself following events there increasingly closely. It is home and it is what first shaped me. If this book sounds angry or harsh at times, it is because I care. I have developed a strong sense that Britain must do better, in its dealings with both its own people and the rest of the world.

Patriotism is a much-abused term but, by any reasonable definition, there seems to me to be plenty of it still in the UK. It is clear many people want the country to improve. Not all of them like to wave flags, but that doesn't mean they feel any less strongly about the society they live in. Many of these shy patriots quietly do good in their workplaces or communities. I salute their example and would like to follow it.

It is worth stepping back to register the rapidity of the change in the story the UK tells about itself. When I left in January 2011, the Conservative-led coalition government had just abolished a project to improve arts teaching as part of wider spending cuts. Chinese Vice-Premier Li Keqiang was starting a four-day visit to the UK, as part of a relationship that later led Chancellor George Osborne to hail the beginning of a 'golden decade'.[4] Demonstrators rallied outside the Iranian embassy in London over attacks[5] on exiles in Iraq, where British troops were pulling out eight years[6] after the invasion.

All those stories look radically different 12 years later, reflecting wider shifts in the UK and its international position. A narrative that the country's public realm is 'broken' has taken hold, as the impact of years of spending cuts has become apparent. The gilded era of Sino-British relations never really materialised and was finally declared dead[7] in late 2022 by Prime

Minister Rishi Sunak. The sense of the Iraq War as a singularly catastrophic act has hardened after an official inquiry heavily criticised then premier Tony Blair.

It was a dramatic shift from the sense of certainty projected by Blair himself as he left Downing Street less than a generation ago. The May 2007 speech he gave on stepping down[8] as prime minister now seems from another world. He timed his departure well – at least for himself. The irresponsible behaviour in the finance industry seeded during decades of deregulation under him and his Conservative predecessors was about to trigger a crisis. Abroad, the bodies of Iraqis and British soldiers would continue to pile up – but that would now be someone else's problem.

Blair presented his decade-long premiership in self-justificatory terms, with a window-dressing of apparent humility. Near the end, he made a homage to the country. It is instructive to read it in full.

> Britain is not a follower. It is a leader. It gets the essential characteristic of today's world: its interdependence.
> This is a country today that for all its faults, for all the myriad of unresolved problems and fresh challenges, is comfortable in the 21st century.
> At home in its own skin, able not just to be proud of its past but confident of its future.
> This country is a blessed nation.
> The British are special.
> The world knows it.
> In our innermost thoughts, we know it.
> This is the greatest nation on earth.

It is quite an achievement that every single point he made is at least highly contestable – and has been proved so by subsequent events. Even allowing for the bombastic register of political elegy, the tone feels alien. Today few Britons, whatever their views, are talking up the country's greatness, specialness or ease with itself.

Within months of being back, I felt that if Britain were a person, it would need its friends to sit it down and deliver it a few home truths. It has had a rough time lately. At an institutional level, it has damaged others, and increasingly itself, with its behaviour. It urgently needs to allow its more positive qualities to flourish.

It is not surprising that much of this is clearer to outsiders than to some of us in the country. Overseas observers are unencumbered by the folkloric stereotypes of Britishness that those of us who grew up here absorb, consciously and unconsciously. Many foreign citizens have experiences of the UK's past actions that contrast starkly with its proclaimed central values of decency and fair play.

That's why this book ultimately concerns something much bigger than Britain. It is about how countries, or at least influential constituencies in them, deceive themselves and become at once grandiose and narrow-minded. It is about the contrasts between our self-images and how we appear to others' eyes. It's about the importance of perspective and focusing on what really matters, rather than wasting attention on distractions. It is about life's many hypocrisies – and its numerous saving graces.

The walk to the National Archives takes me across the River Thames, Kew Green and a splinter of history spanning hundreds of years. The British royal family made Kew their country seat in the 18th century. It was the principal retreat of George III, the erratic king whose forces were defeated in the American War of Independence. During the Second World War, the green was used for vegetable allotments as part of the 'Dig for Victory' campaign to keep Britain fed.

The archives themselves epitomise the UK's attempt to reconcile the country it has been with the nation it wants to be. The facility is housed in an intimidating brutalist building behind an artificial lake populated by swans and herons. It has changed much since it opened in 1977 and was visited by Queen Elizabeth II the following year. It aims to project a more progressive agenda than many of the documents in the imperial-era records it contains.

A panel outside the cloakroom highlights the 75th anniversary in 2023 of the arrival from the Caribbean of the ship *Empire Windrush*. The archives hold many records related to the historic voyage, including the passenger list. The words are inspiring – but they are a reminder, too, that authorities later wrongly persecuted and in some cases deported members of this immigrant generation and their descendants. 'These British citizens faced discrimination despite the long history of Black presence in Britain and its empire,' the text reads. 'Those who settled here had a huge impact on British society, fighting for change to prevent future generations facing the same barriers they encountered.'

I grew up among various provincial southern English environments that reveal something of the good, the bad and the ugly of the country's past. I was born in Royal Tunbridge Wells's Pembury Hospital,[9] which was built on the site of a Victorian workhouse. It is a reminder of a long tradition of punitive official attitudes towards the poor.

Tunbridge Wells itself has become a place emblematic of a bedrock conservatism sometimes said to define the English nation. It is picturesquely located[10] on the sandstone High Weald of wooded hills, fields and farms – classic English landscape, as evoked by J R R Tolkien's Shire, Rupert Brooke's 'The Old Vicarage, Grantchester' or Miss Marple's home of St Mary Mead. The town owes much to the monarchy that has ruled Britain or constituent parts of it for more than a thousand years. It has a Church of King Charles the Martyr, named for Charles I, whose 1649 execution began England's only modern period without a monarch. Its regal prefix was a reward from Edward VII in 1909,[11] because the British royals had long enjoyed its spa waters. The popular Georgian promenade of The Pantiles is still a social centre and a spectacle for visitors.

In modern times, Tunbridge Wells has become a base for commuters with high-earning jobs in London. It is – fairly or not – a byword for cosseted insularity. It has been used as an evocation of pleasant but unadventurous existence[12] in films from *On Her Majesty's Secret Service* to *Lawrence of Arabia*. Perhaps unsurprisingly, the parliamentary constituency has returned Conservative MPs with healthy majorities[13] since its creation in 1974, even during the national Labour landslide of 1997. It was here that Rishi Sunak boasted to Tory members in 2022 how he had diverted money from 'deprived urban areas' to places like Tunbridge Wells.

The town is probably best known for the phrase 'Disgusted of Tunbridge Wells', which has become a popular trope for comments expressing outrage at some progressive social development. Its origins, like other aspects of Britain's history, are vigorously disputed. One claim is that it was the sign-off on a genuine letter to *The Times* from a retired British army colonel. Another is that it was invented by a local newspaper to fill space.

Whatever the phrase's origins, wide usage has turned it into a convenient truism. *Private Eye* magazine used it as a sign-off for satirical letters infused with primness and prejudice. BBC Radio 4 even originally called its flagship listener-response programme *Disgusted, Tunbridge Wells* – although this was wisely renamed *Feedback* not long after. There is even a *disgustedoftunbridgewells.co.uk* website, a self-declared 'political correctness free zone' with content to match.

There is, of course, more to Tunbridge Wells than the stereotype of rich reactionary bastion allows. In 1913, suffragettes campaigning for women to be given the vote burned down[14] the cricket pavilion at the local

Nevill Ground. The mayor even declared the town a 'hotbed of militants'. Political hyperbole aside, the incident showed how in England the radical instinct has often burned stronger than the country's habit of electing Tory governments suggests.

I spent much of the rest of my childhood in the south-west of England, starting in the coastal town of Torquay. That late 1970s and early 1980s period told another story of modern Britain. Torquay became a thriving resort in the Victorian-era early days of tourism, but the advent of mass foreign holiday travel sent it into decline. It was the setting for the TV series *Fawlty Towers* and the former home of the thriller writer Agatha Christie, the best-selling novelist in history. Christie's childhood mansion was demolished[15] in 1962 to make way for a squat modern apartment block, as post-war housing demands clashed with lucrative English heritage. I wonder if local councillors weep today when they think of the tourist revenues forgone from decades of lost literary pilgrimage.

In Exeter, the small cathedral city where I spent my secondary-school years, the economic trajectory was the opposite of its coastal neighbour's. The place has prospered during my lifetime, attracting incomers thanks to its amenities and access to the countryside and sea. The Met Office's relocation there from Bracknell in 2003 gave it a further boost. Growing social liberalism turned a formerly solid Conservative constituency into what was, in 2015, the only English non-Tory seat west of Bristol.

After university I lived in London for a few years, most memorably near Smithfield on the edge of the City. I loved the sense of deep time I felt from walking through it. Next to the 12th-century St Bartholomew the Great church, one of the oldest surviving in London, is a former site of public execution. The 1305 hanging, drawing and quartering of Sir William Wallace, the Scottish independence leader, is memorialised there.

The area is dominated by the vast gaudily coloured meat-market complex. Smithfield has been used for the buying and selling of livestock for more than 800 years. In 1174, Thomas Becket's clerk described a 'celebrated rendezvous'[16] of 'fine horses . . . swine with their deep flanks, and cows and oxen of immense bulk'.

The site has survived the centuries and was rebuilt after a devastating fire in 1958, but its days finally seem numbered.[17] The operation is scheduled to move to a less central location with better traffic access. Even here, English tradition's long reach can be felt: an objection to the plan cited a royal charter on market relocation dating back to 1247. Henry III's rule was being used[18] as sway in the reign of Charles III, almost eight centuries later.

The UK's well-recorded and often embellished history feels like both blessing and curse to the country today. It is an anchor in both senses of the word, offering both security and drag. It feels as if it has contributed to an existential smugness that has run through British politics during most of my adult life.

This worldview held that everything would turn out okay, because it always had in the past. Britain was used to having a certain status. The country had fought and its people suffered in terrible conflicts, but it had not been invaded in the memory of anyone alive today. It had been an imperial power, then a victor in two world wars, then a beneficiary of 20th-century industrial prosperity.

In short, Britain was presented as intrinsically secure and different in nature from other countries that collapse into poverty, lawlessness or war. Until recently, many people with power and wealth in the UK seemed to find it hard to imagine such bleak outcomes. It feels like some still struggle to do so.

This has always seemed to me a dangerous and irresponsible view of affairs. My reporting has taught me how national crises can look distant, until suddenly they explode. During the Arab world uprisings of the early 2010s, countries such as Egypt and Syria seemed calm one day – and then revolutionary the next.

It is not as if eruptions have never happened on British streets in modern times. I was in Libya when riots broke out in 2011 after Mark Duggan, a Black Londoner, was shot dead by police. (An inquest ruled the killing lawful. The Metropolitan Police later settled a civil claim brought by Duggan's family, without admitting liability.) The UK unrest was seized on by Colonel Muammar Gaddafi's Libyan dictatorship, which was being pummelled by domestic rebellion and a Nato bombing campaign. Libya's state TV portrayed the events in Britain as a popular uprising against the government. Like all well-crafted propaganda, it had a kernel of truth.

At my hotel near Kew the evening of my arrival, a screen behind the reception desk flashes up the latest news headlines. One is about an escaped terror suspect who will later be arrested in Chiswick, just a bend in the river down the Thames from where I am. Another concerns a false alarm about a mass murder in Lincolnshire, which turned out to be people lying on the floor during their yoga class.

There seems no better place to start my exploration of my new home, in all its seriousness and strangeness. I talk to the receptionist about the heatwave and then comment that I've been hearing a lot of chatter about how nothing in Britain works. Her response ends the conversation with pitch-perfect diplomacy and a dash of quintessential Englishness.

'I think it's probably the weather,' she says, handing me the key card for my first night back in this at once familiar and exotic land.

1

Britain's Trick Mirror

Winston Churchill did not think he'd do well in modern politics, however great the public admiration for him. At least, that's what he told the conservative GB News channel in January 2022.

'I don't think I could probably survive in the current climate,' he lamented, clad in his trademark black felt suit and spotted bow tie, a homburg hat on the table beside him. 'Although, one would give it a go, of course.'

The real Churchill was, of course, long dead. It was the 57th anniversary of his funeral, which provided the thin conceit for the surreal segment. The impersonator, Stan Streather, didn't quite have the late original's gruff jowliness, but he was game in his pretence. The encounter even ran with the apparently authentic caption 'Winston Churchill, former prime minister', before Streather eventually broke character.

The ersatz interview made me think of the gap between image and reality in British political debate. There is evidence of a gulf between how some perceive the country to be versus what it actually is – and how it is seen abroad. The larger-than-life UK of the Churchill tribute act lives alongside a more nuanced reality.

Polling suggests that, over the years, an appreciable number of Britons have formed a warped picture of their own nation. These mistaken impressions tend to reflect anxieties about social change, often stoked by partisan media coverage. The result is a country that looks in the mirror and, in some respects, sees a caricature of itself.

Some politicians have used this phenomenon as a kind of British trick mirror. It has helped them turn once contentious ideas about the nature of the nation into received wisdom. Assertions including that the UK is 'swamped by migrants', is a 'soft touch' on benefits and needs to 'take back control' have metamorphosed into commonplaces. Those beliefs have then been deployed to build support for far-reaching policies such as Brexit, immigration crackdowns and spending cuts.

The trick mirror effect can make social divisions appear bigger than they are. The non-profit group More in Common has examined how political rifts in the UK are less grievous than some rhetoric might make them seem. The organisation's inspiration is the late Labour MP Jo Cox, who was murdered by a far-right terrorist during the final days of the 2016 Brexit referendum campaign. In her maiden parliamentary speech[1] in 2015, Cox said, 'We are far more united and have far more in common than that which divides us.'

A 2020 More in Common report looking at the UK in the decade to come offered both hope and foreboding. It found that large differences in people's proclaimed beliefs on economics and social conservatism didn't necessarily map on to disagreements over political priorities. Hefty majorities agreed that climate change was important, equality a problem, and racism serious, for example. But the research contained a warning[2] that feels as if it has grown still more pertinent in the time since publication. It said Britain faced a profound choice over its direction, in an era where US-style 'culture wars' increasingly dominate online discourse and political conflicts.

'One path leads to the deepening polarisation that is being experienced in other countries, where "us-versus-them" dynamics shape national debates, causing distrust and even hate between people on either side of the divide,' it read. 'The other path leads to a more cohesive society where we build on common ground and focus on the issues that we agree are more important than anything else.'

The UK has always felt like a notably malleable country. There is a vagueness to how it operates, with its strong emphasis on custom and precedent for both legal and behavioural norms. It has no US-style written constitution, nor an equivalent to the overarching Napoleonic code of law. It is a system that can work smoothly – until one day, under political or other circumstantial pressure, it doesn't.

The UK's very composition is a common source of bewilderment, especially overseas. Its status as four nations has generated a galaxy of online explainers with titles such as 'Is the UK a country?'[3] As one language blogger[4] warns students, 'The first thing to know is Britain and England are definitely not the same.'

The Ordnance Survey even has a webpage[5] devoted to the potential misunderstandings. It has maps to explain the differences between the terms UK, Great Britain and the British Isles. 'So let's clear this up once and for all . . .' it begins, wearily.[†]

Then there are deeper UK politico-geographical mysteries. These include the status of the Crown dependencies of the Channel Islands and the Isle of Man (not part of the UK, but under its protection). Another oddity is the imperial legacy of the UK overseas territories scattered across the world, from Gibraltar to the Falkland Islands (often domestically self-governing, but with London retaining overall responsibility).

These contorted identities can be contradictory and openly grate against each other. I once witnessed the extraordinary spectacle of Peter Johnstone

---

[†] Regrettably, even this book is guilty of the interchangeable use of 'UK' and 'Britain' that the Ordnance Survey scolds is seen 'all too often'. My self-justification is that Britain is the best-known term colloquially and is the seat of UK-wide institutions of power.

arriving as the new governor of Anguilla, a UK overseas territory in the Caribbean. Hubert Hughes, Anguilla's chief minister, greeted Johnstone with a broadside against London. 'Colonial governors . . . promote Britain's interests,' Hughes railed, in a parliamentary welcome speech to ruffle the ostrich feathers on the new emissary's pith helmet. 'Which in most cases are against the interests of the people they are sent to govern.'

Small wonder that the question of what kind of country the UK is should be such a perennial puzzle. Babbel, the language-learning company, attempts to unravel it in a four-minute video slugged 'Is there a difference between Great Britain and the United Kingdom?'

'Are England and Britain the same thing? Are British people from the United Kingdom?' the video's teaser reads. 'Let's get rid of your British befuddlement.'[6]

By the same token, there are things some Britons believe about themselves that may not be as true as they think. Many familiar representations of the country are as revealing for what they aren't as for what they are.

The lion and the unicorn heraldic supporters are so iconic that George Orwell used them to entitle his famous essay on the UK at war, 'The Lion and the Unicorn: Socialism and the English Genius'. Yet the depiction includes an animal never found in the wild in modern Britain and another that never even existed. The symbolism is rich. The UK's royal coat of arms is propped up on one side by a fiction and on the other by a creature grabbed from someone else's country.

Or take Saint George, a fundamental part of English identity from football terraces to literary classics. Shakespeare invokes him in one of his most quoted lines, Henry V's clarion call at Agincourt to 'Cry "God for Harry, England and St George."' Yet George is a promiscuous patron: he is shared with more than a dozen other countries, cities and regions, from Lithuania to Ethiopia. His origins are obscure[7] but he may have been a

Roman soldier whose deeds were spread in England by returning Crusaders. One certainty is that he wasn't English.

The UK's national anthem is similarly portioned out. The melody Britons know as 'God Save the King' is the same as for Liechtenstein's 'Oben am jungen Rhein' ('High on the young Rhine') and the US's 'My Country, 'Tis of Thee'. The tune was formerly used in Switzerland and other German-speaking territories, too.

The UK's 'national drink' of tea is an imperial-era import from Asia. The brand known as Yorkshire Tea[8] comprises leaves from more than 20 places across Africa and India, which are then shipped to Harrogate for blending. The company's website seems to tacitly recognise the incongruity of its name. 'Blends are often named after the place they were born,' it reads, pointing artfully to 'English Breakfast' tea as a famous example.

Britain does have an indigenous tea industry today. A business named Tregothnan[9] produces the leaves from *Camellia* bushes planted in a Cornish microclimate where they can thrive. The company says it began to reap 'the most British tea in history' in 2005 – although the first harvest yielded just 28 grams (1oz). Tregothnan acknowledges that even today its production makes it a 'small player on the global tea market'. It may be quite a while yet before a true British brew takes over the world.

These examples may be trivial and tongue in cheek, but they speak to a wider cultural point. Some of what is proclaimed in Britain as distinctive about the country is not unique, nor even real. These misleading mental props may be harmless – or they may feed into real-world opinions and actions based on a skewed sense of reality.

Outsiders' views of the UK are sometimes revealingly at odds with what some Britons feel about themselves. In 2014, a British Council-commissioned poll[10] of 5,000 18–34-year-olds from Brazil, China, Germany, India and the US yielded both stereotypes and surprises. Asked to pick Britons' three most positive attributes from a list, politeness came top, followed by 'educated and skilled' and 'friendly'. Patriotism, creativity and work ethic brought up the rear.

The choice of negative features made still more sobering – or perhaps that should be inebriated – reading. 'Drink too much alcohol' and 'bad eating habits' loomed largest on the list of Britons' undesirable qualities. They were followed by 'ignorant of other cultures', 'too nationalistic' and 'intolerant towards people from other countries'.

The British Council's analysis of its results contained both regret and optimism. Negative perceptions about British drinking and eating were 'even stronger among those who have been to the UK than among those who have not', it noted, sounding wistful. It continued: 'More encouragingly, those who have been to the UK are less negative about some of the perceived negative traits – including perceptions of nationalism and intolerance. It appears that in these areas the negative British reputation abroad may be remedied to some extent by the direct experiences of people who visit the UK.'

Perhaps the greatest received wisdom in British public life is that the country holds decency, tolerance and fair play dear. These tropes are cited by figures across the political spectrum. In 2005, the former Tory leader Michael Howard quoted them as an antidote to terrorism.[11] Brendan Cox, Jo Cox's widower, did much the same. In 2000, Labour Prime Minister Tony Blair officially declared[12] 'fair play' a key quality of 'British identity'.†

Since then, the government has formally defined[13] what children should be taught as British values. They are 'democracy, the rule of law, individual liberty and mutual respect and tolerance of those with different faiths

---

†   His take still wasn't positive enough for Conservative leader William Hague. In a foreshadowing of Britain's Brexit psychodrama to come, he accused Blair of 'refusing to stand firm against the drift towards a European superstate'.

and beliefs'. Schools' effectiveness in imparting these is evaluated by the inspection agency Ofsted.

Yet the fundamental narrative of British fairness had long seemed odd to me. I grew up in the socially restive 1980s. It was a time of industrial conflict, most notably the miners' strike – and the start of an era of resurgent wealth disparities. The income share enjoyed by the top 10 per cent of earners fell from 34.6 per cent in 1938 to 21 per cent in 1979, according to the Equality Trust.[14] Thirty years later, it was back above 30 per cent again.

My time outside the UK had made an even bigger difference in how I looked at my country's supposed core doctrine of fairness. While I had read plenty about its many dark histories in the world, my experiences in Nigeria in my twenties made my abstract understanding concrete. Imperial oppression had been followed by an era of oil extraction that had mainly benefited local elites and Western companies and consumers, including in Britain.

In hindsight, my time in Nigeria represented a kind of sentimental rupture – and a searing lesson about Britain's views of itself. I still loved many things about the UK, but I found the praise of the benefits it had supposedly given the world to be cant. What everyone who had lived in a former colony knew about Britain was very different from the egalitarian values it proclaimed at home.

The dubious image of Britain's innate progressiveness seemed part of a broader global canvas of questionable social assumptions. Perhaps the most significant of these is the idea that life has, in general, been getting better for most people for decades. This worldview has been endorsed at gatherings such as the World Economic Forum in Davos. It promotes books by thinkers such as the late statistician Hans Rosling and the psychologist Steven Pinker. It has gained traction because in some important respects it is true. Globally, girls' access to education has improved significantly, for example. Life expectancy worldwide rose from 66.8 years to 73.4[15] between

2000 and 2019. In Britain, lifespans increased throughout the 20th and early 21st centuries (though they began to stall from 2011[16]).

Yet the analysis of consistent if bumpy improvement appears increasingly to gloss over deeper countervailing dynamics. There is a growing breach between the positive numbers and people's reported negative feelings about their lives, across continents and social classes. A UN report[17] published in February 2022 warned of the 'startling' contrast between 'improvements in well-being achievements and declines in people's perception of security'. 'People were, on average, living healthier, wealthier and better lives for longer than ever,' the report said. 'But under the surface a growing sense of insecurity had been taking root.'

This dissonance chimed with my own experiences. I have had many inspiring encounters with extraordinary people on my travels. But beyond these episodes, I often found the bigger picture dispiriting. My overwhelming sense was of prevailing cultures of the strong exploiting the weak, from Syrians living under dictatorship to Cambodians toiling in garment factories.

One possible explanation for the contrast between what statistics suggest and how people say they feel is that the measures we use are too narrow. People's incomes may be rising, but in other respects their quality of life may be worsening. Surveys such as the UN Human Development Index tend to ignore stresses such as political repression, lack of health insurance or crippling work hours. They correctly note that the world is better fed – but they don't account for the environmental costs of the intensive farming that made this happen.

Perhaps even more crucial is the way improvements in countries' indicators overall mask increasing divisions within nations. Wealth and other social inequalities have been growing across the world. In the UK, life expectancy continued to rise for the rich in the 2010s even as it fell for women living in deprived areas.

A failure to understand the social realities beneath the headline numbers helps explain why the prevailing pessimism has shocked some people in power. The 'dominant ideology' in politics, business and the media is 'increasingly antagonistic to lived reality', the political essayist and author Pankaj Mishra argued in 2022.[18] His comments certainly seem to resonate in modern Britain. 'The post-truth age has dawned murkily in a chasm,' he wrote. 'Between the way an elite represents the world in which it is flourishing, and the way ordinary people experience that same world.'

The conundrum of how starkly people's feelings can be at odds with apparent realities has kept Bobby Duffy busy for most of his career. He is one of the leading students of the UK's misleading ideas about itself. He has even written a book on it: *The Perils of Perception – Why We're Wrong About Nearly Everything*[19] was published in 2018. Duffy's work draws on polling done globally since 2012 by Ipsos,[20] his former employer. It looked at how people in Britain and dozens of other countries[21] view themselves – and the many mistaken impressions they have.

Duffy speaks to me from his office at King's College London, where he is professor of public policy.[22] During the interview, a distracting procession of people passes back and forth behind him. It creates a sense of ceaseless institutional activity that would no doubt delight the University of London's vice-chancellor.[23]

Duffy, who sports a 1970s-style look with a purple tie and the hint of a quiff, has had a career of more than 30 years in policy research and evaluation. He did a short secondment at the prime minister's strategy unit under Tony Blair in 2001. His focus there was on how to improve people's life satisfaction. That feels like a distant goal in a time of soaring inflation and the struggles facing an increasing number of people simply to survive.

During our conversation, Duffy couples an academic deliberation with a sense of irony, occasionally running his fingers through his hair as he ponders the implications of a point. He often digresses down the many fascinating statistical byways he has travelled during his long career.

His headline conclusion is that we live in a world of misinterpretation. The Ipsos results from almost every country show people's views are sometimes at wild variance[24] with the world as it is. Areas in which they – or rather we – are most wrong are myriad and diverse, including murder rates, connectivity to technology and how healthy people are.

One example of where people commonly get it wrong is in their assessments of how much money their fellow citizens have. Almost all countries surveyed in 2016 thought wealth was more evenly distributed than it actually is. Intriguingly, the UK was one of the few nations to have a reasonably accurate sense of how much money people had. Survey participants thought the poorest 70 per cent of citizens owned 19 per cent of national wealth, against the actual figure of 21 per cent.

Respondents in countries such as India, the Philippines and Italy were particularly adrift from social realities. While Duffy notes wryly that it would be 'British exceptionalism' to see our flawed perceptions as unique, he says we are nevertheless 'quite an outlier' in important respects. The UK may be roughly in the middle of the pack on average, but it does have profound misconceptions in significant areas.

Some of the most grievous UK misapprehensions concern how the country is changing as a result of immigration. The 2016 findings showed[25] Britons thought 15 per cent of the population was Muslim – more than three times the actual number of 4.8 per cent. These errors segue into another set relating to European immigration. On average people thought nationals of other EU countries accounted for 15 per cent of the UK's population – three times the actual level.

In addition, people grossly underestimated the importance of the EU to the UK economy. They thought the bloc accounted for 30 per cent of foreign investment, compared with 48 per cent in reality. By contrast, China was said to be responsible for 19 per cent of investment, as opposed to the actual figure of just 1 per cent.

Even more strikingly, people were grotesquely mistaken about how much UK child benefit[26] was claimed by people from other EU countries. Almost 40 per cent thought the number of children elsewhere in the EU receiving British child benefit was at least 40 times the actual level. In other words, more than a third of those surveyed thought other EU citizens were sucking British resources on a scale massively greater than the reality. They were not just wrong, they were outlandishly in error.

I tell Duffy I am struck by how many of the misperceptions skew to a worldview promoted by right-wing politicians and media. I ask if there are any that tilt leftward. He says he and his team have 'looked hard' but not found much evidence of that.

Duffy offers as an explanation that people see many of the trends relating to immigration and the EU as a threat. It is the same reason that they overestimate the number of people killed annually in both terrorist attacks and other murders. All these subjects provoke feelings of insecurity, which historically conservatives have exploited by portraying themselves as guardians of law and order. This 'may well explain why it's more small-c conservative trends that we get most wrong' in surveys, Duffy says.

Older people, perhaps understandably and unsurprisingly, tend to be the most worried, he adds. This is a crucial electoral point in an aging nation such as Britain. 'There are very strong lifecycle and cohort effects that people just get more worried about change as they get older. The sense of threat, that negative information, we're hardwired into paying more attention to than more calming information. So we inflate that in our thinking and ignore the point that things aren't changing as much as we fear. And that gives a skewed version of reality.'

Average UK social attitudes have grown much more liberal in some areas, but in others they are harsher than those of European counterparts.

Britain generally takes a harder view than its European neighbours on social benefits. The idea that people are getting money without meriting it is more deeply embedded in Britain, Duffy says.[†]

'There is lots of work that shows we are an outlier on thinking welfare recipients are scroungers and don't deserve support,' he adds. '[There's] a much stronger perception here of the undeserving welfare recipient than in other countries.'

That appears to reflect the way the subject is consistently framed in UK politics and media. But Duffy suggests that is not the only reason Britain is 'fertile ground for those types of messages'. Polling suggests the UK is 'very mid-Atlantic in our perceptions', with a view that 'society and progress are basically meritocratic'.

'We are kind of closer to America than we would think,' he goes on. 'And quite different from Europe, mainland Europe, in lots of ways – worrying about political correctness and that type of stuff.'

I tell Duffy I'm surprised to find that a belief in meritocracy is reasonably prevalent in the UK. The US idea of the nation of immigrants all with the chance to live the American dream is deeply embedded, however flawed it may be. The UK, on the other hand, is notorious for its class system and has long been fertile ground for social satirists such as Charles Dickens. Class conflict led to the creation of the Labour Party and animated politics for much of the 20th century.

Duffy sees this as a sign of 'contradictions in our national psyche'. He cites how the belief that hard work and talent lead to success co-exists with structures the UK has set up to lessen inequality. These include the universal healthcare system and other aspects of the welfare state.

[†]   The same scepticism doesn't seem to apply to generous government handouts to high earners. In 2023, the government raised the personal pension investment annual tax-free allowance from £40,000 to £60,000 – a perk worth up to £9,000.

Evidence suggests that Britons hold mixed views about the extent to which inequalities in the country are caused by individuals or institutional structures, Duffy says. These opinions do not necessarily map neatly on to the existing political parties, especially now. The EU referendum exposed this, as Leave was backed mostly by Conservative voters but by a significant minority of Labour supporters, too. Since then, both parties have wooed swing voters whom they style crudely as socially conservative, but economically left wing in their support for state intervention.

'This is a really important division where you get about a third of people that are more individualist, a third of people are more structuralist and a third of people that are kind of in the middle on this,' Duffy says. 'And that relates to political identities, but it's not the same as being a Labour supporter, a Conservative supporter and so on. There are quite a lot of Conservatives who have got a more structural view – and a fair amount of Labour supporters who've got more individualist views. So it's slightly different from left/right political ideologies.'

Duffy dates greater hostility to welfare recipients not to Margaret Thatcher's governments of the 1980s, but to the 2000s. It may be linked to the rise of EU immigration after the bloc enlarged in 2004 – and a sense that the new arrivals were getting something for nothing.

'If you characterise the perception overall, then it got a bit too generous and a bit too open to others,' he says. 'The very real reaction against the big increases in net migration in the early 2000s and mid-2000s kind of colours people's views of benefit recipients.'

Overestimates of immigration and misapprehensions about its negative impact can open the way to harsh policies. This is what appears to have happened in the UK.

It is not only the Conservatives who have been responsible. The preceding 'New Labour' governments of Tony Blair and Gordon Brown attempted to project a sense of toughness. Anti-immigrant sentiment grew under Labour,[27] fuelled by statements such as insisting people spoke English in the home, according to the National Centre for Social Research. In 2015, Labour's online merchandise included an election campaign mug[28] bearing the message 'controls on immigration'.

Under Conservative rule since 2010, the UK has been plagued by immigration scandals that reflect both callousness and maladministration. The Windrush affair is perhaps the most infamous example. It emerged after years of the avowedly 'hostile environment' created by the government towards people with no official permission to stay in the country. People of Caribbean heritage who were British nationals or had settled in the country for decades were suddenly told they had no right to remain. More than 160 were wrongly detained or deported, according to an official review.[29] They included a 61-year-old grandmother who had worked in the House of Commons for 30 years. She was wrongly held in a detention centre for a month and avoided expulsion from the country only because her MP and a charity intervened.

The Windrush injustices may have harmed hundreds or even thousands more people, who lost the right to work, benefits or medical treatment. It is a shameful counterpart to the celebrations of that group I had seen on the walls of the National Archives.

Whether this kind of policy actually worked seemed secondary to the image of firmness it was intended to project. As the journalist and author Adam Serwer has written of the appeal of Donald Trump's language targeting oppressed groups, 'the cruelty is the point'. Over time, it helps to establish meanness as an unexceptional characteristic of the nation.

Many saw this logic as underpinning the move the UK government announced in 2022 to send prospective refugees to Rwanda.[30] This was a response to people arriving irregularly in small boats across the Channel. Delays to considering their asylum claims meant that they sometimes ended up living in hotels for extended periods. About 45,700 people came to the UK this way in 2022. That's a significant number, but also a fraction of the millions of refugees who have, for example, fled the Syrian War for Turkey.

The story had a Brexit angle, too. The UK's departure from the EU meant it could no longer automatically return asylum seekers to fellow countries in the bloc. Under the EU's so-called Dublin regulation, arrivals into any country could often be sent back to the first member of the bloc in which they had entered. This tended to favour Britain, since people making the journey to the UK across the Channel had self-evidently been in another EU nation first. In practice, the system has often not worked smoothly during the EU's big internal battles over migration – but the rules are there.

This loss of UK rights due to Brexit was understandably not something the Leave side chose to highlight in its campaigning materials on immigration. In September 2023, Labour announced that it would seek an agreement with the EU to return asylum seekers – essentially an attempt to recreate something like the former status quo.

The British government could have responded to the uptick in Channel arrivals by speeding up processing, but it decided on a more hostile approach instead. It leased a barge[31] named the *Bibby Stockholm* to house male asylum seekers off the Dorset coast, although it had a capacity of only 500 people.

The more ambitious part of Westminster's plan was a deal under which it would pay an initial £140m to Rwanda to take an undisclosed number of asylum seekers. From there, they could apply for refugee status there or in another 'safe third country'. One thing they would not be able to do is quit the East African country to make another attempt to enter the UK.

The plan reminded me of a similar case[32] I reported on in 2014, while based in South-East Asia. It concerned Australia's move to send refugees to live permanently in Cambodia. The outcome was a cautionary tale for the UK government and those who support its Rwanda policy. Australians would know that this is an unwise path for Britain to take.

The backdrop to the Australian Cambodia venture had resemblances to the UK Rwanda deal. Australia has long had draconian immigration measures, including sending asylum seekers to offshore camps in Nauru and Papua New Guinea's Manus island. Governments have stoked public fears that, without such measures, too many people will come. In 2019, almost half of Australians said immigration levels were too high, according to a survey by the Lowy Institute think tank.[33]

Like the British government Rwanda policy, Australia's deal with Cambodia was an attempt to get refugees off their hands. Under the agreement Canberra would pay Phnom Penh more than A$50m,[34] comprising A$40m of aid and A$15.5m in resettlement costs for programme participants. That in itself was striking. Cambodia had a reputation for official corruption and had been ruled by the authoritarian Prime Minister Hun Sen since 1985.

The policy lurched almost immediately towards dark farce. In April 2015, the Australian government was condemned by rights groups over a video it produced for potential resettlers. In it, Peter Dutton, immigration minister, said Cambodia offered a future 'free from persecution' and rich in jobs. 'Cambodia provides a wealth of opportunity for new settlers,' he announced in the four-minute film. 'It is a fast-paced and vibrant country, with a stable economy and varied employment opportunities.'

A separate information letter drawn up by Canberra made further questionable claims about life in Cambodia. It said the country offered good-quality housing and healthcare, plus 'all the freedoms of a democratic society'. At the time, Cambodia ranked 148th of 190 countries[35] in the UN's annual Human Development Index. Hun Sen had just marked 30 years in power after a disputed election two years previously.

Refugee rights groups branded the video and letter misleading. Their content even jarred with the Australian government's own travel advice, which warned those visiting Cambodia of 'reports of assaults and armed robberies against foreigners'. It highlighted the limited access to emergency assistance in some areas of the country and flagged 'violent clashes between security forces and demonstrators'.

Initially only four refugees travelled[36] to Cambodia under the programme – three Iranians and one Myanmar national. The deal expired[37] in 2018, by which time it had resettled a grand total of ten people. A year later, only one of them[38] – a member of Myanmar's persecuted Rohingya minority – remained. The man, Mohammed Roshid, said he felt 'hopeless and broken' and was 'stuck in limbo without a future in sight'. He remained stateless and denied basic rights like access to housing and work. Roshid eventually married and had a child with a fellow Rohingya in Cambodia, according to later reports.[39]

There seemed few reasons to think the outcome of the Rwanda deal would be much different for the UK. The first challenge for the government was to persuade the courts that the scheme was lawful. It was allowed by the High Court but struck down in June 2023 by the Court of Appeal.

In November 2023, the Supreme Court ruled the policy unlawful. It said there were 'substantial grounds' to believe Rwanda would send asylum seekers back to their home countries, exposing them to the risk of persecution.

It was a comprehensive repudiation of Boris Johnson's claims about the scheme when he launched it as prime minister in 2022. He asserted then that Rwanda was 'one of the safest countries in the world, globally recognised for its record on welcoming and integrating migrants'.[40]

Refugees sent to Rwanda would face many of the difficulties their counterparts faced in Cambodia. They would be foreigners seeking employment in a poor country where good jobs are scarce. In 2021, Rwanda ranked 165th[41] out of 191 countries in the UN Human Development Index – 19 places behind Cambodia.

Like Cambodia, Rwanda is an authoritarian state. Paul Kagame, a former rebel leader, has been president since 2000. Michela Wrong's 2021 book *Do Not Disturb: The Story of a Political Murder and an African Regime Gone Bad* documents how Western governments have overlooked the persecution of Kagame's political opponents, including murders of dissidents overseas.

In December 2022, UK Home Secretary Suella Braverman decried[42] what she branded the 'great deal of misinformation about Rwanda'. Her response had strong echoes of Australian minister Dutton's justification of the Cambodia plan. Braverman described Rwanda as a 'safe and dynamic country with a thriving economy' and an 'excellent record of supporting refugees and vulnerable migrants'.

'It is what the overwhelming majority of the British people want to happen,' she claimed about the plan, without elaborating. 'The sooner it is up and running, the sooner we will break the business model of the evil gangs and bring an end to the illegal, unnecessary and unsafe channel crossings.'

Immigration is just one example of how misperception can drive public debate and policymaking in modern Britain. I put it to Duffy that another much misunderstood phenomenon is the Brexit vote. Its presentation as a revolt against the elite has been widely absorbed and internalised in how the parties deal with the aftermath.

The portrayal of the Leave vote as an uprising by the oppressed is politically helpful for various factions. It is advantageous to right-wing Brexit campaigners who want to present themselves as tribunes of the people. It works well, too, for those on the political left who want to style the referendum as an indictment of inequality in the UK. It receives another helping hand from the contemptible behaviour of some Remain supporters, who have disdained Leave voters as stupid.

Boris Johnson evoked this dubious David-versus-Goliath narrative before the Brexit vote, when he was both Mayor of London and an MP. It is worth noting in passing that what he said would surely – and rightly – have been condemned as condescending had it come from a Remain supporter. It surfaced after the referendum, in the leak of an unpublished anti-Brexit article he had written when he was still deciding which side to take. In it, he fantasised about the bucolic celebrations that would greet concessions the then prime minister David Cameron had wrung out of the EU. Johnson imagined 'peasants blind drunk on non-EU approved scrumpy[43] and beating the hedgerows with staves while singing patriotic songs about Dave the hero'.

The problem with this portrayal of yeoman English Euroscepticism is that polling suggests the single biggest group of Brexit voters were comfortably off. They were described as 'affluent Eurosceptics' in research published after the referendum by the National Centre for Social Research.[44] This demographic comprised almost 25 per cent of Britons – and three-quarters of them backed Brexit.

Brexit presented a lower risk to this group than to others, making it easier for them to vote for it. Many were retired and owned their own property, so they were insulated from some of the impact of leaving the EU. Trends that affected the working population – such as rising unemployment or interest rates – would not hurt them to the same degree.

Duffy agrees it is notable that the idea of Brexit being in good part a movement of the financially secure hasn't gained more traction. After all, British public life is increasingly awash with resentment of members of the post-war 'baby-boom' generation and the assets they have acquired. Yet somehow – perhaps reflecting the effectiveness of the Leave campaigners' propaganda – Brexit was still mostly seen as a rebellion of the deprived.

'We managed to keep those thoughts very separate in our heads,' Duffy says of the apparent disconnect. 'It's a different sort of narrative across the two, rather than one that joins up.'

Duffy sees Brexit and its fallout as reflecting the first stages of a move in the UK towards the culture wars that are seen across the Atlantic. As is the case in the US, the tendency of social media to create bubbles of the like-minded and incentivise outrageous statements is corrosive.

'The problem is that our information environment only shows and amplifies the very extreme ends of that progressive and traditionalist argument,' he says. It creates the false impression that 'this is the entirety of one side, versus the entirety of the other.'

Surveys still show 'a huge amount of overlap' between Labour and Conservative supporters on various questions of political and cultural identity, Duffy says. But he notes ominously that the degree of agreement is beginning to shrink. 'That's the worry right now – that we are tripping into quite a lot of these culture-war methods and approaches. Which means emphasising these divisions, only focusing on the extremes – and it's very hard to stop once you've started, because it becomes quite self-reinforcing.'

One troubling sign is the way needed debates over policies have been hijacked into culture-war weapons. Duffy cites as an example the parliamentary byelection that, at the time of our conversation, has just taken place in Boris Johnson's old constituency of Uxbridge and South Ruislip. The Conservatives held the seat against expectations, by exploiting opposition to the extension of London's Ultra Low Emission Zone (ULEZ) levy on some older cars. Within days, Prime Minister Rishi Sunak had seized on the opportunity to promise drivers he was 'on their side' against 'anti-motorist Labour'. He brushed over the fact that a Conservative mayor, Boris Johnson, had introduced the first ULEZ[45] in London. The Tory government had also encouraged cities[46] up and down the country to set up the zones.

This creation of what Duffy terms 'mega-identities' among voters covering many subjects may bring parties short-term political wins, but it is destructive in the longer run. It makes it harder to discuss change – and it makes people contemptuous of each other.

'The more things that are rolled into that identity, the harder it is to see the other side as normal,' Duffy says. 'The more that's rolled in, the easier it is to activate those identities on anything. And the more you activate them, the more they strengthen – and it becomes this cycle that you are quite stuck in.'

Duffy smiles at my suggestion that Brexit seems to have been a kind of a gateway drug for these culture wars. He says the battle over EU membership revealed and reinforced existing tensions over subjects such as immigration.

'Brexit is much more about how you see the country and your vision culturally for it,' he says. 'In the drug analogy, it's less the start than the switch to heroin – or something – after some soft drugs.'

This is why the consequences of Brexit are about much more than how close Britain should be to the EU. Neither main party is prepared to be fully honest about the costs of leaving, whatever the perceived benefits may be. Brexit campaigners thrived by creating misperceptions, which have 'worsened our inability to be truthful to ourselves', as the academic Will Jennings has put it. Since many high-profile Brexit supporters have always been loath to admit that leaving the EU has any intrinsic downsides, no policy can ever take account of this. In the same way, ill-founded or inconsequential post-Brexit initiatives are given centre stage, as long as they can be spun as supporting the decision to leave.

The government's 'Benefits of Brexit' paper published in January 2022 is a prime illustration of this damaging dynamic. The first item the government's business department tweeted about it was the opportunity that Brexit gave to return Britain to greater use of imperial measurements. 'Imperial units like pounds and ounces are widely valued in the UK and are a core part of many people's British identity,' the paper claimed, without quoting evidence.

The very origins of the proposal were based on a popular misconception that the EU had stopped the use of the imperial system. In fact, the European rules said only that the metric number should be displayed on packaging with at least the same prominence as its imperial counterpart. Other traditional British measures, such as miles on road signs and pints of beer in pubs, are still in use. The government paper was self-evidently wrong to claim that there was an 'EU ban on imperial markings and sales'.

The politics of the misleading imperial measurement plan play to the country's basic demographics. The zeal some Conservative politicians have shown for culture wars has its roots in the country's aging population. Older voters turn out in higher numbers than younger people – and they tend overwhelmingly to support the Tories.

This stark age divide in British elections is something new. In 1979, the Conservatives led Labour among voters under 35. Yet by 2019, well under 30 per cent in that age group[47] backed the Conservatives, compared with almost 60 per cent of those who were 65 and above.

'On the conservative side, you've got this shrinking base, because the generational age differences in voting are the biggest we've seen,' Duffy says. 'So there is a motivation there to pull your base as close as possible to you and emphasise the threat on the other side. That's a difficult mechanism to get out of once you're in it, because you end up getting more extreme in pushing that.'

What the intensity of these culture wars and demographic skirmishes has obscured is the amount of agreement among British people. The sense of a country divided may be helpful to the government, but it does not necessarily reflect what people think – or how they are. Polling suggests wide agreement on what citizens value in society, including healthcare, education and attractive public spaces. Social attitudes have become profoundly more liberal[48] in areas such as same-sex relationships and women's access to abortion.

Duffy says his research supports suggestions that people share many more values than much political and media coverage would suggest. Indeed, he says that Britain scores highly compared with many other countries surveyed.

'We actually quite like each other as a whole,' he affirms. 'We are the most tolerant on many, many measures, the most open and the most relaxed with each other.'

But he warns that people's opinions about the way the country is run are a different story. Evidence from UK polling showed a 'decline in confidence in key institutions', he says. The police and courts have seen 'terrible falls'. This had fed an even bigger problem of a loss of belief in the power of democracy to deliver.

'This is not an authoritarian reflex where we're going, "This is the wrong system",' he says. '[The percentage of people] thinking democracy is the best system has actually gone up. The thing is more how it's being delivered to people – and it's just not working for them.'

Other studies have found that this disillusionment is particularly grievous among younger generations. Minorities in all age groups thought democracy addressed the interests of people like them, according to a 2022 study[49] by the IPPR think tank. That figure plunged to 19 per cent among 18–24-year-olds, compared with 46 per cent of those aged 65 or over.

Duffy argues that these trends show a desperate need to get back to policies that yield results. His response is hardly rocket science, but it seems almost revolutionary at a time when the idea that Britain has become fundamentally dysfunctional is widespread.

'That focus on delivery – and not all of this creating division from nothing – is what it's crying out for,' he says. 'In that sense, switching back to that kind of focus would be a real benefit for the country.'

The UK's misreadings of itself are deep-seated and have been formed over an extended period of time. As long as they remain, this will be a nation that continues to live with a trick mirror vision of itself. Churchill cosplay won't help efforts to make the country better.

I ask Duffy about the damage that ever more entrenched misperceptions of the world around us can do. Does a nation become the ghoulish version of itself it sees in its reflection? Do our negative opinions of each other eventually become so calcified that they are impossible to shift?

He laughs and replies that he is more optimistic because of 'studying public opinion for so, so long'. He points to the inherent plurality and contradictoriness of most people's worldviews, even when massaged by politicians, the media and the internet.

'We can hold these different impressions in our heads, so when you look in the mirror, in that analogy, you also see beauty, or great potential, or something else,' he says. 'It feels like one perception should be completely at odds with and unable to live with the other – but we're very good as humans at having both of those.'

He also points out that his polling suggests many people still feel 'a lot of pride and a lot of connection to Britain'. That endures despite the political rancour of the recent past. The country may increasingly see a twisted and bleak vision of itself – but it is not too late to change that.

'I think it is right that this is not a very productive self-reflection that we've had, because it's so caricatured and extreme,' he says. 'But equally, I suppose, I would be more hopeful that we also see the good in our national image as well – and that is just as authentic as all the bad.'

2

The Nostalgia Trap

Frank Trentmann has been a student of Britain's history ever since he moved to the country from Germany as an undergraduate. So when he had to answer questions about the UK's past as part of the government's official citizenship exam, he was shocked by what he found.

The first tell was a chapter title in the handbook for what is known as the Life in the UK test. It declared that Britain had a 'long and illustrious history'. Other material styled the British Empire 'a force for good in the world'. The D-Day landings by the Second World War allies in Nazi-occupied France were described as exclusively the 'British invasion of Europe'.

The content dismayed Trentmann, who had wanted to become a UK citizen for 'practical and family reasons' because of Brexit. It offended him on 'personal, political and, you might say, moral or ethical' levels, he tells me.

'When I read this history chapter, it hit me in a variety of ways,' says Trentmann, a professor at Birkbeck, University of London, and author of a book on Germany's post-war experience. 'First of all, as a person who has lived in this country, but also as a historian. And then thirdly, as someone who is particularly aware of issues of historical memory and how countries and societies deal with difficult bits in their past, because I'm a German national.'

Trentmann had stumbled into one of the many murky rivers of nostalgia that flow through and beneath modern British life. It is an undertow that we perhaps underestimate because we are so used to it in the public discourse. Sometimes, it takes an insider-outsider like Trentmann to highlight the oddness of certain things we can all see.

Trentmann sees the Life in the UK test as pernicious to Britain's understanding of itself. He has written about being particularly disturbed by what he has branded the 'false and distorted account of slavery and decolonisation in its pages'. He argues the historical material follows 'a consistent pattern in which key events are bowdlerised and manipulated'. This 'feeds new citizens myth, which it requires them to remember'.

It is the mentality that enables ministers such as former home secretary Suella Braverman to present a sanitised version of British history. In a September 2023 speech in the US, she argued that the UK has 'a proud history of human rights dating back to Magna Carta'.[1] At a stroke, she eliminated entirely the country's responsibility for crimes of the past eight centuries.

Trentmann decided to act on his experience of the Life in the UK test. He drafted an open letter calling for reforms. More than 600 historians signed it. The letter is part of a building effort to force the Home Office to revise the citizenship test material. It is a campaign that, as of December 2023, the government had mostly resisted. It has become another attritional battle over how deeply Britain is prepared to engage with and account for its past.

Trentmann sees the 'very low historical sensitivity' of the UK citizenship handbook as part of this important broader conflict. It is about a nostalgic strain in British public life that is shaping the way the country conducts itself today.

'It's about . . . society trying to find its place in a radically changing world,' Trentmann says. 'And so the past is a kind of resource for self-assurance in the present.'

*

Nostalgia for a past real or imagined is a powerful emotion that is prone to manipulation. It can be trivial and benign, but some strains of it are most definitely not. It can be a hugely effective political tool for rulers in dictatorships and democracies alike.

Leaders across continents and cultures deploy nostalgia and its darker twin, atavistic historical grievance. The drive to restore Russia's lost empire is crucial to Vladimir Putin's framing of his 2022 invasion of Ukraine. In China, the Communist Party and ultra-nationalists of today draw deeply on the so-called century of humiliation by Western powers and Japan. In the US, Donald Trump harks back to a social order of even greater domination by white men.

I gained a deeper appreciation of the power of nostalgia during my years reporting abroad. Physical absence creates longings for what you no longer have, from bracing walks in cold weather to summer nights when it seems to stay light forever. The pandemic heightened these feelings: I was surely not alone in looking back more than usual at the films and music of my younger days. The older we get, the more tempting it becomes to try to revive the spirit of our youth through recreating its cultural and emotional furniture.

It sometimes seems as if longing for a past real and imagined has become an industry in Britain. It has a special potency for an aging electorate. 'Classic' or 'retro' styles in music, television or food are acclaimed and sometimes revived, with more problematic aspects airbrushed or softened. In politics, advocates of both right and left look to rekindle the country's supposedly lost glories, whether in international influence or industrial capacity.

This wistfulness is apparent to many onlookers with at least one foot beyond the country's shores. It has been documented by Ian Howorth,[2] a photographer born and raised outside the UK by a Peruvian mother and English father. His pictures range from seaside kitsch to abandoned red telephone boxes.[3] They capture what he described in 2023 as 'a cultural nostalgia that has engulfed all facets of life'.

'While nostalgia reigns, modernisation cannot be completed, and therein lies the contradiction of Great Britain – why attempt it at all?' Howorth wrote.

It is little surprise to find that David Frost is one of the people at Britain's nostalgic vanguard.[4] The former diplomat turned hardcore Brexiter is increasingly vocal about how life in the UK isn't what it used to be.

'Do you remember when TV adverts were funny?' he bemoaned in a July 2023 *Daily Telegraph* column. 'John West salmon, Hamlet cigars, Heineken and Castlemaine 4X. Nowadays it's all virtue signalling: feel-good tweeness from John Lewis, subtly political slogans like HSBC's "We are not an island", or just deadly earnest tedium from virtually everyone else.'

I remember these old commercials well from my own childhood. They came over as amusing and cool, at least to a pre-adolescent boy. Catchlines like 'Australians wouldn't give a XXXX for anything else' seemed like the height of edgy wit. So did Heineken helping a posh young woman say, 'The water in Majorca don't taste like what it ought to' in a Cockney accent.

Frost's nostalgia is, however, highly selective. A former head of the Scotch Whisky Association, he doesn't consider the darker side of his wistfulness. Three of the four commercials he mentions were for harmful products – alcohol and tobacco. (The fourth, for John West, involved a more outré kind of risk, depicting a man brawling with a bear over a freshly caught salmon.) In those days, the devil certainly had the best advertising tunes – or at least the biggest marketing budgets. Cigarette commercials drenched sport: in cricket alone, I grew up watching the John Player Special League and the Benson & Hedges Cup. Now tobacco sponsorship and promotion are almost entirely banned, while those for alcohol are more restricted. Few would surely argue that this is a bad thing.

A consequence of greater maturity and the lapse of time ought to be the realisation that some things you once cherished had ugly aspects. I've looked back at some pop cultural phenomena of my childhood during research for this book. The results are often not pretty.

I grew up in an era of routine stereotyping in the UK. This was a country where the jams and preserves maker Robertson's didn't drop the golliwog from their branding until as late as 2001. The company even used the character in badges made for promotions.

It's worth underlining just how insidious this was. Robertson's marmalade has had a Royal Warrant since 1933 – an endorsement by the British monarchy. 'Gollies' first appeared in a book published in Britain at the tail end of the Victorian era, according to the Jim Crow Museum[5] in the US. They are 'grotesque creatures, with very dark, often jet black skin, large white-rimmed eyes, red or white clown lips, and wild, frizzy hair'.

Some Britons still revel in these offensive caricatures today. In 2023, UK police seized a collection of them[6] from an Essex pub, after someone reported feeling racially harassed, alarmed or distressed by them. YouTube videos of old adverts for Robertson's Golden Shred marmalade featuring a golly have hundreds of thousands of views between them. 'I can watch this over and over. It's just adorable,' reads one comment.[7] 'Such a shame these kinds of adverts are not on the tv today they are so simple heart-warming adverts full of nostalgia,' says another.

Hain Celestial, the US company that took over Robertson's in 2012, says, 'The use of the golliwog in historical advertisements does not reflect the values of Hain Celestial or Robertson's. The golliwog is not associated with the Robertson's brand today.'

The Robertson's commercials were part of a pattern of offensiveness in British advertisements during the 1970s, 1980s and sometimes beyond. Food and drink publicity alone contained multiple examples of derogatory racial imagery and cultural appropriation. Commercials for Kia-Ora orange squash featured various stereotypes of Black people – and didn't acknowledge that the brand took its name from a Maori greeting. An advert for the soda Lilt was set in the Caribbean and had a reggae soundtrack, but not a single Black person in sight.

Lilt's rebranding by its current owner, Coca-Cola, in 2023 drew out the rearguard that still exists in the UK to combat such changes. The conservative *Daily Mail* asked, 'Has Lilt been cancelled?' and quoted 'Lilt fans' decrying the decision – although one of the fans opined that the ads were 'a tiny bit racist'.[8] (Coca-Cola didn't respond to a request for comment.)

My favourite childhood comic the *Beano* has become part of the nostalgia culture wars. In July 2023, right-wing news outlets ran headlines[9] on the 'woke' makeover there. They pointed to the use of 'sensitivity readers' to vet new characters.

The 'woke' jibe ignored how the *Beano* had already changed many times over the years to reflect shifts in social attitudes. The comic had made its message less anti-school and had recalibrated the balance between cool bully Dennis the Menace and pathetic swot Walter 'the Softy'. Walter, for so long the fall guy, has even been reinvented as a much meaner character for the CBBC TV series *Dennis the Menace*.[10] I almost feel sorry for him, forced to atone for the sins of the strip's previous authors.

The *Beano* has made several revisions to weed out racial stereotypes. I remember reading a strip devoted to Little Plum, a Native American boy catchlined 'Your Redskin Chum'. It was dropped for a 2002 revamp – although it returned for a while and appeared in reprints as late as 2010.

What I found most surprising was how late the *Beano* made some of its changes. The anchor centre-spread strip *The Bash Street Kids*, about an unruly school class, is a case in point. It was only in 2021 that Spotty's name was changed to Scotty and Fatty's to Freddy. Fatty's rebranding prompted criticism from then government minister Jacob Rees-Mogg (himself a bit of a Walter the Softy lookalike).

The first non-white Bash Street Kids, Harsha and Mandi, arrived in the same year. The *Beano* has since introduced others and is eager to position itself as progressive. Mike Stirling, its creative director, has said the comic had never seen 'woke' as a pejorative term. 'What would be easy to do would be to sleepwalk and keep the *Beano* the way it had always been done for ever,' he told *The Times*.[11]

The UK was hardly alone in the questionable material it was turning out for children – and its European neighbours could be worse. Even in the 1980s British publishers balked at *Tintin in the Congo*, with its grotesque caricatures of the country's people (and the hero's wildlife shooting sprees). Still, all the other books in Hergé's series, featuring myriad racist stereotypes, were available to be devoured by me and many other kids. *Tintin in the Congo* was eventually published in the UK, too.

Even cult TV shows popular with children could be problematic. One was the Japanese series *Monkey,* based on a Chinese folk tale about a band of wanderers comprising a monk and three outcasts from heaven. A British cast including Miriam Margolyes and Andrew Sachs dubbed it – with a stereotypical imagining of how nationals of East Asian countries might speak English.

I saw how egregious it was on rewatching, after a friend of Chinese heritage mentioned it. A largely affectionate appreciation[12] of the show published in the Australian cultural magazine *Blunt* made the same point. Tellingly, the author was tentative in his conclusions, perhaps anticipating the backlash that often seems to be triggered by even measured reappraisals of the past.

'[The] thing about the stuff we loved back in the day is that it stays the same while we and our culture continue to grow and develop,' the piece read. 'Look, I'm just gonna come out and say it, and you can drag me for it in the comments: in the cold light of 2021, the English dub is pretty racist.'

*

The author's nervousness is a sign that the currents of old prejudice still run stronger in society than some of us may like to think. Boris Johnson's rise to lead the country highlighted how easy it is still in Britain to avoid real responsibility for past offensive behaviour.

Johnson has long traded in a kind of nostalgia for Britain as an imperial power. It echoes in some of the language he uses. In a 2002 piece ridiculing Tony Blair's globetrotting, he described people in Commonwealth countries as 'flag-waving piccaninnies' and referred to the prospect of Congolese 'tribal warriors' breaking out into 'watermelon smiles'. He has written about 'Papua New Guinea-style orgies of cannibalism and chief-killing' and compared Muslim women wearing burqa face-coverings to 'letterboxes'.

Johnson has never been held to account in any meaningful way for these remarks. They mattered the more acutely because they showed how he saw, or was perceived to see, much of the world and many UK citizens. In some cases, he has belatedly offered apologies and argued that he was deploying tropes in the cause of satire.

Johnson may be a particularly crude example, but he is far from unique among UK leaders who have indulged discredited attitudes. Labour's Gordon Brown used a trip to Tanzania in 2005 to declare[13] that 'the days of Britain having to apologise for its colonial history are over'. Tony Blair reached for a verbal contortion to gloss over Britain's imperial past. The Labour premier praised Britain's 'outward-looking approach to the world', which he said flowed from its 'unique island geography and history'. There is, to put it mildly, a great deal to unpack in the phrase 'outward-looking approach'.

The nostalgist style of British politics extends far beyond the treatment of race and empire. Some conservative commentators scorn the emergence of what they see as pettifogging rules governing health and safety. Their mockery of the culture of 'elf and safety' has become familiar linguistic currency. Strangely, these advocates for freedom and adventure focus less on the sharp fall in fatal injuries to employees, as laws have tightened and practices improved. Such deaths declined by well over two-thirds, from 495 in 1981 to 135 in 2022–3, according to the Health and Safety Executive.[14]

This type of nostalgism often ends up harking back to the Second World War, the formative event in so much British myth-making. The so-called 'Blitz spirit' is hailed as a sign that people were tougher and more generous in those days. In 2021, the former Tory leader Sir Iain Duncan Smith used it to sneer at people who wanted to continue to work from home post-pandemic. The *Mail on Sunday* piece [15] was headlined: 'In the 1940s they kept coming to the office – even when Hitler's bombs were raining down.'

Duncan Smith and his ilk pay less heed to the body of scholarship that has exposed various bits of war fabulism, including about the Blitz. For example, the 'Keep Calm and Carry On' posters that epitomise British resilience were never actually shown in public during the conflict. As for the Blitz, interviews with hundreds of air-raid survivors in Hull revealed a reality far removed from the stoicism of legend.

'These case studies showed that people developed serious psychosomatic conditions, including involuntary soiling and wetting, persistent crying, uncontrollable shaking, headaches and chronic dizziness,' wrote Richard Overy,[16] a professor of history at the University of Exeter and author of *The Bombing War: Europe 1939–1945*. 'The government papered over the evidence of the physical and psychological effects of being bombed and focused instead on the stories of British resolve.'

I had become something of an accidental student of officially sanitised histories during my time away from the UK. All countries are guilty of it – and authoritarian states are particularly assiduous. Government decisions were portrayed as almost universally wise in countries from the United Arab Emirates to Vietnam, with no fear of contradiction. Democracies do historical house-cleans, too – and they can take more work to spot. These generally, though not universally, avoid overt censorship or the arrests of dissenters who tell inconvenient truths. Instead, as in the UK, history is often shaped through such means as factual omissions, rewoven narratives and the elevation of certain voices over others.

The Philippines, where Bobby Duffy's research has pointed to a big gulf between perceptions and reality, is a case in point of historical revisionism. It is a starker case than Britain – but there are parallels in how a national story has been reworked.

The extraordinary resurgence of the Marcos family to reclaim the Philippine presidency in 2022 relied heavily on their wielding dubious nostalgia as a political weapon. The clan, driven into exile by the 1986 popular uprising against the dictatorship of President Ferdinand Marcos Sr, was able to return to power after rewriting the past.

I'd seen the prelude to this during the time in office of former president Rodrigo Duterte, who took power in 2016. Official propaganda and online trolls had justified his bloody backstory, including a regional war on drugs that he then rolled out nationally. It worked: he won the election by pitching himself as a hard man bent on cleaning up the country. He remained popular until the end of his six-year term, despite overseeing thousands of killings by police and shadowy militias.

The 2022 election for Duterte's successor took the revisionism over past rights abuses to another level. On the campaign trail, presidential candidate Ferdinand Marcos Jr, known by the nickname Bongbong, praised his late father[17] as a 'political genius'. After he won by a landslide, he thanked Marcos Sr for teaching him 'the value and meaning of true leadership', according to a statement by his team. These were striking comments on a man who ran a tyranny accused of thousands of killings and stealing up to $10bn.

Marcos Jr's supporters used an array of signature tricks, many of which have echoes in UK politics. He and his supporters unleashed a sea of misinformation to portray his father's rule as a wonderful time for the Philippines. They ignored not only the human rights abuses, but the economic troubles that led the country to be branded 'the sick man of Asia'. A vote for Bongbong was portrayed as a return to a better past – both financially and culturally.

The return of the Marcoses is especially painful for people like Loretta Rosales, a veteran activist, politician and human rights campaigner. Rosales, now 84, was one of an estimated tens of thousands of victims detained, physically abused or murdered under Marcos Sr's regime. She was involved in street protests against the government and says she was arrested in 1976[18] by agents seeking information on a Communist insurgent leader.

Rosales has told of being held for a month, during which she was raped and tortured with candlewax, electric shocks and simulated drowning. These kinds of atrocities were not always known about by those who didn't experience them – and they have been only partially exposed since.

'During the time that Marcos Sr was in power, there was no media,' Rosales tells me. 'So the people, they did not know what was going on. It really shocked me and I would say: "You mean to say you don't know about what happened?"'

Rosales, a former chair of the national Commission on Human Rights, is speaking to me from her home in Manila. She is a charismatic presence, offering rapid-fire thoughts from her decades of activist experience. Her swept-back grey hair exudes the energy of a breaking wave, while her spherical earrings jiggle as she makes her points. A book on the shelf behind her is entitled *People Politics Power*, evoking memories of the protest movement that successfully toppled Marcos Sr in 1986. The campaign, known as People Power, resonated around the world just a few years before the fall of the Berlin Wall.

The aspect of the Philippine uprising perhaps most lodged in global folk memory is First Lady Imelda Marcos's shoe collection. When demonstrators stormed the presidential palace after the family fled, they found thousands of pairs in a wardrobe of grotesque luxury. The stash became an international byword for dictatorship's corruption of both money and spirit.

How times have changed. Hundreds of Imelda's shoe pairs are now on display in a museum in the capital, Manila. The former first lady herself toured it, apparently without embarrassment (shamelessness is a crucial attribute for the power-hungry). She even lived long enough to fulfil – at 93 – her long-held dream that her son would emulate his father by leading the country.

Rosales is aghast at the revisionism she has seen. She describes a recent trip to the north of the Philippines' main island of Luzon, the Marcos family's home region and political stronghold. She attended a rally where they played the song in praise of the Marcoses that used to be ubiquitous during the father's time in power.

'I was really shocked,' she says. 'How dare they? I said, "How can you do this – there was a revolt against you?"'

Marcos Jr himself is 'suave' and 'knows how to play the game' of airbrushing his family's dark history, Rosales observes. She says there is only one way of dealing with the misleading nostalgia that has enabled his return. It will require a big effort on behalf of the public – and particularly those who weren't around during the dictatorship.

'How do you combat it? You tell the truth!' Rosales says, animatedly. 'If you have young people who are bright and independent, you have better chances.'

One of those smart young Filipinos is Fatima Gaw,[19] who has studied the Marcos family's reinvention closely. Gaw, born seven years after the father fell, is a researcher specialising in the interplay of technology with politics. She led a project called Digital Public Pulse to analyse the 2022 Philippine elections that brought the son to power.

Gaw's account highlights many tropes familiar from the politics of nostalgia in Britain. The story of how Ferdinand Marcos Jr reinvented his family is one of distorting the meaning of events and weaponising failures to present them as successes. Most of all, the Marcos resurrection shows how fictions of a glorious past can often find a ready audience eager to escape the very real discontents of the present.

I speak to Gaw from her new perch at Northwestern University in Illinois, where she has just started a PhD. The late-summer morning light squeezes through a window in her digs. Gaw sports a grey cardigan, big round glasses and a neat black bob. She talks with the clarity and economy that have made her a highly respected analyst of online campaigning.

We are chatting on a day ripe with symbolism. A controversy has erupted in the Philippines over a Department of Education edict to rewrite historical references to Marcos Sr's time in power. Instead of talking about 'the Marcos dictatorship', textbooks will now simply refer to 'the dictatorship'.

'In the campaign he whitewashed history,' Gaw says. 'Now the president is institutionalising nostalgia in the history books.'

The way Marcos Jr's supporters have attempted to disinfect the past carries lessons for political debates worldwide, including in the UK. Gaw says the Marcos camp's key insight was the opportunity offered by the digital world to disseminate its own version of history. The internet has offered a previously unavailable means to quickly circulate entirely recrafted stories.

Political movements quite often blame online disinformation for their defeats. But the Philippines has been a particularly intense battleground. Filipinos had the highest average daily screen time[20] on phones out of almost 50 countries examined in a 2023 survey. The army of online warriors for Marcos Jr's predecessor Duterte showed the power of the internet for gaining and shoring up power.

Gaw says Marcos saw the consequences of this trend – and how it could be developed even further. 'My suspicion is that he realised, "If there's demand for this information, then we can create a whole new set of assets that people can look up online and do their own research," ' she says.

Marcos had already learned from his narrow defeat in the 2016 race for the vice-presidency. In the Philippines, this is elected separately from the top job. The contest revealed two important facts. The first was that Marcos was not a good loser and seemed to feel entitled to power. In a foreshadowing of Donald Trump's efforts to cling to office after losing the 2020 US presidential election, Marcos attempted to discredit his loss. He persisted all the way until 2021, when the Supreme Court rejected his claims that he was the victim of ballot fraud. The second crucial point was that the 2016 defeat led Marcos to decisively switch strategies. During that campaign, he had made some efforts to distance himself from his father's time in power. Afterwards, by contrast, he reversed course to embrace it.

Part of this was out of necessity, since Marcos Jr himself is deeply implicated in this history. He was no child bystander in the dictatorship, but an active participant in it. By the time the father's regime collapsed, the son was already in his late twenties. He held the post of provincial governor of Ilocos Norte, the family's home area. Marcos Jr even appears in an infamous February 1986 family photo on the balcony at the Malacañang presidential palace. Dressed in military combat gear, he stands alongside as his father roars in defiance of the tide about to sweep him away. Later that day, Marcos Jr fled the country with the rest of the immediate family.

Marcos Jr conjured a narrative of his father's rule as a 'golden age'. The story contains strands familiar in type from Britain's own politics of nostalgia. It traded on an image of the Philippines as an economic and cultural powerhouse. In 1975, it was the venue for the climax of the three-fight boxing epic between Muhammad Ali and Joe Frazier, the so-called Thrilla in Manila. In 1966, the Beatles had visited on tour at the height of their popularity, though that had ended less happily, when Marcos loyalists harassed the band and their entourage after they skipped an event hosted by Imelda.

The problem with the Marcos campaign's account of past national glory was the economic calamity of the father's time in power. In 1984,[21] gross domestic product fell 7 per cent and inflation topped 50 per cent. 'There was a claim that if Marcos had stayed in power, we would be a First World nation, we would be as rich as the US,' Gaw says. 'So that's the first false nostalgia about the Marcos era.'

A key part of the 'golden age' story was that Marcos Sr's clampdown had helped bring order to the country. While the son and his supporters denied the worst of the alleged human rights abuses, they portrayed the father's strong government as a boon to the nation.

'The way they whitewashed that version of history was to say that martial law was good because it promoted peace,' Gaw says. 'If there were people who were victimised . . . it is because they didn't follow the law. They were positioned as troublemakers – and so they deserved to be locked up and harassed.'

At the same time, Marcos supporters attempted to neutralise allegations of corruption by floating sometimes fantastical alternative tales about the family's wealth. In one particularly outlandish scenario, Marcos Sr was said not to have needed to steal money because he was independently rich. His fortune supposedly came from his work as a lawyer for a tycoon family who paid him in gold bars. In some versions of the yarn, the precious metal would be redistributed to the poor when Marcos Jr took office.†

A host of smaller details in the Marcos reinvention were themselves telling. Some, such as CV inflation, will be familiar enough from British politics. The Marcos camp once said he had graduated[22] from Oxford University. They downgraded that claim after St Edmund Hall, the college where he studied politics, philosophy and economics, said he

---

† As of October 2023, this does not yet seem to have happened.

had not completed his degree. He instead received a 'special diploma in social studies' – an unusual arrangement that the college no longer offers to students.[23]

Like many successful nostalgists, including in the UK, the Marcoses have capitalised on a disappointment with how things are. For many, the dividends of the post-People Power era have not been what they hoped. Except for a brief period between the mid-2010s and the Covid-19 pandemic, more Filipinos than not told pollsters their quality of life was falling.[24]

'Economic policies haven't really helped people improve their lives,' Gaw says.

All this gave the Marcos campaign room to perform its final breathtaking sleight of hand – one that is again characteristic of the nostalgist style. They portrayed themselves not as the aggressors, but as the aggrieved. 'What made it really sellable was the victim narrative,' Gaw says. 'The Marcoses are not at fault – they are the victims here.'

The return of the Marcoses has turned into a culture-war topic. The second coming of the clan has been about splitting the country into 'sides', says Gaw. Once you are on their team, you will stay with it whatever their opponents may claim. 'It's not about truth or factual or historical evidence any more. It's about allegiances and your identity somehow.'

Those words chime loudly in the UK, where skirmishes over the stories the country tells itself about its past have become ever more common. As in the Philippines, these often involve disputes over which version of history should be used. Some of the clashes have brought the British government into conflict with other well-established national institutions.

Few of these have deeper roots than the National Trust, the charity that is the custodian of historic buildings and estates across the country. In 2020, a report it had commissioned found that nearly a third of about

300 properties reviewed were linked to colonial activities, including slavery. The Trust now more fully reflects the imperial dimensions of homes including the former residences of the writer Jane Austen and Winston Churchill. The initiative is part of a larger project called Colonial Countryside, which focuses on links between UK assets and the profits of slavery and empire.

The project has triggered a strong reaction from the political right, including the Conservative government. The academic who led the project received death threats.[25] Tory MPs pushed for a Charity Commission investigation into whether the Trust had breached the law by acting outside its charitable purposes. The commission ruled in 2021[26] that it had not.

It is worth reflecting on how extraordinary the conservative position on this is. It was not challenging the National Trust's action on any factual basis. It was simply unhappy with the information being disclosed. The Tory reaction looks like the kind of attempted suppression of uncomfortable truths more normally associated with dictatorships than with democracies.

It might seem ironic to see institutions like the National Trust at the centre of these cultural storms. The Trust is, after all, deeply associated with a conservative vision of England. Yet it seems likely that it has received so much flak precisely because of this status. A Tory government can safely dismiss avowedly radical organisations with which it has no sympathy. That is much harder to do with a body whose membership must surely overlap significantly with its own. For a right-wing political partisan, it is a sign of team discipline breaking down.

The Trust spat is part of a wider government revolution against re-evaluation. One of its leading voices is Oliver Dowden, who was promoted to deputy prime minister in April 2023. In a speech as culture secretary to the conservative US Heritage Foundation in Washington,

DC, in 2022, he warned of a 'pernicious new ideology . . . sweeping our societies'. These 'woke warriors' were 'engaged in a form of Maoism' and 'determined to expunge large parts of our past in its entirety', he claimed. 'For them, nothing is sacred. Winston Churchill was central to the Allied victory in a fight for survival against Nazi tyranny. Yet some seek to trash his whole reputation and deface monuments to him in wanton acts of iconoclastic fury.'

Dowden's choice of Churchill as a rallying point is both predictable and revealing. The reverence with which the man who led the UK through the Second World War is treated sometimes ignores the controversies of his life before that time. It is historically uncontroversial that Churchill expressed many highly bigoted sentiments, as academics such as Richard Toye have noted.

'Churchill is often the subject of false or exaggerated allegations,' Toye has written. 'But in truth, he said enough horrifying things that there is no need to invent more. He said that he hated[27] people with "slit eyes and pig tails". To him, Indians[28] were "the beastliest people in the world next to the Germans". He admitted[29] that he "did not really think that black people were as capable or as efficient as white people".

Even though it is true that racism was more deeply embedded generally in Britain in Churchill's day than it is now, his prejudices were notably strong and wide-ranging. Not everyone shared them – and some even attacked them contemporaneously. It's strange that it's perceived as less acceptable to criticise Churchill almost 60 years after his death than it was when he was alive. It seems that a constituency in the UK still struggles to consider the man in full, capable of both extraordinary accomplishments and darker deeds.

Dowden went even further in his attack on the so-called 'woke' agenda. He suggested that 'social justice warriors' threatened the 'unity of purpose' needed to combat authoritarian states. 'We risk a collapse in resolve,' he said.

'If all we hear is that our societies are monstrous, unjust, oppressive, why on earth would anyone fight to sustain them?'

The minister decried critics who 'by their own shallow logic' would consider him privileged because he attended Cambridge University and was now a cabinet minister. He was, he said, the son of a shop worker and a factory worker who went to a state school. 'But even to question my supposed privilege is deemed to be proof of how privileged I am,' he lamented.

I assume Cambridge University taught Dowden, who studied law there, how to structure a persuasive argument. In which case, he doesn't really seem to have absorbed the lessons. His suggestion seems to be that a necessary step to enable democracies to stand up to autocratic states is to suppress internal criticism. In other words, one can beat dictatorships by becoming more like them and adopting the same uniformity of views. This does not seem an effective method of mounting the 'vigorous defence of the values of a free society' that Dowden said he desired.

In addition, Dowden seems to have a strange view of what privilege is. He doesn't appear to see the advantages that a Cambridge education gives him, even if he wasn't to the manner born. The uplift offered by Oxbridge is considerable in terms of access to social networks and opportunities – and obvious to people far beyond the rank of 'social justice warriors'.

There is something deeply patronising about this kind of rhetoric. It appears to be founded on an idea that people in the UK cannot cope with conflicting ideas or uncomfortable truths. 'In Britain, one of the most depressing things about the purported defenders of history is that they seem to view school pupils, university students and indeed the general public as brainless receptacles for any old story,' wrote Richard J Evans, Regius Professor Emeritus of history at Cambridge University, in 2021.[30] 'In reality people are more than able to think for themselves.'

*

Evans was one of the hundreds of historians who denounced the version of the past presented in the official Life in the UK handbook and test. A big shift towards the sanitisation of the material appears to have occurred during the 2010–15 Conservative-led government, when Theresa May was home secretary. The changes proved to be well suited to the atmosphere of tub-thumping nationalism after the 2016 Brexit referendum, when she became prime minister. May herself promised a 'red, white and blue Brexit' – although even the hard withdrawal she proposed wasn't tough enough for the right-wingers who toppled her in 2019.

The citizenship exam was originally the creation of Tony Blair's Labour government. It is a requirement not just to become British, but for some applications for a permanent right of abode. Failing it can have life-changing consequences.

Taking the Life in the UK test is, by many accounts, far from an inspiring experience. In 2023, Brian Klaas, associate professor in global politics at University College London, wrote about his own journey to do it in a 'bleak office building'.[31] It was the culmination of a process in which he said he had spent about £13,000 on visas and appointments.

'I was greeted not with a smile, but by being told to empty my pockets, stand spread-eagled, and await my ritualised once-over with a metal detector wand,' wrote Klaas, who was born in the US. 'Once they had carefully checked both ears for hidden earpieces (I'm not kidding), I sat down to take the test.'

Klaas found parts of the exam obscure or odd. None of his British-born friends knew that Saint Augustine became the first Archbishop of Canterbury. He queried why there should be a question about the day Jesus died in an exam for UK citizenship. He challenged the historical accuracy of a practice question that named Alfred the Great as the king who first unified England.

Once Klaas had finished, the official supervising the test told him he had succeeded. When he asked if he got any questions wrong, she said she didn't know: the computer only told her whether the applicant scored the 18 out of 24 pass mark. Klaas pointed out that this seemed an odd approach to take to history that was supposedly foundational to living in the UK.

'This was the final ingenious flourish, to never let future citizens know the correct answers to questions about knowledge deemed essential for one's ability to thrive in Britain,' he wrote.

Klaas's account echoes the criticisms made by Frank Trentmann and others about the test. In a piece[32] published in 2020, Trentmann documented in detail the way the Life in the UK handbook creates a pastiche version of the country. Good deeds are exaggerated and bad ones suppressed. The handbook claims falsely that 'slavery was illegal within Britain' by the 18th century, Trentmann wrote. It says that 'for the most part, an orderly transition from Empire to Commonwealth' took place after the Second World War. That ignores the conflict and violence in many countries that led to hundreds of thousands of deaths during the 1947 South Asian partition alone.

These are the mere 'tip of an iceberg of distortions and falsifications', Trentmann wrote, adding that the result 'does violence to our basic understanding of history and raises fundamental questions for a liberal society'.

'In the recent debate about the removal of statues of slave traders and imperialists, Prime Minister Boris Johnson tweeted "we cannot now try to edit or censor our past. We cannot pretend to have a different history",' Trentmann went on. 'Unfortunately, his own government does precisely that in the Life in the UK handbook.'

During my conversation with Trentmann, he points out how loose some of the handbook history is – sometimes on matters unrelated to

Britain. The section on Hitler's rise omits the role of appeasement, which was UK policy during the pre-war years under Prime Minister Neville Chamberlain. Much more grievously, it does not mention the Holocaust, or other mass murders of civilians by the Nazis during 'fierce conflict' on the eastern front.

The handbook is often narrow and exclusionary in its storytelling, Trentmann says. It proclaims the involvement of Britons in innovation, and plays down the contribution of outsiders. Trentmann cites as examples the accounts of the development of DNA sequencing and the Cern particle-physics research facility.

'Instead of telling a story of Britain as a globalising place with transnational exchange and linkages, what you get is a story where all the inventions, all the greatness, is kind of insular,' he says. 'It comes out of the British Isles and then it's exported to the rest of the world.'

All countries – and in particular those with a history of conquest – wrestle with an honest accounting of their past, as Trentmann acknowledges. Germany's treatment of the Nazi era is often held up as a good example of how to reckon with monstrous past crimes. But Trentmann points to his country's failure to fully address its colonial record, which includes the early 20th-century genocide[33] in what is now Namibia in South-West Africa.

Nor is Britain alone in the tendency of some citizens and institutions to wallow in nostalgia. In the former East Germany, the feeling even has its own portmanteau name. *Ostalgie* comes from the German words for 'east' and 'nostalgia' and is a product of the Berlin Wall's fall in 1989 and German reunification the following year. 'The tremendous social and economic shock made many Easterners nostalgic about the world they had lost, and forget the injustices, oppression and frustration against which they rebelled in 1989,' Trentmann says. 'It does not mean that people wanted a dictatorship back, but it led to a selective, prettified memory which obscured the dark side of the past.'

Trentmann suggests that the UK's nostalgic constructs are more durable than many because they have so much historical bedrock to build on. The narrative of the country as a world civiliser and enlightener is increasingly contested but still deeply embedded in political life, particularly in England.

Whereas the Philippines' Ferdinand Marcos nostalgia-makers are rewriting history's first draft, their British counterparts are drawing on long-existing material about the country's liberal reforming spirit.

'You read 19th-century or early 20th-century accounts, Britain is leading the world, Britain is the place which frees the slaves, Britain is liberty and progress,' Trentmann says. 'So there is this older story that they can build on.'

In some cases, these tales go back centuries. The first Elizabethan age in particular is full of stories of the country as a formidable power, epitomised by the Spanish Armada's defeat. It is also part of popular culture and education. My generation was taught the legend of how cool-hand Sir Francis Drake finished his game of bowls on Plymouth Hoe before beating the approaching Iberian fleet. The Ship Inn in my home town of Exeter displays prominently a quotation supposedly from Drake declaring it a favourite watering hole.†

Historical periods such as Tudor England have become hugely popular in books and television programmes. These tend almost subconsciously to reinforce an idea of long-standing national greatness. It is this sensibility that government ministers draw on when they lash out at reassessments of the past.

I ask Trentmann whether he thinks that British politicians really believe that the country's history is as lustrous as they claim. He says he is glad of the question, as it illustrates a sentiment that has been troubling him.

---

† It turns out that this suspiciously convenient 'historical fact' may have been invented centuries ago by the owner of a neighbouring coffee house to attract visitors.

'I have some very, very clever journalist friends who said, "Oh, come on, Frank – really, no one quite believes that." And I'm not sure about that. If I'm a minister and text goes out under my name which gets the origins of the Second World War wrong and erases the Holocaust, I would think I should be deeply embarrassed and do something about it.'

Trentmann points to what he sees as a double standard in the treatment of history. Politicians responsible for the Life in the UK test wouldn't dare be as cavalier in their approach to information about the law, he argues. 'Imagine if there were serious howlers about what the chapter on law says about Scotland,' he says. 'Scottish lawyers would be up in arms. You would be in trouble.'

He notes that the government has made some minor changes to the Life in the UK materials since he began his campaign. Practice questions about D-Day and Queen Elizabeth I's relationship with Parliament have been reworded. But he is dismayed that authorities have still not launched the more thorough reform he and many other historians have advocated.

'History is seen as something that you make suit your purposes for the day,' he says. 'And that is troubling. History is not some sort of chewing gum that you can just bend in whatever direction you like.'

The push for the government to change its approach to the Life in the UK test has gathered growing support. In 2022, the House of Lords Justice and Home Affairs Committee launched an inquiry into the matter. Chaired by Baroness Sally Hamwee, a lawyer and Liberal Democrat peer, the committee took evidence from a wide range of people, including Trentmann. In its conclusions, it pointed to the importance[34] of the test for people who wanted to stay indefinitely in the UK. 'If they fail the test, they may face deportation, the loss of their livelihoods, and separation from their families,' Hamwee said in a 2022 letter to Kevin Foster, minister for safe and legal migration.

The letter – written with the approval of the committee, whose membership comprises four Conservatives, four Labour, two Liberal Democrats and two unaffiliated 'crossbenchers' – made a series of criticisms. The committee was 'astonished' that the government had not yet held its 'long overdue' review of the test, Hamwee wrote. She pointed out that such a move had been proposed as long ago as 2018 by a previous Lords committee. 'The current handbook was described as a "mockery" trying to create "a particular image of British traditions and values" in evidence we received,' Hamwee wrote. 'Its content was described to us as "impractical", "inconsistent", "trivial", "outdated" and "false" to such an extent that the handbook is "undermining British values".'

The test appeared to cause puzzlement – and amusement – outside the country, the letter said. A US law professor noted that a widely noticed question 'related to the appropriate action to take after spilling a beer on someone at the pub'. (That question has since been removed.)

'The handbook, in other words, is not respected at home or overseas,' Hamwee wrote.

Aspects of the Life in the UK material are simply obscure. Hamwee's letter went on to query the relevance of a string of questions on seemingly scattergun subjects. Examples include 'early Scottish poetry, 18th-century furniture design [and] the country where the founder of the UK's first curry house eloped with his wife'.

Some questions are 'confusingly phrased' or 'fall well short of inviting candidates to reflect about their rights and responsibilities', the letter continued, with pointed understatement. It highlighted a practice question that asked 'which TWO rights are offered by the UK to citizens and permanent residents?' It offered the following multiple-choice possible answers:

1 'Free groceries for everyone and a right to a fair trial'
2 'Long lunch breaks on Friday and a right to a fair trial'

3 'Freedom of speech and a right to a fair trial'

4 'Freedom of speech and free groceries for everyone'.

The letter's final verdict is scathing. The Life in the UK handbook content comes across as a 'random selection of obscure facts and subjective assertions that most people would not know'. This trivialises the process of becoming a UK citizen. 'The content of the history chapter is so insensitive as to be offensive,' Hamwee concluded. 'It urgently needs replacing.'

When I catch up online with Hamwee a year after she wrote that letter, she is in her snug offices at the House of Lords. She and ten other Liberal Democrat peers are crammed there among pastel-coloured box files, though thankfully not everyone shows up at once. Hamwee has one eye on the screen showing parliamentary proceedings, as she awaits the call to vote.

Hamwee, a 76-year-old former chair of the London Assembly, talks with urgency and vigour. She wears a floral top, her mane of grey hair fronted by a dashing streak of blue. She pauses from time to time, as if weary of dealing with controversies that have changed too little over the years.

I ask about why she thought it important to launch an inquiry into the Life in the UK handbook. She shoots back that it is a 'portrayal of the UK as if the atlas was still largely coloured pink – and I hate that'. This is a reference to the way occupied British colonial territories were depicted in imperial-era maps. 'I've never put it quite in those words in the [Lords] chamber,' she reflects. 'But I have said that we're not all ancient Britons – and a lot of us are very recent Britons.'

Hamwee's own family illustrates that point. One branch of it has origins in the Baltic region. Another traces its roots to the Syrian city of Aleppo, where its members were in the cotton business and forged links to other cities important in the trade. 'My grandfather went from Syria to Cairo to Manchester, which is probably quite a normal path,' Hamwee says of how her family ended up in the UK. 'They came here for commercial reasons. They were economic migrants.'

That is a reference to the dehumanising modern official terminology often applied to people seeking a better life in the UK. Hamwee points to how anti-migrant sentiment in official policy is of a piece with the carelessness about history in the citizenship test. It doesn't help, too, that the Home Office is a 'mess', with high staff turnover and recruitment problems.

'I don't know whether it's a collective defensive mindset on the part of government,' Hamwee says, speaking about the refusal to amend the Life in the UK materials. 'I find it difficult to believe that Home Office officials are really persuaded by all this.'

I ask Hamwee why she thinks there is such a strong appetite for nostalgic fantasy in some parts of UK public life. It seems to run counter to the many positive ways the country has changed – or perhaps it is a response to precisely that. Hamwee sees in it a desperation to 'return to the sort of life when we were ruling the waves', a sentiment she says is 'so alien' to her. ' "We need to defend the British way of life", whatever that is,' she says, characterising what she sees as the mindset of her opponents. 'And then it's incorporated in these really quite astonishing publications.'

Hamwee offers some hope on how wider attitudes might alter. She points to how the National Health Service's multinational staff has given people more sense of their dependence on more recent British citizens – and non-citizens. 'I have heard so many people comment on that,' she says. 'I think it's quite a salutary experience actually – that they see Britain as changing because of this.' She is heartened by how many people still persist in their efforts to gain citizenship, notwithstanding the various obstacles and deterrents. These include concerns about its cost and the requirement to travel to testing centres. 'It wasn't encouraging,' Hamwee says of her committee's findings. 'But what of course was encouraging was that one met people who wanted to become British despite all this.'

Hamwee is still pressing the government for action over the Life in the UK materials. In August 2023, she asked a parliamentary question about the reaction to her committee's work. In September 2022, Home Office minister Kevin Foster had said the government would respond within 12 months. That time was up. In reply, the government told Hamwee that a timetable would be set by the end of the year. The latest delay was hardly a surprise. It seems that, officially, it is always too soon to reassess Britain's historical legacy. One day, it may be too late.

It is notably hard to obtain information about how the handbook and test are put together. Frank Trentmann says he received nothing of substance when he put in a Freedom of Information request to the Home Office. The department does not appear to publish details of how the content is decided.

I submitted a short list of questions to the Home Office about the Life in the UK handbook and test. I asked why the commitment to producing a timetable to review the content had slipped. I inquired who was responsible for setting and reviewing the handbook, including any historians or other external advisers.

A Home Office press officer replied a couple of days later. Her response was brief. 'Unfortunately, we do not provide statements which will be used in books, hope you understand,' she wrote.

I replied requesting clarification. I said that my queries were factual and would help me write about the Life in the UK test as fully and accurately as possible. I asked why the Home Office would decline to engage with such questions. I received no further response.

The phenomenon of political nostalgism takes many forms. In the Philippines, the government is rewriting the history books. In the UK, it is refusing to do so.

Frank Trentmann says many people have contacted him about their dislike of the Life in the UK test. Some are people who have heritage in countries formerly colonised by Britain and feel their family histories have been 'erased from the story'. The test 'should be a kind of welcoming handshake, which both sides want to conduct', he says – but many people saw it very differently. 'They felt sort of repulsed, and either laughed at some of the statements, or felt they were dealing with authorities they had very little respect for. So it's just the opposite, actually, of what you want a citizenship test to do.'

3

Heavy Reigns

A week after Britain's King Charles III was crowned in May 2023, Chonthicha Jangrew was elected to Thailand's parliament. The 27-year-old new MP already had an eventful history of activism. She faced the threat of a long jail term over criminal charges of sedition and insulting her country's royal family.

Now Chonthicha is an elected official, she has swapped her campaigner's street gear for business attire. When we speak, she wears a dark skirt suit and a lapel badge of her Move Forward Party's distinctive orange triangular emblem. The criminal charges against her are a sign of how Thai authorities use the law to 'control activists' and keep them quiet, Chonthicha says. 'But certainly, I haven't been quiet,' she adds, with a laugh, in a video interview from her new home in the legislature in Bangkok.

The story of Chonthicha and other Thai campaigners like her is a cautionary tale against complacency for Britons. Like the UK, Thailand is notionally a constitutional monarchy. In reality, any questioning of the royals and their role is ruthlessly suppressed.

Modern Britain has nothing like the decades-long prison sentences imposed on some Thais supposedly guilty of lese-majesté, or libelling the monarchy. But the UK does show warning signs of intolerance towards criticism of the royal institutions – as illustrated by a spate of arrests around the time of the coronation.

This matters greatly as a point of free speech. It is important, too, because the UK throne is – like its Thai counterpart – more than the benign ornament of popular portrayal. Questions swirl in both countries about the sources of the royals' wealth, the public spending on them and the transparency of their political influence.

In Britain as in Thailand, royal opulence contrasts increasingly noticeably with the growing deprivation suffered by many people. This dynamic has been noted outside the country. It was evident to foreign news outlets at a time when many inside the UK were gripped by coronation fever. Days before Charles's investiture, a CNN piece[1] headlined 'It's not a good look' reported on how some Britons were critical of the 'glitzy' event. An article in India's Firstpost[2] declared, 'It's time to question the extravagant cost of King Charles's coronation.'

In Thailand, Chonthicha thinks it no coincidence that street demonstrations for regal reforms first erupted in 2020 at the height of the Covid-19 pandemic. The suffering of that time focused people's minds on the divergence between how they lived compared with society's better off. The pressure on the monarchy was a microcosm of discontent with how the country was governed.

'So many Thais lost their jobs – and some died on the street,' she says. 'They questioned a lot why they didn't have a better life. They thought about the government and tax – and the monarchy is part of that as well.'

The sense of poverty amid royal plenty that Chonthicha evokes chimed with feelings I'd had while watching the British coronation pageant from my perch in Tokyo. The proximity of the ceremony to Thailand's general election may have been coincidence, but it resonated with me. I had been living in Bangkok in 2016 when King Bhumibol Adulyadej died after 70 years on the throne, passing power to his son Maha Vajiralongkorn. In Thailand, the end of an epic reign seemed unintentionally to reveal uncomfortable truths about a country. The same would be true for Britain when Elizabeth II died six years later.

In the post-Elizabethan UK, the cry that 'Britain is broken' was now growing across society. Many indicators of the health, wealth and happiness of citizens were in decline. Polls showed that a clear majority[3] of Britons thought the country was heading in the wrong direction.

The pessimism was also being noticed beyond the nation's shores. In September 2022, the London correspondent of *Le Monde* recounted the many elements[4] of what he understatedly called the UK's 'bad patch'. 'For months now, the country seems to have been sinking into the doldrums, with one problem after another, at an impressive rate,' he wrote.

It was all a far cry from the mood of national reincarnation summoned to mark Elizabeth's coronation in 1953. That celebration, after years of war and painful recovery, constituted 'a vast prize package that made up for the long years of drabness', *The New Yorker* wrote at the time. While Britain's imperial age was coming to a close, it was being replaced by what would become a decades-long period of Western industrial prosperity.

As the day approached, a UK-funded expedition made the first recorded ascent of the world's highest mountain. The *Daily Express* famously summed up the events with the headline of its 2 June edition: 'All this – and Everest too!'[5] A banner above exhorted: 'Be proud of Britain on this day, Coronation Day.'

Other front-page stories recounted a kingdom united in joy. One was titled 'Police furl a Royal Standard'. A photo showed people waiting for the ceremony huddled under mackintoshes and the headline 'When time and rain mean just nothing'. The scene may have looked thoroughly miserable, a classic British holiday washout, but the newspaper's craft rendered it a delight. 'Despite the rain, defying the rain, singing in the rain, the People surged into London all day yesterday and equally sat or lay down in its streets,' its correspondent enthused.

More than 70 years later, the organisers of the coronation of Elizabeth's son attempted to restitch that tapestry of positive sentiment. The ceremony was modernised to include non-Christian faiths and performances from a gospel choir, but its core was the same as in 1953. It remained an ornate and arcane affair, founded on the assumption that the royals have a birthright to rule over the rest of us.

Superficially, the symbolic grandeur of the modern coronation may have matched that of its post-war predecessor, but something important had changed about the country. As I'd seen in other places I'd reported from, the magic of monarchy didn't work in quite the same way in the modern age. Even as people were encouraged to cheer royal pomp and circumstance,[6] a former Bank of England economist told them they needed to 'accept' becoming poorer.

The *Daily Express* front page[7] for the coronation day of 6 May 2023 struck a dour note compared with its 1953 counterpart. There were no gushing words, no reports of public celebration or illustrations of a young and energetic new monarch. Instead, there was simply a picture of the empty 14th-century oak chair where the 74-year-old Charles was to be crowned. At its foot was a three-word slogan as ominous as those used to flag bloody battles ahead in *Game of Thrones*: 'Day of destiny', the sunken headline read.

The idea that life in the UK was deteriorating badly had become a commonplace by the time King Charles III was crowned. For those who had long been poor, this was already a familiar story. What was new was that the impact of spending cuts and crumbling public services was being felt increasingly by the better off. Sewage in waterways, councils going bust and ballooning National Health Service waiting lists affect almost everyone. The result is what some observers have waspishly described[8] as the 'Great Noticing' of the country's long-standing problems by those previously insulated from them.

The dysfunction has even affected those outside the UK. During the summer of 2022, one of my relatives was caught in the vortex of delay in issuing new British passports – and many people had far worse experiences. The wait is particularly nervous if you live overseas. You have to send the old document to the UK, and so you can't travel anywhere until the new one arrives, perhaps many weeks later.

Those who disputed Britain's sharp national turn towards gloom found themselves mocked or portrayed as out of touch. A commenter[9] on a *Guardian* opinion piece deploring the quality of Britain's governance unwisely observed that 'overall the UK is pretty brilliant really'. One of the many retorts to this, under the user name ROBDOLPHIN66G, gave a long list of counterpoints with which innumerable other Britons would agree.

> Brilliant?
> Is that if you ignore, schools and hospitals in danger of collapse, the NHS, public transport outside of London, vast swathes of workers taking industrial action, food banks, FPTP [the first past the post election system], corruption amongst the government, routine discharge of sewage into our waterways, falling living standards, increasing levels of inequality, the [Metropolitan] police, social care, the monarchy, the cost of living and companies profiteering from it.

Those who have been watching closely have chronicled how the roots of the UK's current malaise stretch back to supposedly more benign times. In June 2023, a group of academics highlighted Britain's structural shortcomings in a book called *When Nothing Works: From Cost of Living to Foundational Liveability*.[10] It examined the long-term stagnation of the economy and wages – and the lack of action to deal with it.

'The current "cost of living crisis" has a prehistory in the 2010s and it's about more than household disposable and residual income,'

Karel Williams, one of the book's authors, has written.[11] 'The three pillars of household liveability – income, essential services and social infrastructure – are all crumbling. This requires some thought about our political response because we cannot expect too much from the central state.'

Important aspects of the country's finances have benefited the better off most. In an era of growing hardship for poorer people, governments have often prioritised cutting taxes at the expense of funding public services. Almost 30 per cent of children lived in poverty[12] in 2021–2, according to the Child Poverty Action Group. This was in a country where the number of billionaires had soared during the pandemic,[13] a 2022 report by the Equality Trust charity said.

The decaying buildings of Parliament itself have become a crushingly obvious metaphor for the breakdown of British public life. The Palace of Westminster is leaking and spending up to £2m a week on fixing problems. There was a 'real and rising risk' it would be destroyed by a catastrophic event, the House of Commons public accounts committee warned in May 2023.[14] The implementation of a planned refurbishment kept being deferred, just like the wider changes a growing number of people felt the country needed.

The only answer many politicians seem to have to the scale of the crisis is to deny or play down problems. Some have responded to concerns about the cost of living or decaying social services by suggesting people get used to it. It seems to be a way of deflecting responsibility by implying there is something pampered in making the complaint.

The UK's departure from the EU accelerated this trend towards a tyranny of low expectations. As far back as 2018, Brexit secretary Dominic Raab adopted the language of disaster emergency. He promised that authorities would 'make sure that there's adequate food supplies' if no deal were reached with the EU. Such modest ambitions were a far cry from the Brexit bonanza promised by the Leave campaign.

Perhaps the most vivid example[15] of recalibration of ambitions came from David Davis when he was Brexit secretary. In February 2018, he denied that leaving the EU would mean the UK would be 'plunged into a Mad Max-style world borrowed from dystopian fiction'. It seemed unusual to offer reassurance by linking the consequences of Brexit to a film series about war, societal collapse and deadly fights for resources. That his speech was delivered to a group of Austrian business leaders added to the weirdness.

It all serves the political purpose of lowering the bar for what constitutes success – and thus normalising what might otherwise be seen as objectionable. In May 2023, the discharge of sewage by water companies into rivers and the sea was causing widespread public outrage. Former minister Damian Green reminisced on national television about how he used to swim in sewage in South Wales as a youngster. His tone was gentle and nostalgic, giving a strangely soothing edge to his tale of kids wading through shit. It was 'sort of regarded as acceptable', he reflected, even though 'of course it wasn't'.

'I am absolutely not denying it's a big issue,' he said. 'But it always has been.'

Whether Green intended it or not, the connection he drew between pollution more than 50 years ago and today looked like sophistry. It gave the impression of a problem that had existed continuously between then and now. In fact, the cleanliness of UK coastal waters had improved dramatically[16] over the preceding decades. By omitting that crucial context, Green seemed to lessen the government's responsibility for the decline since. The fact that the higher standards had been driven in part by the EU's Blue Flag scheme – which promoted quality of beaches, safety and environmental education – added to the political piquancy.

A similar blame-shifting can be seen in responses to the rise in food poverty as wages have stagnated and inflation has surged. Some politicians have proposed cheap menus for people to make at home. In May 2022, Tory MP Lee Anderson claimed householders should be able to prepare meals for 30p, but couldn't because many were unable to cook. Less than a year later, Anderson was rewarded with the post of Conservative Party deputy chairman.

Anderson's framing inverts Jean-Jacques Rousseau's fictional princess saying of poor people, 'Let them eat brioches' (the advice commonly – if probably wrongly – attributed to Marie Antoinette). But Anderson's comments are just as contemptuous in their way. That they come from an MP who is able to dine in heavily subsidised Westminster canteens adds to the insult. A parliamentary restaurant menu widely circulated[17] on social media, apparently from 2019, offers every main course for less than £10 – including ribeye steak.

Disturbing but remediable developments in Britain are sometimes portrayed as catastrophes that require radical spending cuts. Reframing problems in apocalyptic terms in this way frees the space for policies that would otherwise be widely opposed. It is a tactic commonly deployed by advocates for axing public services they claim Britain can no longer afford. The Conservative–Liberal Democrat coalition formed in 2010 used it brutally as they sought to justify slashing basic services after the 2008 financial crisis. That year Prime Minister David Cameron claimed Labour had 'maxed out our nation's credit card'.[18] It was an absurd assertion, since much government debt had long repayment terms and interest rates were falling to near zero.

The coalition was helped hugely by a piece of grotesquely misjudged flippancy by Labour Treasury minister Liam Byrne. He wrote, 'I'm afraid there is no money' in a note for his successor. The paper was later flourished publicly by Cameron as evidence of Labour's supposed irresponsibility. It helped the Conservatives prepare the ground for billions of pounds of cuts, making it surely one of the most costly jokes in British political history.

The habit of embellishing crises to drive through measures many voters would otherwise find repellent is now deeply entrenched in British politics. A May 2023 *Telegraph* column headline declared, 'The NHS already gives Britain third-world healthcare.' It added that the health service's performance was 'set to get worse'.

To describe Britain as 'third world' is both unserious and offensive to the countries to which the writer was referring (in addition, the term 'third world' is widely seen as derogatory in itself). It seemed to be a way of suggesting that the NHS is irredeemably flawed. That in turn lays the ground to argue that the service is 'just not working any more' – and so needs to be privatised.

Whatever the NHS's problems, the argument fails to acknowledge the reality of state healthcare provision in some poor countries. Affording services and accessing basic drugs is an impossibility for some. When I lived in Nigeria in the early and mid-2000s, how to pay for healthcare caused anxiety to everyone outside the moneyed elite. Having access to £100 could literally be a matter of life and death. I ended up funding what were then revolutionary antiretroviral drugs for HIV for someone I knew.

A more valid lesson to draw from Nigeria is how financial inequalities leave a disturbing number of citizens living on the brink of disaster. One of the most shocking figures I remember learning early in my *Financial Times* career was about how many Britons have no or negligible savings. More than a quarter have less than £100, according to a survey[19] published in 2022 by the Money & Pensions Service (MaPS). This suggests about 14 million people living without a financial safety net, said MaPS, which is sponsored by the government's Department for Work and Pensions. That is millions of people who are one life setback – or even a sudden gas bill increase – from catastrophe.

*

It all provided a disturbing backdrop to the nine months of ceremonials between Elizabeth's death and Charles's coronation. The period reminded me of Thailand's long handover from King Bhumibol to his son. Bhumibol's regal history had a striking congruence with Elizabeth's. For many years, the pair stood together atop lists of the world's longest-reigning living monarchs, far ahead of any other competition. In the end, her reign would surpass his by just 88 days.

The duo's simultaneous extended rules led to a personal entwinement that built on long-standing links between the two royal houses. In the 19th-century Queen Victoria had corresponded with King Mongkut – the subject of the book and film *The King and I* (long banned in Thailand). Elizabeth had welcomed Bhumibol[20] to Britain on his arrival at London's Victoria Station in 1960. She visited Thailand in 1972 and 1996, watching a procession of royal barges on the Chao Phraya river in Bangkok. Thailand's royal platinum jubilee congratulations to Elizabeth noted the 'cordiality and mutual esteem' that existed between the two monarchs.

The extended reigns in Bangkok and London offered other telling consonances. Like Elizabeth, Bhumibol was projected to the public as a source of continuity and stability for the nation. In 1992, he had famously ended a protest against military rule by lecturing both the demonstration leader and the junta chief on live TV. Both Bhumibol and Elizabeth demonstrated how longevity is perhaps the crudest but most effective tool monarchies use to build legitimacy. The more time you stick around, the deeper you penetrate into the minds of the public – or, in royalty's demeaning language, your 'subjects'. This constant background presence is crucial to inspiring devotion, or at least acquiescence. Royal events became waystations in everyone's own experiences of aging and mortality.

This applies whether or not you support the idea of monarchy. Queen Elizabeth provided one of my earliest memories, whether it is innate or has lodged in my mind through being recounted to me. I attended a street party in Bingham near Nottingham for her silver jubilee in 1977. I was just under three years old and wore a pirate hat.

Whatever the ultimate source of the 'memory', the point is that it is permanently in my consciousness. So are the wedding of Charles and Diana in 1981 and the journey of Diana's funeral cortege along London's Finchley Road in 1997. I even briefly met the Queen herself during her visit to Nigeria for the 2003 Commonwealth summit.[†]

All this meant that I watched the reaction to Bhumibol's death in Thailand with a sense of foreshadowing. It struck me that it would be like what would follow Elizabeth's passing in the UK. I thought her departure would have a more profound effect than many people seemed to realise. People spoke of Bhumibol as a father figure much as some British mourners would later honour Elizabeth as a kind of mother of the nation.

I was not surprised by the size of the queue extending along the River Thames to see Elizabeth's coffin in Westminster Hall. Long lines to honour Bhumibol had stretched outside Bangkok's Grand Palace, where a monarchist mob had lynched protesters against the military dictatorship in 1976. Just as for Elizabeth's coronation, waiting in the rain became a marker of loyalty – and a way of binding people to the royal institution.

The acclaim for Elizabeth and Bhumibol had further common threads. Both drew wide praise for avoiding public scandal and supposedly exhibiting exemplary conduct. Even some foreign visitors to Thailand would confidently recount how Bhumibol was universally loved, just as the country's politics turned deadly under army rulers he had backed. Like Elizabeth, he was discreet in his public statements, allowing people to project on to him any qualities they wanted – or were told.

[†]   Elsewhere in the line of royal introductions was a Nigerian oil-state governor who later fled the UK to avoid money-laundering charges.

The truth in both cases was more complicated. The two monarchs operated sharply to protect the status and wealth of their families. Bhumibol signed off on his country's frequent coups by the military, including the 2006 ousting of a premier elected with a big mandate just the previous year. Meanwhile, an opaque organisation called the Crown Property Bureau was estimated to have tens of billions of dollars' worth of property and shareholdings. The amount was unknown because it never published full accounts.

In the UK, the law-making process quietly worked in the monarchy's favour. Elizabeth received advance warning of bills going through Parliament and had the right to push for changes to them. She appeared to have successfully lobbied[21] the government to stop details of her riches being published.

Like Elizabeth for the British, Bhumibol had been the only monarch most Thais had known. He had journeyed with them from the aftermath of the Second World War to the digital age. But the country's political realities – and his role in them – were becoming more difficult to ignore. In 2010, soldiers killed more than 90 people to end the occupation of part of central Bangkok by anti-government protesters. No one was held accountable – and in 2014 the king approved another military putsch.

The tensions had intensified because Thailand's 'South-East Asian tiger' boom had faded. The country had enjoyed rapid expansion during decades of Bhumibol's reign as a production centre for goods from autos to computer hard drives. The surge had since ebbed and the worry was the country would be caught in the so-called 'middle income trap', as its population aged. It would – in a term now used by economists sceptical about China's growth prospects – get old before it got rich. As the old king ailed in a Bangkok hospital, it felt like the whole country was gripped by anxiety about what would follow him.

*

By the summer of 2022, the political mood in the UK was similarly grim. In July, Prime Minister Boris Johnson succumbed to an uprising by his own ministers and resigned, ending three tumultuous years in power. In August, *The Economist* ran a piece headlined 'Almost nothing seems to be working in Britain. It could get worse.' The very next month, Liz Truss took power. Two days after that, Queen Elizabeth II died.

Once the mourning period was over, Truss was forced to quit within weeks over her financial programme. It was an inauspicious start to the reign of King Charles III. At his first audience with Truss after the budget debacle, the monarch did not appear able to contain his feelings.[22] 'Back again?' he remarked to the prime minister as she entered the room. When she replied, 'It's a great pleasure', he muttered, 'Dear, oh dear. Anyway . . .'

Many would have echoed the king's gut reaction, but it still seemed an odd way for a supposedly neutral monarch to greet the premier. This mattered because of the often unfavourable comparisons made between Charles and his mother. He would always struggle to match her popularity – in part because of his divorce from Diana, but also because of his outspokenness.[†]

This aspect of Charles's ascent to the throne had echoes of Thailand's succession story. Maha Vajiralongkorn, King Bhumibol's son, had been Crown Prince and designated heir since the 1970s. Since then, the prince, who was educated at the UK's Millfield School, had generated public dislike and even fear over many incidents of erratic behaviour. Less than two years previously, he had divorced his third wife, Srirasmi. Several of her family members were jailed under the country's lese-majesté laws.

The scrutiny of Vajiralongkorn showed how modernity and the technological advances it had brought threatened the image of the Thai

---

† This included writing letters in distinctive 'black spider' handwriting to lobby government ministers.

monarchy. The same applied to their British counterparts. Both royal families have had to reckon with the way the internet has taken their behaviour global. Vajiralongkorn's luxurious life in Germany, where he has increasingly based himself, has attracted growing attention thanks to digital devices. Smartphone cameras, flight tracking data and social media commentators have made a public record unlike any that could be assembled during the analogue age.

Over in London, a photo circulated widely online fuelled criticism of Elizabeth's second son, Andrew, over his association with the late child abuser Jeffrey Epstein. It showed the royal with his arm around the waist of Virginia Giuffre, who accused Epstein of trafficking her for sex as a teenager. The prince paid an undisclosed sum in 2022 to settle sexual assault allegations brought against him by Giuffre. (Andrew has denied any wrongdoing.)

Prince Andrew attended his brother's coronation despite having been stripped of his military titles and royal patronages in 2022.[23] He was far from being the only jarring presence at the event. The invitees showed how the world's monarchs stick together on the global stage, whatever controversies they may be entangled in at home.

Coronation guest Sultan Hassanal Bolkiah took the throne of the tiny South-East Asian nation of Brunei in 1967, following his father's abdication. He has ruled with absolute power since. When Elizabeth died in September 2022, he became the world's longest-ruling living monarch. His reign has been marked by scandals involving the country's finances. He was once embroiled in an embarrassing legal dispute in which he alleged his brother Prince Jefri had embezzled $14.8bn from the country's investment agency. (Prince Jefri denied wrongdoing and settled the case in 2000 by agreeing to return assets.)

The extravagant lifestyles of the sultan and his family have for decades raised questions about how oil-rich Brunei's revenues are managed. The

Daily Mirror pointed to this in a preview of the UK coronation.[24] 'As absolute monarch, there is a lot of confusion around where the sultan's private wealth ends and the national finances of Brunei begin,' it said.

The observation is hardly unique to Brunei. The British monarchy's finances lack transparency – and receive preferential treatment. The family has acquired enormous land and property holdings over years. UK royals started paying some taxes in the early 1990s, but are still exempt from levies that apply to all other citizens – including inheritance tax.

The world's monarchies help each other out financially, with Gulf royals a particular source of largesse. In 2022, claims emerged that the then Prince Charles had received €3m[25] in cash in bags and a suitcase from a former premier of Qatar. Charles's office said the money from Sheikh Hamad bin Jassim bin Jaber al-Thani in 2015 was immediately deposited with one of the royal's charities. (Neither Charles nor Sheikh Hamad are accused of any illegality.)

The transaction was a small example of how little is known about the finances of the UK royals, compared with other public bodies. A *Guardian* investigation published in the weeks before the coronation estimated King Charles's wealth at about £1.8bn. Charles's spokesperson dismissed the figures as a 'highly creative mix of speculation, assumption and inaccuracy', but offered no further detail. (Buckingham Palace didn't respond to a request for comment for this book.)

The *Guardian* claimed Charles and his mother, Elizabeth, had received an inflation-adjusted £1.2bn in share dividends since she took the throne in 1952. This is all in addition to the annual £86m public grant to the family and the big tax breaks on income from the hereditary estates. In addition, the royals have received fabulous gifts from governments and other monarchies, ranging from mint South-East Asian stamps to a Salvador Dalí etching.

The status of royal possessions remains, as in other monarchies, a grey area in some cases. The Royal Collection, which contains more than a million objects, describes itself as being held in trust by the sovereign 'for his successors and the nation'.[26]

A sense of indulgence hung heavily over the planning for the coronation ceremony. The media was full of stories about the golden tunic and other extravagant clothes worn by King Charles. Instead of using the opportunity to inject a dose of humility into the rituals, the monarch flaunted excess. Informational articles on objects such as the bejewelled coronation coach risked having an unintended subversive effect. They provoked comparisons that the British state might have been better off not inviting. The swords and sceptres made a gilded counterpoint to the hardships facing people who were struggling to put food on the table.

Some of the efforts that were made to update the event highlighted the difficulties in reinventing the royals. For the coronation of Queen Camilla, the ceremony's organisers had opted not to use a crown that contains the Koh-i-Noor diamond. The gem was taken from what is now India during British imperial rule – and is the subject of growing calls for its return. But the designated alternative created problems of its own. It contained diamonds cut from the so-called Cullinan stone mined in South Africa in the early 20th century. The gem was the booty of empire, since it was gifted by the country's colonial government to King Edward VII.

In Thailand, royal riches have increasingly become a touchstone for dissent. In 2018, the Crown Property Bureau announced that all its assets would be transferred to King Vajiralongkorn personally. This appeared to contradict the Thai government's long-standing insistence that the bureau held wealth in trust for the people, rather than the monarch.

In 2020, the Crown Property Bureau became a major focus of the unprecedented street rallies for reform of the monarchy. Protesters called for a reversal of the 2018 asset transfer to the king. Many demonstration leaders were arrested and an apparently rattled Vajiralongkorn began spending more time in Bangkok. He even made a rare public remark, telling a foreign journalist who asked about the protesters that 'we love them all the same'. Thailand was a 'land of compromise', he added – a twist on the cliche that the kingdom is the 'land of smiles'.

Vajiralongkorn's seemingly mild response carried a lesson for how both the Thai and the UK authorities have tried to deal with criticism of the monarchy. Public relations are the preferred option, but state coercion looms in the background if needed. The oppressiveness is much greater in Thailand than in the UK – but the difference seems one of degree, not substance.

That's why experiences like those of the Thai MP Chonthicha are relevant to Britain. Her matter-of-fact manner belies the seriousness of the subjects she is confronting – and the risks involved. It is sometimes disconcerting to hear her give a little peal of laughter as she talks about campaigns that could see her imprisoned for decades.

Chonthicha started her campaign for political rights young. She was a student of barely 20 when she joined protests against the 2014 military coup that had ousted the elected government. In 2015, she was one of a group of activists charged with sedition for demonstrating against the junta. The case had still not been brought to trial eight years later.

By 2020, Chonthicha had years of activist experience to draw on. She quickly established herself as a charismatic spokesperson when the street demonstrations for reform of the monarchy broke out. Her yellow rain poncho stood out with cinematic intensity[27] against the darkness as she gave interviews during a November 2020 march to Bangkok's Grand Palace.

Like fellow advocates of royal reforms, Chonthicha stresses that she has never campaigned for the abolition of the monarchy. In common with many others, she calls instead for the scrapping of the lese-majesté law that stifles discussion of the royals. In September 2023, the law was used to jail Arnon Nampa, one of the country's most high-profile activists, for four years.[28]

The two lese-majesté charges Chonthicha faces relate in part to subjects that have resonances with UK debates over royal powers and privileges. One concerned a letter she wrote to King Vajiralongkorn raising questions about how the monarchy uses public funds and exercises power under the constitution; the second was about a speech she gave concerning a 2019 decree that gave the palace direct control[29] over two military units.[†]

There are further parallels with Britain in the ten royal reform demands issued by demonstrators during the Thai protests. The list, compiled by students at Thammasat University,[30] includes calls to cut royal propaganda and public funding for the family. Other items highlight how sinister repression related to royal matters has become in Thailand as it has been allowed to grow unchecked. The campaigners wanted investigations into disappearances and murders of critics of the monarchy. In one notorious case, the cement-stuffed corpses of two activists who had fled to neighbouring Laos were dredged up from the Mekong river in 2018.

Chonthicha continues to walk a perilous path as she tries to campaign while avoiding crossing red lines of criticism. These are not defined and can be set arbitrarily. She is finding life in Parliament quite an adjustment, she laughs. 'I have more power and more responsibility,' she says. 'I have to be careful of everything I say – and I have to be careful of everything I do.'

The Thai establishment's hard-line reaction to the rallies for reforms of the monarchy has come as no surprise to her. There seems very little sign of authorities following King Vajiralongkorn's injunction to love the protesters the same as everyone else.

[†]   UK monarchs technically remain commanders-in-chief of the armed forces, although they do not exercise those powers.

Chonthicha says she runs the risks she does because she believes people deserve the right to talk about the monarchy and its position in society. She sees no reason why royals should be spared the accountability expected of others.

'I never thought we would be able to organise mass protests in the centre of Bangkok to call for the reform of the monarchy,' she says. 'Many, many people want to change the country in the same way as us – and it gives me hope.'

Britain's flurry of royal events in 2022 and 2023 offered a snapshot of how the state buttresses the monarchy – and heads off criticism. Queen Elizabeth's platinum jubilee, her funeral and Charles's coronation triggered a rush of publications in honour of them. A book on Charles called *The Boy Who Would Be King* was billed in its publicity as a 'poetic celebration of our new monarch'. It was the work of a heavyweight duo: the writer Sir Michael Morpurgo and the artist Michael Foreman.

Morpurgo had penned a book the previous year for the Queen's platinum jubilee. At the time, the government also sent schools millions of copies of a book that emphasised Elizabeth's charitable works and 'dignity and commitment' to the public.

The publicity on Amazon for the King Charles tribute purred about its subject's virtues. It claimed his 'devoted' conservation work would 'continue to inspire the protection of our planet for future generations' (it didn't mention his contentious advocacy of homeopathic medicine). The blurb continued:

This allegorical story tells how – with the help of a tiny acorn – a wise old woman gives a lonely boy, who would be king, the courage and determination to change the world for the better, for everyone.

This sentimental treatment jarred with the harshness shown to those who wanted to protest against Charles's crowning and the system of birthright privilege it represented. In the run-up to the event, authorities had insisted that they would respect the right to demonstrate. Yet two days before the ceremony the Metropolitan Police warned that its 'tolerance for disruption' and 'undermining the celebration' would be 'low'.

The police detained a number of people before the ceremony. Those arrested included women distributing rape alarms under a government-funded initiative, as well as demonstrators from the pressure group Republic. An Australian fan of the monarchy who happened to be standing near the protesters was picked up by mistake. It added to the sense that no one was to be allowed to cause embarrassment to Charles on his big day at Westminster Abbey. The Met later expressed 'regret'[31] over the Republic arrests. Five months later, it said no further action would be taken against any of the 21 people detained at the time of the coronation.[32]

Inside the abbey, Archbishop of Canterbury Justin Welby provided religious justification for the new monarch's temporal power. Welby, an old Etonian, had himself made an interesting journey to the spiritual life, from the very material world of the extractive industries. He once worked for the oil companies Elf Aquitaine and Enterprise Oil, including on projects in West Africa.

I had met Welby in Nigeria in the mid-2000s, including over dinner in Lagos. He was working there as a Coventry Cathedral canon on resolving community conflicts with the oil industry. It was a world of violence, corruption and mass deprivation amid riches for the few, in which Western multinationals were deeply implicated.

As archbishop, Welby had appointed a special representative for conflict in sub-Saharan Africa. His choice was Precious Omuku, a former head of public relations for Shell in Nigeria. It felt disorienting to find these former oilmen embedded at the heart of the Church of England, now headed by Charles III.

Welby's office, Lambeth Palace, had drawn criticism ahead of the coronation for its efforts to promote vocal enthusiasm for the new monarch. It 'invited' the audience to join for the first time a public 'chorus of millions' during the ceremony, pledging allegiance to Charles. It hoped this 'homage of the people' would yield 'a great cry around the nation and around the world of support for the King', though the call for the pledge was toned down at the last minute.

Commentators made much of the beauty of the coronation service, although it should hardly have been otherwise at an estimated cost of at least £50m. People were certainly prepared to be swept away. As one *Observer* writer put it,[33] 'Only a stone-hearted person could fail to have been moved by the multifaith parts of the service, and if you felt nothing when the choir sang Handel's *Zadok the Priest* at the king's anointment, you are either an algorithm or half dead.'

The singing was indeed stunning and evocative, even via a slightly dodgy internet connection in a densely packed Tokyo neighbourhood of modern apartment blocks. But it should be possible – and indeed normal – to appreciate great art without necessarily endorsing the political ideas it is promoting. It is surely hardly news that it is possible for a performance, or indeed a person, to be both beautiful and highly manipulative.

The crucial part of the coronation ceremony was how – even well into the 21st century – it reasserted the divine right of British monarchs to rule. At one point, a screen was erected to hide Charles from view as the Archbishop of Canterbury anointed him with a perfumed oil. The unguent came from groves on the Mount of Olives in Jerusalem, near the burial place of Charles's grandmother, Princess Alice of Greece. It demonstrated the 'strong historic link between the Coronation, The Old Testament and the Holy Land', according to the ceremony's official notes.

The straining for symbolism served only to illustrate that there is nothing inevitable about hereditary rule. Beneath the Coronation Chair lay the so-called Stone of Destiny. It was transported from Edinburgh Castle for the occasion and is an ancient symbol of Scotland's monarchy.[34]

Yet the name is misleading. It is not fate that royalty exists – nor indeed the union between England and Scotland. Their legitimacy is highly contingent. It depends on sufficient people accepting, or at least tolerating, their continued existence.

Much of the coronation pomp hides similarly mundane realities. Online commentators enjoyed the fancy outfits and florid names of the attendant pursuivants, an ancient heraldic title. But the holders of offices such as Unicorn, Bluemantle and Portcullis have lives far removed from the high regal diplomacy of their predecessors. The Rouge Dragon pursuivant, for example, is a graphic designer[35] who has worked at the British Academy of Film and Television Arts (BAFTA).

Opinion polls suggest a majority of Britons still want the country to retain the royal family. But support has been shrinking and is lowest among younger people. Meanwhile Commonwealth countries including Barbados and Belize are either ditching the British monarch as head of state, or considering doing so. The premier of the Caribbean island nation of St Kitts and Nevis offered a tart response to the coronation. He commented that his country was 'not totally free' while Charles was its head of state.

The pressure on the established royally-headed order has been growing in Thailand, too. In the May 2023 general election, voters delivered a humiliation of the traditional conservative establishment. The two main opposition parties, Move Forward and Pheu Thai, won more than two-thirds of the votes.

As the wheeling and dealing to build a governing coalition unfolded, rumblings about the role of royalty continued to be heard. Thai authorities banned a forthcoming book[36] on King Vajiralongkorn, who is known as

Rama X, through an order published in the royal gazette. The notice said that *Rama X: The Thai Monarchy under King Vajiralongkorn* showed the authors' intention to defame the royals or 'undermine national security, social stability or good morals'. The book's editor, Pavin Chachavalpongpun, an academic living in exile in Japan, highlighted the absurdity of the situation. 'My book has been banned despite the fact that nobody has read it,' he wrote plaintively on Facebook.

The Thai monarchy was embroiled deep in politics again a few months later. I was in the northern city of Chiang Mai when the king cut the jail sentence of the billionaire former Prime Minister Thaksin Shinawatra. This was big news. Thaksin, who used to own Manchester City, had just returned after 15 years of self-exile and been imprisoned for eight years on corruption charges that he claimed were trumped up. Vajiralongkorn commuted that to one.

Hours after the king's move, Thaksin's Pheu Thai party agreed to form a government with parties linked to its long-time enemies in the army. The deal sparked cries of betrayal from some Thaksin loyalists, who had long seen him as being on the people's side against the traditional military-monarchy establishment. The sequence of events looked choreographed – and the king played a crucial role in it.[†]

Few Thais dared to talk to me plainly about the king's role in the political developments – and certainly no one wanted to be quoted on it by name. Some made veiled references to the influence in the Thaksin case of 'another person' or 'someone else'. It underlined that, while Thailand is officially a constitutional monarchy, there is a lot going on behind the apolitical façade.

[†]   The UK monarch still retains a power of criminal pardon. It has been used in cases such as that of Alan Turing, the mathematician and Second World War codebreaker convicted of gross indecency for consensual gay sex.

On my last night in Chiang Mai, I went to buy mango and sticky rice. The server asked where I was from. When I told her, she said, 'King Charles? Like our king.'

'Why?' I asked.

'Many wives,' she said with a twinkle in her eye.

Her judgement was a bit hard on Charles. He only has one divorce behind him, whereas Vajiralongkorn is on to his fourth marriage. The comment was a measure, perhaps, of how the split with Diana – and her death a few years later – had become a global story. It showed, too, how monarchs club together not only among themselves but in the public mind.

The two reigns in the UK and Thailand say something about both royalty's enduring power and its underlying fragility. The long tenures of previous incumbents have held the status quo together, but perhaps at the expense of delaying necessary reform. That has created a misleading aura of unchangeability and unending stability.

From King John's 1215 agreement to Magna Carta on, British monarchs have learned the value of making limited political concessions to ensure their long-term survival. They have ruled for all but the 11 years after the 1649 execution of Charles I – or King Charles the Martyr, as per the Tunbridge Wells church (see page 8). They have fought, ousted and killed each other, but the institution has remained intact.

Now the third Charles faces the more subtle threat of withering legitimacy. Whatever the arguments for and against monarchy in Britain, its special financial status and privileged protocols feel increasingly uncomfortable in a modern society. Shows of material excess like the coronation jar at a time of suffering for many citizens. Even the pared-down pomp stood out.

If royalty is a barometer of the health of UK public life, then the coronation did not feel like a particularly auspicious event. The ceremony seemed to speak to an official desperation to be seen to be 'putting the great back into Britain'.[37] One British journalist argued the occasion was a 'reminder that, as a nation, we seem to be infinitely better at staging public spectacles than at governing the country'.[38] In other words, the UK was a nation that increasingly excelled at diversions but failed at essentials. I found myself wondering if it was possible that these two phenomena were somehow linked.

Britons are at least able to debate the royals' role and behaviour. It is crucial to make the most of that freedom as Charles's reign unfolds. It doesn't exist in Thailand or in the authoritarian Gulf monarchies where I have worked, such as the United Arab Emirates, Saudi Arabia and Qatar.

The British police excesses at the coronation were a lesson about the direction events could take without vigilance. The arrests came after the 2022 Police, Crime, Sentencing and Courts Act and the 2023 Public Order Act widened official powers to crack down on demonstrations. The joint parliamentary human rights committee has warned[39] that such recent legislation is likely to 'have a chilling effect on the right to protest in England and Wales'.[40]

Thai campaigners for royal reforms are all too familiar with the risks of what they do. Chonthicha Jangrew says she and fellow activists have looked at how monarchies work elsewhere, including in Japan and the UK. When I ask what she thinks about the British situation, she says she is 'a little jealous'. No one is being handed jail terms – although she's aware of the coronation arrests and she regrets that it's 'not easy' for campaigners for change.

It's a reminder both of the latitude for dissent Britons still enjoy and of the importance of maintaining and using it. The existence of robust debate around a royal family says something about the health of a country – and its ability to adapt to changing times.

'If the monarchy doesn't have transparency, people will have questions, people will gossip,' Chonthicha says, in remarks about Thailand that could apply to the UK. 'If we have checks and balances, maybe we will have a better relationship between the monarchy and the people.'

4

Flawed Prophets

Liz Truss swept back into British politics as if she were an aspirant prime minister rather than the shortest-ever holder of the office. Almost a year to the day after her disastrous seven-week tenure began in September 2022, she offered little sense of self-reflection – and certainly no apology.

During her brief time in Downing Street, Truss had vowed to 'ride out the storm' of economic crisis and turn Britain into an 'aspiration nation'. Instead, the tempest easily outpaced her. Financial markets took fright at the unfunded tax cuts she and her Chancellor Kwasi Kwarteng proposed – and the chaos forced both of them out. Truss left power quoting the Roman philosopher Seneca[1] to suggest the country had failed to show sufficient daring to succeed.

The commentary from outside Britain was not so highfalutin – and much less forgiving of the role played by Truss and her predecessors. A column in Canada's *Globe and Mail*[2] thundered that the UK's political system had in recent years thrust 'dunces and charlatans into command'. The *Washington Post* editorial board[3] offered the painful damnation of pity to the rulers of what it said 'looks increasingly like an isolated Atlantic island state'. 'Britain should be more than an exporter of royal gossip and lurid political news,' it wrote.

A year on, Truss had a very different take on events. She seemed to have developed a strong sense of herself as the victim of a fiasco rather than its lead author. She attacked a nebulous 'anti-growth coalition' for opposing her plans and causing her leadership to flame out.

'The anti-growth coalition is now a powerful force, comprising the economic and political elite, corporatist parts of the media, and even a section of the Conservative parliamentary party,' she told an audience[4] at the Institute for Government. 'The policies I advocate simply are not fashionable on the London dinner-party circuit.'

Truss is not stupid. Her speech included the minor apparent self-criticisms key to making self-exculpation plausible. She regretted that she hadn't communicated her ideas better. Some of her points doubled as humblebrags. She said she perhaps moved too fast because – she claimed tendentiously – her proposals were popular with the British people. In other words, her biggest mistake was trying too hard to give the public what they wanted.

'The reason we were in a rush was because voters wanted to see results,' she said.[5] 'I knew with the level of resistance and the lack of preparation time, that things weren't going to be perfect.'

Truss seemed undeterred by failure on a scale that would have left many people scarred with a deep sense of shame and humiliation. She even used her return to the public eye to announce she was working on a book called *Ten Years to Save the West.*[6] She said it would show the 'stark choices' needed to avoid 'managed decline' of a Western institutional architecture that has 'presided over generations of relative peace and prosperity'.

She did not note the obvious irony. The 'stark choices' she had made during her brief premiership had tipped the country into an unmanaged – and rather sharp – decline. She was proposing a ten-year programme for the West even though her leadership of the UK had not lasted ten weeks.

Truss's bold political re-entry is worth looking at in detail because it ticked off quite a few behavioural tropes in contemporary politics. She offered to reheat ideas that had already been tested and discredited. She attributed error to others, not herself. She portrayed herself as the prey of the country's establishment, rather than a member of it.

The alternative explanation of Truss's mayfly premiership is that it was a particularly vivid example of profound British political elite failure – and subsequent denial. By some strange neuron pathway, my mind went back to a memorable exchange from the cult 1980s children's BBC TV school soap opera *Grange Hill*. Cool kid Ant is consistently late for scary French teacher Mr Bronson's lessons. He claims as an excuse that another teacher, Mr Baxter, has made him late, exploiting the mutual dislike between Bronson and Baxter. The problem is that he overuses the ploy and in the end makes Bronson suspicious. 'Aaaaaah, Mr Baxter! That explains everything,' Bronson says. 'Every time you are late it is Mr Baxter's fault. Why?'[7] Bronson finally arranges a meeting with Baxter and Ant's cover is blown.

Britain's politics feel ever more Baxterised. Whatever goes wrong is never the responsibility of ministers. They blame it on someone else: lefty lawyers, woke charities, anti-Brexit civil servants or whatever other enemy it is useful to conjure up that day. The most important rule of government in the early 2020s seems to be that it is always someone else's fault.

Brexit and the ensuing years of political chaos magnified many pathologies of elite dysfunction – but the trend has been going on a lot longer. What some look back to wistfully as a better age of so-called 'grown-up politics' seems in important respects anything but. Supposedly wise elites gave us the entrenched inequalities of Thatcherism and the bloody folly of the Iraq War. These were on a continuum with the cavalier politics that yielded Brexit and the ensuing Tory leadership melodrama. Each represented a kind of hubris – and a failure to mitigate predictable negative consequences.

This top-level foundering seems a symptom of problems with UK democracy that look institutional as well as individual. From the outside, there appear to be damaging shortcomings in the country's basic systems of government. These include a lack of representativeness in the voting system and the political parties. Nor is Parliament itself immune, particularly the unelected House of Lords. A jibe heard from abroad is that the UK and Iran are the only countries that give religious leaders automatic seats in their legislatures. The observation has been repeated in the House of Commons.[8]

The flaws in British governing institutions long spoken of pridefully are becoming increasingly clear, inside the country as well as abroad. Quality democracy is supposed to be one of the UK's defining strengths, but mounting evidence seems to throw that into question. The crisis of faith has caused palpable shock among those who once basked in Britain's apparently high international reputation for how it runs itself.

'How did the birthplace of parliamentary democracy, the "mother of parliaments", and a respected voice of sense on the world stage find itself in such an unaccustomed place?' a senior executive from the public relations firm Edelman lamented in 2020, in an article entitled 'The UK: a parable of distrust'. 'What exactly precipitated this fall from grace?'[9]

Britain had early warning of the Truss experiment and its likely consequences. She was once part of an ambitious quintet of new Conservative MPs who promised their country harsh revolution followed by liberation. The others were Kwarteng, Priti Patel, Dominic Raab and Chris Skidmore.

The five outlined their tough recipe in their 2012 book *Britannia Unchained*. It is a radical text that attacks the 'bloated state, high taxes and excessive regulation'. It says Britain must 'stop indulging in irrelevant debates about sharing the pie between manufacturing and services, the north and the south, women and men'. It includes the following eye-catching passage:

The British are among the worst idlers in the world. We work among the lowest hours, we retire early and our productivity is poor. Whereas Indian children aspire to be doctors or businessmen, the British are more interested in football and pop music.

The five accused the British people they were supposed to serve of displaying a 'diminished work ethic[10] and a culture of excuses'. Promotional material for this political polemic warned that the UK 'must learn the rules of the 21st century, or we face an inevitable slide into mediocrity'.

The group's attacks on the very people they relied on for votes did them no apparent harm. All rose to ministerial office, four of them to top-level government jobs. Then, for the quartet who had flown highest, it all went wrong. Kwarteng's double act with Truss meant he lasted just 38 days in office. Raab had to resign as justice secretary after being found to have broken the ministerial code over bullying allegations, which he denied. Patel survived a finding of bullying (which she too has denied), but was brought down as home secretary after her draconian migration policy failed to reduce arrival numbers.

The fifth author, Chris Skidmore, eventually took a contrasting path. He supported Truss in the 2022 Conservative leadership election, but later that year announced he would stand down as an MP. In 2023, he warned that some Tories wanted to take the party 'in a very dark direction'.[11]

Britannia Unchained was a significant waystation in the evolution of an important trend. Its authors presented themselves as disruptors to conventional thinking, yet were very much of the establishment. All except Patel went to Oxford or Cambridge universities (Raab attended both). All worked in conservative think tanks or as aides to Tory politicians before entering Parliament.

The five are not Britain's only self-proclaimed scourges of the status quo to have strong establishment ties. This inconvenient truth runs counter to an image of the UK as less prone to nepotism and groupthink than countries with more obviously dynastic politics. Britain's political elite is in some respects strikingly narrow, even if the ties within it tend to be ones of culture rather than kin.

British politics seem to me to suffer from the same dangerous disconnect that I have seen in other places I've lived and worked in. Many privileged people are alienated from the lives of their fellow citizens. This can hobble efforts to redress social injustices. In Thailand, I listened to urban pro-monarchist 'yellow shirts' dismissing their rural 'red shirt' political opponents as ignorant – or even 'buffaloes'. In Nigeria, the poverty and pollution of the oil-producing Niger Delta were remote from Lagos's high society.

The UK is one of many democracies worldwide that draw their ruling classes from shallow pools – until it gets too much for voters to stomach. In Sri Lanka, five members of the Rajapaksa family sat in the same cabinet until 2022. Then public protests at economic hardship erupted and forced President Gotabaya Rajapaksa from office.

The modern political history of India, often touted as the world's largest democracy, is interwoven with that of the Nehru-Gandhi family. Jawaharlal Nehru became prime minister on independence in 1947. He, his daughter Indira Gandhi and his grandson Rajiv Gandhi held the top job for all but a few years until 1989. Nehru's Indian National Congress party has since been led by Sonia Gandhi, Rajiv's widow, and their son Rahul Gandhi. (Mallikarjun Kharge has been president of the party[12] since October 2022 – the first non-member of the family for 24 years to hold this position.)

Congress's clannishness helped enable the rise of the Hindu nationalist Bharatiya Janata party prime minister Narendra Modi. He was once banned from the US for 'severe violations of religious freedom'. More than a thousand people, most of them Muslims, died in religious riots[13] in the state of Gujarat in 2002 when he was chief minister there. (He has denied any wrongdoing.)

The US has its own dynastic politics problem. It clearly helped Donald Trump in the 2016 election that his opponent was the wife of a former president. If Hillary Clinton had won, the country would have had a modern-day roster of presidents that read Bush, Clinton, Bush, Obama, Clinton. The posture of privileged characters like Trump against the political establishment is sustainable in part precisely because such an elite manifestly exists.

In Britain, an already pronounced social hierarchy is in some ways becoming even starker. I remember reading Anthony Sampson's landmark book *Anatomy of Britain* and being struck by the closed establishment world it described. It first came out in 1962, the year before Alec Douglas-Home became the country's third successive old Etonian prime minister.[†]

There followed a period when *Anatomy of Britain* seemed less on the mark. Five prime ministers in a row – Harold Wilson, Edward Heath, James Callaghan, Margaret Thatcher and John Major – didn't go to private schools. Callaghan and Major didn't go to university either.

But British politics has returned to type – and even more strongly than before. This has remained true even as the number of women and ethnic-minority holders of top cabinet jobs has grown. Tony Blair went to the prestigious Fettes private school in Scotland. David Cameron and Boris Johnson are both old Etonians.

Oxford University has entrenched its already extraordinary run in Downing Street, through Blair, Cameron, Theresa May, Johnson, Truss and Rishi Sunak. As of late 2023, all but one of the country's 14 university-educated prime ministers since the Second World War

---

† Churchill, the premier before that trio, went to Harrow.

have been to Oxford – only Edinburgh graduate Gordon Brown briefly broke the pattern.

The plausible manner that private schools and Oxbridge help instil can be a dangerous thing. I should know, having attended both. Extreme policies may seem more credible if they are put forward by self-confident characters such as Blair or Cameron. Private-school polish has given some tinpot ideas a fatal dazzle. People who present well and speak fluently tend to command attention,[14] even if they are advocating dubious policies.

Boris Johnson's premiership epitomised the style of spurious elite eminence – and perhaps tested it to destruction. His schtick was to create the impression that his roguishness is both human and understandable – and, crucially, more honest than other politicians. The argument has a compelling, if misleading, humility: I am no better than you, but I'm also no worse. If you convince people that everyone else is in the gutter with you, it lessens your own misdeeds.

The idea of Johnson as an almost loveable rascal became ingrained. One revealing moment came in a February 2022 edition[15] of the BBC's flagship political discussion programme *Question Time*. The journalist Tim Stanley compared the prime minister to a character in the heist film *Ocean's 11*. 'Technically he may well be a con-man and he might be the bad guy but you want to see if he gets away with it and how he did it,' Stanley said.

The show's host Fiona Bruce replied in the same indulgent spirit. 'Are you saying he's like George Clooney or Brad Pitt – which one are you choosing?' she asked.

The tongue-in-cheek tone was of a piece with Johnson's easy media ride during his rise to power and early time in office. After his December 2019 election win, *The Atlantic* ran a piece[16] headlined 'It's Boris Johnson's Britain Now' in which it predicted he could 'remake the country'. In June 2021, it followed this up with a profile slugged 'Boris Johnson knows exactly what he is doing'. It described its subject as 'a tornado of bonhomie in a country where politicians tend to be phlegmatic and self-serious, if not dour and awkward'.

It's no coincidence that Johnson's most uncomfortable interview[17] was one in which the questioner simply refused to engage with his well-practised bluster and charm. The encounter with the BBC's Eddie Mair happened way back in 2013, when Johnson was still London mayor. Mair pointed to Johnson's sackings by *The Times* for making up a quote and by Conservative Party leader Michael Howard for lying about an affair. He then questioned him on why he gave his friend Darius Guppy the address of a journalist Guppy wanted to have beaten up.

What was remarkable was that, skilful as Mair was, he was armed only with publicly available information rather than sensational new disclosures. Deprived of his most potent weapons, Johnson floundered. Mair's conclusion – 'You're a nasty piece of work, aren't you?' – seemed a rhetorical statement of the obvious given the available facts.

Mair's grilling stands out as the exception in the indulgence that helped Johnson's rise. The author Jonathan Coe sketched this out in a prophetic 2013 piece headlined 'Sinking Giggling into the Sea'. The title references words used by the late comedian Peter Cook when he warned in the 1960s of a fundamental unseriousness in British public life.

Johnson's appearances on the BBC TV comedy show *Have I Got News for You* 'cemented the public image of him as a lovable, self-mocking buffoon', Coe wrote. He continued:

In an age when politicians are judged first of all on personality, when the public assumes all of them to be deceitful, and when it's easier and much more pleasurable to laugh about a political issue than to think about it, Johnson's apparent self-deprecating honesty and lack of concern for his own dignity were bound to make him a hit.

It seems no coincidence that what did for Johnson's premiership was a matter of such seriousness he couldn't sidestep it. He was ousted after it emerged Downing Street had hosted parties that broke its own national rules against gatherings during the Covid pandemic. It was impossible to put a benign spin on illicit drinking and dancing while fellow citizens died painfully and isolated from their loved ones. Giggling was, for once, not a viable option.

Johnson's rise was an example of the considerable rewards British-style elitism has offered many of its members for failure. The year after the Brexit vote forced David Cameron's resignation, he showed up in Bangkok[18] when I was still living there. He came to give a speech to the World Travel and Tourism Summit on the subject of 'Altered states: has globalisation had its day?' He spoke about the need to listen to people's concerns on culture, border control and immigration – a Brexit campaign talking point. He 'enthralled' gathered executives on 'political and social changes in Europe and the Brexit process that he initiated as prime minister', according to one testimonial.[19] The use of the word 'initiated' made it sound as if Cameron had made a considered decision, rather than gambled the house and lost.

Liz Truss earned £80,000 from a Taiwanese think tank for delivering a speech during a visit to the island in May 2023. In it, she called on Western countries not to work with China. Her bullishness went beyond her party's policy and was condemned by Beijing. In short, it seemed like the former prime minister was being paid handsomely for a diplomatic incident. 'This is the most consequential place in the world for what is the most consequential struggle of our time,' she told her audience.

The emergence as prime minister of unsuitable candidates such as Truss and Johnson highlights a fundamental flaw with how Britain chooses its leaders. The quality of those individuals is a reflection of the troubled institutions that choose them. Both Johnson and Truss were originally the selections not of the nation, but of a Conservative Party membership numbering fewer than 200,000.

Labour has a similar problem that is only slightly less grievous. It, too, chooses its leaders by a vote of members (and supporters), under a contentious 2014 rule change.[20] It had about 432,000 members[21] as of December 2021 – or less than 0.7 per cent of the UK population.

Johnson was part of a run of four Tory leaders – and counting – who have bypassed the public on their journey to Downing Street. (Theresa May and Rishi Sunak would have faced a membership vote had they not been unopposed.) At least two of that quartet – Johnson and Truss – stoked grave doubts even among many of their own MPs about their fitness for office. This did not stop those same MPs picking them as their top choices to put before the party membership – another marker of Britain's crisis of leadership.

The modern Conservative Party's rank and file is narrow as well as small. The Tories could almost be the product of an exercise in constituting a political organisation unrepresentative of modern Britain. Statistical data on the membership is limited, but it's undisputed that it is on average significantly older, maler and whiter than the adult population at large.

The paradox is that Conservative members had no power to pick their leaders when they were part of a truly mass party. Tory membership was estimated at almost 2.9 million in 1951 and 1 million as recently as 1990, according to the House of Commons Library.[22] But now that it has shrunk to a small fraction of that size, activists have an authority of which their forebears could only have dreamed.

This is not the only aspect of the modern UK Conservatives that an outsider might find shocking. In 2019, *The Economist* ranked them the world's most successful party, in good part because of their adaptability over two centuries of frequent political dominance. The Tories ruled, alone or in coalition, for almost two-thirds of the 20th century. Labour, by contrast, never grabbed more than six years at a stretch until the governments of Tony Blair and Gordon Brown between 1997 and 2010.

Yet the Conservatives' brutal effectiveness at the polls belies a sense in which they are being hollowed out as an institution. Just as the party's membership has dwindled to a glimmer of former glories, so it is financed from a strikingly narrow base. During Johnson's first two years in office, a quarter of the Tories' individual donations came from just ten people, according to the *Independent*.[23] Most made their money in finance or property.

In 2023 the billionaire businessman Mohamed Mansour announced he had gifted £5m[24] to the Conservatives. It was the biggest individual donation they had enjoyed in more than 20 years, and more money than they had received from all sources for the last quarter of 2022. Mansour, who had been named the party's senior treasurer in December 2022, said Rishi Sunak was a 'very capable prime minister'. He added that Sunak could 'make the modern economy work for all UK citizens'.

Mansour, a naturalised British citizen, has an interesting history. He was born in Egypt and served as transport minister[25] under the dictatorship of President Hosni Mubarak from 2006 to 2009. The Mubarak regime, which had ruled since 1981, was notorious for corruption and repression of the opposition using detention, torture and other rights abuses. Barely a year after Mansour quit, Mubarak was toppled in a popular revolt after more than 30 years in power. I reported from the streets of Cairo in early 2011 as crowds chanted for the president's fall. Little did I imagine that one of his ministers would soon bankroll and hold a position in the ruling party in my home country.

Mansour's business interests have also attracted attention. His Caterpillar dealership Unatrac drew fire in 2023 when it emerged it was supplying Russia's oil and gas industry despite Western-led sanctions. Mansour later said the company had suspended its Russian operations.

Perhaps the most revealing aspect of the Mansour story is how little comment it provoked. While there is no evidence he was involved in the abusive aspects of the Mubarak government, his presence helped add to the regime's credibility. That is a matter of personal choice – but there is certainly an argument that it should be a bar to involvement in democratic politics. (A spokesperson for Man Capital, the global investment arm of the Mansour Group and the family office of Mohamed Mansour, declined comment for this book. The Conservative Party didn't respond to a request for comment.)

It is a sign of Britain's democratic institutional troubles that relationships like the Tories' with Mansour have become normalised. There is an obvious read-across with the world of English football, where takeovers by affiliates of authoritarian states and oligarchs are now commonplace. In the end, money seems to count most in the race to win, whether you are Chelsea or the Conservative Party.

Political parties, like countries, are all hypocritical to some degree about any values they claim to hold. But at the same time, they ought to have *something* other than the pursuit of office to offer to voters as a meaningful choice. Otherwise, they become empty shells to serve vested interests that may offer little or no benefit to the country at large.

When I reported on Nigerian elections in the 2000s, I was struck by the honesty of the then-ruling People's Democratic Party. The party had a call-and-response routine that well summarised its purpose. It went as follows:

Candidate: PDP!
Crowd: Power!
Candidate: PDP!
Crowd: Power!

Candidate: PDP!
Crowd: Power, power, power!

The PDP illustrated a whimsical, though surprisingly useful, rule in politics. Sometimes, a party's name can be a good indicator that its policies tend towards the opposite. The PDP wasn't as popular as it made out and it certainly wasn't very democratic: the two presidential elections it won that I covered were marred by serious ballot fraud, according to rights groups and other observers.[†]

In the same way, Britain's Conservative and Unionist Party is no longer well defined by either of those labels. Since Brexit, it has become the party of radical change and of disruption to relations between the UK's constituent nations.

Similarly, on the opposite side of the aisle, the Labour Party is in some ways moving far from its original branding. Politics professionals hold increasing sway. The number of working-class MPs on its benches has halved since the 1980s, according to the Institute for Public Policy Research.[26]

The political parties' identity crises are part of a deeper electoral malaise. The mechanisms Britain uses to choose its governments are coming in for increasing criticism. As parties multiply in number and the public's loyalties become more fluid, the outcomes yielded by the country's crude electoral system look increasingly unrepresentative.

The 'first past the post' voting arrangements have become ever more inadequate for reflecting the nation's range of opinion. It was not always so. Historically, winner-takes-all races have worked well enough in an environment of more or less two-party politics. In 1951, for example, the Tories and Labour between them secured 96.8 per cent of the vote.[27] Even

---

†   In the southern state of Rivers in 2003, I didn't witness a single vote being legitimately cast all day.

here the method introduced a distortion: Labour scored 230,000 more ballots than the Conservatives, but secured 26 fewer seats. In more modern times, first past the post has given ever more warped outcomes, reflecting political fragmentation and the significant vote hauls secured by third, fourth and fifth parties.

Labour actually benefited in the most striking modern case, which perhaps explains the leadership's reluctance to welcome calls for proportional representation. In 2005, Tony Blair's Labour government faced voters after the Iraq invasion and two terms in office. It limped in[28] with a distinctly unimpressive 35.2 per cent of the vote to the Conservatives' 32.6 per cent. Yet the alchemy of first past the post turned this into a crushing 355 seats for Labour – almost 55 per cent of the total. The Tories captured only 198, even though their vote share lagged by fewer than three percentage points.

The general election of 2015[29] is another case study of first past the post's weaknesses. This one highlighted the unfairness of the system to parties other than the big two. The routinely under-represented Liberal Democrats won barely 1 per cent of the seats on their 7.9 per cent vote share. The Greens won well over a million votes – 3.8 per cent of the total – yet took only one seat out of the 650 available.

Most eye-catching of all was the fate of the United Kingdom Independence Party (UKIP). It won just one seat – 0.0015 per cent of the total – on a 12.6 per cent vote share, or almost 3.9m ballots. How much more democratic – and better for everyone – it would have been for UKIP to have had its voice in Parliament and be tested there. Instead of having the EU membership debate at length in the House of Commons, it was turned over to the crapshoot of the referendum.

First past the post has become even more twisted with the rise of the Scottish National Party. Just as the system penalises parties like the Liberal Democrats with fairly evenly spread support, so it rewards nationalists focused on one region. In 2015, the SNP scored just 4.7 per cent of the nationwide UK vote, yet won 56 seats – 8.6 per cent of the total.

The sickness of the UK's governing institutions extends to Parliament itself. It remains an object of international amazement that Britain's upper house should still contain scores of people there by hereditary right. It is one of the sharpest retorts other countries can give when they are lectured by the UK about becoming more democratic.

Plenty of countries I've worked in have problems with their upper houses. In Thailand, all 250 members were appointed by the country's military. In Myanmar, a quarter of them *were* the country's military.[30] But, grotesque as these situations are, there were at least criteria for selection. In the UK, the qualification was simply being born.

The Blair government reduced the influence of hereditary peers without extinguishing it. Today 92 are still permitted to sit in the House of Lords out of a total of about 800 hereditary peers. They are voted in by various selection processes of the whole house or the political parties. Some even rise to become ministers. Gilbert Timothy George Lariston Elliot-Murray-Kynynmound, the 7th Earl of Minto, is one example. He was appointed a minister of state in the business department months after joining the Lords in 2022.

The earl's main business experience was as chief executive of the stationery company Paperchase between 1996 and 2018, then deputy chairman from 2018 to 2021. The business collapsed into administration in January 2023.[31] In the government reshuffle in November that year, Minto was made a minister of state at the ministry of defence.[32]

Further restrictions to hereditary peers' rights in the Lords have been resisted by the government, though such efforts enjoy considerable support in the Commons. 'Peers of all parties and none, both appointed and hereditary, agree it's time to change the system,' the Electoral Reform Society wrote after a failed 2021 effort for change.[33] 'But until the government backs reform it stands no chance of being passed in the upper house.'[†]

Hereditary peers are far from the only problem with the Lords. The shortcomings in the practice of creating life peers, which was introduced in 1958,[34] are increasingly evident. They are seen as emblematic of a rot in British politics, through which leaders reward their friends and financiers.

The appointments seem to be doing increasing damage to Britain's global standing. In 2020, Darren Hughes, the Electoral Reform Society's chief executive, posted a piece on the society's website headlined 'The unelected House of Lords is undermining Britain's reputation'. It highlighted the reaction abroad to Prime Minister Boris Johnson's creation of 36 new peers, including his own brother. 'Corruption in England deepens,' declared one Czech newspaper. Agenzia Italia noted the 'abnormal number' of members in the Lords, who it pointed out 'sometimes do not even go there'.

'There were dozens more headlines like this internationally and at home,' Hughes wrote. 'All with one clear message: Britain's unelected chamber is turning the mother of parliaments into a laughing stock.'

One of the most contentious ennoblements in that batch was Evgeny Lebedev, owner of the *Evening Standard* media organisation. Johnson was reportedly warned[35] that intelligence officials had serious reservations about the plan, though Lebedev, the Russian-born son of a former KGB officer, has denied being a 'security risk' to the UK.

The Conservative life peer Lady (Michelle) Mone, founder of the lingerie company Ultimo, has faced questions over her business dealings. It has emerged that she is linked to a company that made millions from official contracts to supply personal protective equipment during the pandemic.[36]

---

†   Labour has said it will abolish the Lords and replace it with an elected second chamber – although it may appoint new peers at first to pass the necessary legislation.

(Mone has denied any wrongdoing and has not been accused of any offence. The controversy centres on a company named PPE Medpro, which won government supply contracts worth more than £200m during the pandemic. In November 2023, Mone and her husband acknowledged for the first time[37] that they were involved with PPE Medpro. They had previously denied any link.)

None of this controversy is new, nor the sole province of either main party. In 1976, Labour premier Harold Wilson used his resignation honours list to name the textile tycoon Joseph Kagan[38] a life peer. Wilson was a friend of Kagan and wore his company's distinctive Gannex fabric raincoats, which he gifted to other world leaders. In 1980, Kagan was convicted of theft – essentially tax evasion – and sentenced to ten months in prison. He was stripped of his knighthood, but there was no mechanism to remove his peerage.

Another criminally convicted life peer, the writer and former Conservative Party deputy chairman Jeffrey Archer, is still a member of the House of Lords. In 2001, Archer was sentenced to four years in jail for perjury and perverting the course of justice. He gave false evidence during a successful 1987 libel case against the *Daily Star* newspaper after it alleged he had paid a prostitute for sex. He remains a peer and, as 'Lord Jeffrey Archer', an ambassador for Visit Somerset.[39]

The House of Lords Reform Act passed in 2014 disqualifies a peer sentenced to a year or more of imprisonment from attending parliamentary proceedings. A further law in 2015 gives the house powers to expel a member by a resolution – though, again, they cannot remove the title. The former Labour politician Lord (Nazir) Ahmed of Rotherham remains a peer despite his 2022 conviction for sexual offences.[40] The parliament website describes him as having 'retired'[41] from the House of Lords.

Peerages are sticky,[42] no matter how badly the holders of them behave. They can't be relinquished voluntarily by the person in question, although a peer can effectively retire by saying they will no longer attend proceedings. The honours cannot be removed even by the monarch who created them.

The titles can only be cancelled by an Act of Parliament. There hasn't been one since a 1917 law to remove peerages from lords deemed 'enemies' of the UK during the First World War. The lack of any similar actions since suggests Britain's leaders don't consider this kind of self-policing of Parliament to be very important.

The elite negligence that has long plagued British politics found perhaps its fullest recent expression in Brexit. Whatever one's views about its wisdom as a project, there is now a widespread view that its execution has been botched. Even Nigel Farage, former UKIP leader and the person who did perhaps more than any other to deliver Brexit, has said it has been 'mismanaged' and has 'failed'.[43]

Despite the portrayal of Brexit as a popular insurgency, many of its leading advocates had deep establishment roots. Dominic Cummings, director of Vote Leave, and Michael Gove, its co-convenor, are both Oxford graduates, as is Boris Johnson. Farage was educated at Dulwich College, a top private school.

One of the most committed if lesser known Brexiters was Daniel Hannan. The referendum result was the culmination of his quarter-century campaign of Euroscepticism – which had started, perhaps inevitably, at Oxford University. He churned out columns, books and speeches over many years. It is a rich record that shows how flawed many of his – and other elite Brexiters' – core predictions turned out to be. (Hannan didn't respond to requests for comment submitted to the contact email on his House of Lords webpage.)

Hannan approached Britain as an insider-outsider. Like several leading Brexit campaigners he had grown up in part overseas, with a sense of the homeland developed from afar. His parents ran a poultry farm in Peru and sent him to boarding school in the UK. As a student in the early 1990s, Hannan set up the Oxford Campaign for an Independent Britain, whose small membership met in a coffee shop. It was dismissed in the contemporary student media as a marginal, slightly cranky cause. This was the same mistake David Cameron would make years later when he disdained UKIP[44] as 'fruitcakes', 'loonies' and 'closet racists'.

Hannan and his fellow Eurosceptics did seem far removed from mainstream British political opinion during those early days. This was a time when John Major, a Conservative premier, was signing Britain up to the Maastricht Treaty that deepened EU integration.[†]

After Hannan graduated, he built his profile in politics and again benefited from the complacency of both opponents and party rivals. He became a Tory member of the European Parliament and understood – as Nigel Farage did – that it provided a great platform for making viral videos. Footage of him berating[45] Labour premier Gordon Brown on a 2009 visit to the parliament drew more than a million YouTube views.[46] It earned him the 'Speech of the Year' prize at the Spectator Awards the same year.

Hannan was early, too, to recognise the power of right-wing cable TV in the US. He levered his long-time hostility towards the National Health Service[47] to delight conservative Fox News hosts who were campaigning against President Barack Obama's health reforms. In 2009, he branded the NHS a 'mistake' that 'made people iller', telling Fox's Sean Hannity,[48] 'If you see a friend about to make a terrible mistake, you try and warn him. And we've lived through this mistake for 60 years now.'

[†] Major did, however, secure and trumpet opt-outs to initiatives such as joining the single currency and the social chapter.

Hannan's political interventions sometimes had an obsessive and even maniacal edge. Like Boris Johnson, he used classical allusions as a means to project a sense of learning and authority. He closed European Parliament speeches by calling in Latin for the EU's Lisbon Treaty of 2007 to be put to a vote. In 2008, he compared proposed changes to the parliament's procedural rules to Germany's infamous Enabling Act of 1933, which had allowed Chancellor Adolf Hitler to bypass the legislature.[49] Hannan's remarks would find an echo in the run-up to the Brexit referendum, when Boris Johnson compared the EU's integration aims to Hitler's.

The referendum campaign gave Hannan an opportunity to indulge his tendency for dramatic overstatement in pursuit of much higher stakes. Just two days before the 23 June vote, he published a piece[50] about how Britain would look in 2025. It began with an image of a sky ablaze with fireworks to celebrate the country's new annual Independence Day celebration, on 24 June. In this fantasia, the people of the UK 'wonder why it took us so long to leave' the EU.

> The years that followed the 2016 referendum didn't just reinvigorate our economy, our democracy and our liberty. They improved relations with our neighbours.

In reality, those years would be characterised by bitter fights with the EU, new barriers to trade with the bloc, and government dysfunction at home. There have been scant signs of Hannan's predicted 'new industries, from 3D printing to driverless cars . . . around the country'. His dream of older heavy industries such as steel and cement thriving again due to falling energy prices proved similarly off the mark.

Hannan's concluding paragraph began with a bold claim about what Brexit would mean for the psychology of the country:

Perhaps the greatest benefit, though, is not easy to quantify. Britain has recovered its self-belief.

As a piece of fluent political campaign propaganda, it scored highly. As a predictor of what would actually happen after Leave won the Brexit vote, it was abysmal.

All through the tempests of the Brexit battle there was a strange sense that it was a game to some of its elite protagonists. Cameron called the referendum in good part to quell Eurosceptic opposition to him in the Conservative Party. This opened the way for any of his opponents – Brexiters or not – to try to take his job. Boris Johnson famously wrote pro- and anti-Brexit newspaper columns while he decided which stance would better serve his ambitions.

These were the politics of Oxford University, where Johnson and Gove had both been presidents of the Oxford Union debating society. The union is a 'nursery of the Commons',[51] wrote Simon Kuper, author of *Chums: How a Tiny Caste of Oxford Tories Took Over the UK*. The difference is that events within the union's walls are almost irrelevant, whereas Brexit is one of the biggest political changes in Britain's modern history.

Even at the referendum campaign's climax, leading players seemed calmer than many ordinary voters. Michael Gove was so tired – or relaxed – that he went to bed before the results, according to a column published later by his wife, Sarah Vine. When he was woken up by a call to tell him the outcome he replied, 'Gosh, I suppose I better get up!' Vine responded with similar insouciance. ' "You were only supposed to blow the bloody doors off," I said, in my best (i. e. not very good) Michael Caine *Italian Job* accent,' she wrote. 'In other words, you've really torn it now.' [52]

The flippancy grated with some readers. The first comment under the piece, under the name Fridays Child, was scorching.

Whilst the rest of the country was awake to see what their future would hold, Mr G was soundly sleeping with nary a care in the world because he never wanted the leave campaign to win and 'gosh' was surprised when it did. Your comment about only blowing the doors off speaks *volumes*.

The sense of shock pervaded a sombre press conference Gove held with Johnson later that day. Many observers felt the strong vibe that the two most senior Conservative leaders of the Brexit campaign hadn't really meant to triumph. Gove looked, said one commentator,[53] 'like a man who had just come down off a bad trip to find he had murdered one of his closest friends'.

Even Cameron's behaviour did not seem to reflect the seriousness of a situation that had convulsed the country and ended his premiership. Just hours after the result became clear, he arrived at Downing Street and made a joke. 'Well, that didn't go according to plan!' he said, according to Craig Oliver,[54] his former director of communications. When Cameron announced his resignation date a few weeks later, he hummed chirpily to himself as he walked back into 10 Downing Street.[†]

Daniel Hannan's response to his side's referendum victory was considerably more theatrical. He stood on a table at the Leave campaign headquarters to recite Shakespeare's St Crispin's day[55] oration. It is the 'band of brothers' address given by Henry V before the Battle of Agincourt in 1415. The choice of speech adds to the idea that, for its architects, Brexit was a kind

---

† He had reason to be cheerful. In November 2023, he returned to government as foreign secretary and was elevated to the House of Lords as Baron Cameron of Chipping Norton. This was despite a 2021 Treasury select committee inquiry finding that he showed a 'significant lack of judgement' in his post-premiership lobbying work for Greensill Capital bank.

of cosplay that they suddenly had to apply to real life. Shakespeare's speech is a monarch's motivation to men about to win a war or die in the attempt. Hannan's homage was to celebrate the success of a campaign to activate the voluntary withdrawal procedure from an international organisation. The words show the absurdity of the juxtaposition:

And gentlemen in England now a-bed
Shall think themselves accursed they were not here,
And hold their manhoods cheap whiles any speaks
That fought with us upon Saint Crispin's day.

It is part of a strand of preposterous self-aggrandisement that runs through the rhetoric of the most devoted Brexit ideologues. It should have been a tell of both a lack of seriousness and a susceptibility to delusion. A parliamentary researcher once declared that Eurosceptics' work[56] during the thankless decades of EU membership was 'like the monks on Iona' in the Inner Hebrides. Both were 'illuminating their manuscripts and waiting for the Dark Ages to come to an end', he explained to the *Guardian*. In the same piece, Hannan compared his status in the European Parliament to the outcast son of the biblical patriarch Abraham. 'Here I am, Ishmael,' he said. 'Every man's hand is against me.'

Hannan further described an occasion when he had compared himself to the heroic defender in the poem 'Horatius at the Bridge'. That triggered a telling memory for me. The person I had previously heard cite 'Horatius' was Chukwuemeka Odumegwu Ojukwu, leader of the ill-fated breakaway of Biafra from Nigeria in 1967. The difference was that Ojukwu had fought an actual war of what he saw as liberation, rather than a pretend one against the EU's supposed tyranny.

Hannan's visions of the UK's post-Brexit future grew ever more lyrical in the wake of victory. At times, they seemed almost to take on the qualities of rapture. He evoked the sunlit uplands that have since become mocking bywords for the gap between the promises of Brexit and its reality. In his book *What Next: How to Get the Best from Brexit*,[57] published a few months after the referendum, he wrote:

> After 43 years, we have pushed the door ajar. A rectangle of light dazzles us and, as our eyes adjust, we see a summer meadow. Swallows swoop against the blue sky. We hear the gurgling of a little brook. Now to stride into the sunlight.

Amid the florid prose Hannan churned out over this period, he made significant claims that turned out to be misleading or flat wrong. He said it was 'irresponsible to scare EU nationals in the UK by hinting their status might change after Brexit'.[58] But after a long period of uncertainty, their status did indeed change and they had to apply to stay in the country. Hannan said before the referendum that 'absolutely nobody is talking about threatening our place in the single market'.[59] In 2020, the UK duly pulled out of the single market, as a result of Boris Johnson's Brexit deal.

It should be no surprise to find that Hannan later lavished praise[60] on Liz Truss during her successful 2022 Tory leadership campaign. He 'found her one of the most impressive of our ministers', he said, adding, 'She cajoles and encourages anti-Tory officials into bold actions.' So impressive was this minister that she set a new record for brevity in the top job.

Hannan is far from alone in his wonky Brexit-era soothsaying. In the run-up to the referendum, Michael Gove declared[61] that, the day after voting to leave, Britain would 'hold all the cards'. In July 2017, international trade secretary Liam Fox predicted[62] that the trade deal with the EU would be 'one of the easiest in human history'. The agreement took another three and a half years, by which time Fox and his predictions were long gone.

*

In the end, the most powerful criticism of Hannan and the other flawed prophets of Brexit is not about their ideology. It is about the fact that they have been proved consistently wrong on crucial aspects of Britain's future. In trades other than politics and the media, such a record of misjudgement would mean you forfeited your credibility.

Instead, there often seem to be surprisingly small penalties in Britain for such poor performance. In the UK's increasingly rickety version of democracy, members of its elite often move on to different roles and continue to thrive. The country's politics are in their way as clannish as those of countries where office-holders are actual blood relatives.

Hannan has certainly been well compensated by his peers. His success, like Boris Johnson's, is an example of how certain traits and tricks offer a good chance of success in British public life. Confident rhetorical and writing skills can go a long way towards camouflaging shaky arguments. Projecting a sense of cussed eccentricity appeals in a country that often revels in the idiosyncratic. Evoking a sense of 'deep England', by deploying cultural reference points such as Shakespeare and fabled classical heroes, can be seductive.

It is appropriate that Johnson himself set Hannan up for the rest of his life, making him a trade adviser and a member of the House of Lords. Baron Hannan of Kingsclere, a Hampshire village, has the right to vote on Britain's laws as long as he can make it into Parliament.

Kingsclere is known for a story that, like so much ancient lore in Britain, reaches so far back in time it can't be substantiated. It relates to King John, whose signing of Magna Carta in 1215 Hannan celebrated in an 800th-anniversary *Wall Street Journal* essay.[63] The monarch was reputedly bothered by bedbugs[64] on a visit to Kingsclere in 1204. He is said to have marked his suffering by commissioning a weathervane in the shape of the insect on the village church. There it still stands, a permanent fixture in Hannan's parish of choice.

Whether truth or myth, the symbolism seems fitting. Bedbugs do not kill, but they debilitate their hosts daily with their unsightly bites. And once they have a foothold inside a home, they are notoriously tenacious.

5

Reversal of Fortune

The UK seemed in a grim place – and it took an overseas onlooker[1] to offer encouragement. *Time* magazine's London bureau chief did so after investigating the country's essential attributes and its prospects for improvement. In a piece headlined 'Great Britain: Weakness and Strength', he concluded that the country's 'problem can be solved; it is not hopeless'.

'Britain has a lot of industrial know-how,' he wrote. 'Americans who think they have a national copyright on that term would do well to abandon the illusion. Britain has tangible industrial resources. Not all plants are worn out. Not all management is behind the times. Britain is not literally broke.'

The American correspondent, John Osborne, was not writing about the UK's distress during the later days of Rishi Sunak's government. He penned those lines in 1947, about a nation shattered by war and groping its way towards recovery.

The rhetorical similarity with current narratives says something about the condition of contemporary Britain. It reveals an economic arc that the country has traced over the past three-quarters of a century. Post-war deprivation gave way to industrial expansion and then a growing bubble as the finance industry became ever more important. Now both those booms are over and the country's difficulties are as plain to outsiders as they were to Osborne's American eyes.

Most of these drawbacks are not unique to the UK, but there is a case to argue that they are particularly acute there. From abroad, some of Britain's apparent natural advantages are starting to look at the very least double-edged – and even like full-blown weaknesses.

The offshore status that for centuries protected against invasion is increasingly a problem in a world of dwindling resources and supply-chain logistical problems. In 2018, Brexit secretary Dominic Raab inadvertently drew attention to the frailty.[2] He divulged that he 'hadn't quite understood the full extent' of UK reliance on the Dover–Calais seaway for goods supplies. It was a darkly comic moment, as if comedian Harry Enfield's slow-witted 1990s TV character Tim Nice-But-Dim had been handed the reins of government. As one columnist put it at the time,[3] 'Has nobody told Dominic Raab that Britain is an island?'

This era is proving a particularly awkward one for the UK to be quitting the EU and putting up trade barriers to it. In the years since the 2016 referendum, powerful countries and groupings have increasingly weaponised trade as political tensions have risen. The deteriorating US–China relationship, Russia's invasion of Ukraine and financial measures to combat climate change have all had an impact on international commerce.

At the same time, the global spread of the English language is a hindrance as well as a help. Its adoption for much international business and diplomacy is a great privilege for Britons, but it has an unfortunate side-effect. It has reduced the pressure and incentives for Britons to learn other languages. Two-thirds of state secondary schools offer pre-teens and early teens just one additional language, according to British Council research[4] published in 2023. That risks further stoking UK insularity at a time when it urgently needs to look beyond its shores.[†]

[†] The word 'insular' derives simply from the Latin for 'island', but it is perhaps telling that its modern meaning is pejorative.

The UK's vulnerabilities feed into a bigger story of post-war economic rise and fall, at least in relative terms to emerging international powers. Britain's trajectory is in part a cautionary tale of failure to plan properly during the good times. Once the country lost its imperial power to pillage resources and coerce trade, it had to reimagine how it would sustain growing prosperity. There seems to be a case that in some important ways it has squandered resources and taken for granted an elevated position in world politics and business.

The apparent flaws in the British model are contributing to a pessimistic national mood. The question now is whether, as *Time*'s correspondent Osborne asked among the ashes of war, the country can make the changes needed to prosper again.

'The British spirit could slough into disastrous quiescence and defeatism,' Osborne wrote. 'I am betting that Britain will come through.'

Almost 30 years after Osborne's elegy to UK recovery, the country received an extraordinary windfall. On 18 June 1975, energy secretary Tony Benn[5] turned a metal wheel[6] that unleashed a torrent of money for the British government.

The unpromising setting was the Isle of Grain, a marshy Thames Estuary outpost that Benn later described as a 'ravaged, desolate, industrial landscape'. His action opened a discharge valve that started the flow of North Sea oil into a nearby refinery. He was watched by the captain of the *Theogennitor*, the tanker that had transported the oil from Scottish waters.

It was not the only apparently favourable portent. That day was also the 160th anniversary of the Battle of Waterloo. The symbolism was irresistible to a top executive in the five-company consortium developing the first North Sea field. He told guests that the date coincidence meant the maiden oil flow was already assured of a place in the history books.

Benn himself didn't shy away from hyperbole. He compared the moment to the first journey of George Stephenson's pioneering *Rocket* locomotive (though, in a contradictory omen, the *Rocket* had hit and killed an MP on the opening day of the Liverpool and Manchester Railway). According to *Time* magazine,[7] Benn brandished a souvenir bottle of newly piped crude and declared, 'This is much more significant and historic than the moon shot, which only brought back soil and rock.'

The Labour minister pointed to how North Sea oil would make Britain a world top-ten oil producer and give it 'infinitely greater' energy resources than its European counterparts. It was the government's duty to make sure the oil benefited the country as whole and gave its people a 'full and fair return from its development'.

There was some political irony that it was Benn, one of the country's most left-wing MPs, who turned on the taps. The greatest beneficiaries of the oil would be the Conservatives after they ousted Labour in the 1979 election. North Sea oil would play a key role in enabling Prime Minister Margaret Thatcher's tax-cutting agenda – anathema to Benn's socialist beliefs.

Almost half a century later, with North Sea oil all but exhausted, it is surely time to interrogate properly how the money was used. It promised to be a transformative event for the country, as the discovery of energy reserves has been for other nations. Sadly, it is hard to argue that Benn's hoped-for 'full and fair return'[8] to the British public has been achieved.

The comparison with the oil experiences of other wealthy nations is chastening. Resource-rich places from Norway to Abu Dhabi set up sovereign wealth funds to invest their energy wealth for financial returns or later projects. The UK never bothered, either during the Conservatives' 18-year rule or the spike in North Sea production after Labour took power in 1997.

'Almost all of the places that had significant resource finds of oil and gas had these sovereign wealth funds – and yet we didn't,' says John

Hawksworth, an economist who has examined the fate of Britain's oil windfall. 'So we stick out a bit for not having one.'

I have reported during my career from many countries that have had oil riches or were searching for them. They range from Nigeria and its West African neighbours to the Gulf nations and the South-East Asian petrostate of Brunei. I saw first-hand how oil money could be both economically revolutionary and immensely destructive to the very fabric of society.

Natural-resource wealth is particularly prone to being misused, given that it is abundant and governments don't need to make much effort to reap it. If they hire multinationals to do the drilling, piping and shipping, they can just watch as the royalties pile up.

That income is often poorly monitored and accounted for, creating many possibilities for corruption. That is enabled by institutions of the world's powerful nations, including the UK. I once toured the London apartment off Hyde Park owned by a Nigerian oil-state governor who stashed almost £1m in cash there.†

Oil loomed large in the scandal of Malaysia's 1MDB state investment fund, which I had covered when I was based in South-East Asia. Two former senior executives of Abu Dhabi's International Petroleum Investment Company helped divert $3.5bn of 1MDB money,[9] according to the US Department of Justice. The two men, Khadem al-Qubaisi and Mohamed Ahmed Badawy al-Husseiny, were reportedly jailed[10] in the United Arab Emirates in 2019.

In time, I came to realise that I had experience of another oil-rich country that had used its wealth dubiously: my own. Britain's oil money did not go

---

† The official, Diepreye Alamieyeseigha, was the one who met Queen Elizabeth II in the same greeting line as me.

directly into the pockets of its rulers,[11] at least to public knowledge. But there is a strong argument that it was frittered away,[12] much of it benefiting the most well off, rather than being used for social good.[13]

It is remarkable that there is not more debate about what was done with Britain's historic resource windfall. It barely resonates outside the occasional discussion among economists and the narrow section of the media that covers them in detail. I cannot recall it being picked up as an election campaign subject by Labour or the Liberal Democrats in a way that achieved significant publicity.

The story is, by contrast, well understood outside of the UK and in specialist circles. A cursory internet search reveals plenty of articles with headlines unflattering to Britain. 'Why The UK Lost Its Oil Wealth (And Why Norway Didn't)', reads one.[14] 'North Sea oil: A tale of two countries', says another.[15] 'Did the U.K. Miss Out on £400 Billion Worth of Oil Revenue?' asks a 2015 paper[16] from the US-based Natural Resource Governance Institute, referring to the British decision to sell off its equity stake in the state-owned British National Oil Corporation.

The political silence in the UK itself is neatly summed up in a 2013 openDemocracy piece. It is headlined[17] 'Thatcher and the words no one mentions: North Sea Oil'. The article points out that the circumspection is the more surprising because some observers saw the energy reserves' importance early on. As long ago as 1987, one UK politician argued that the oil and gas bonanza was crucial to the Thatcher government's fortunes. He said it had boosted government revenues by the rough equivalent of 7p on the basic rate of income tax (which was 20p in 2023).

'The importance of this windfall to the Government's political survival is incalculable,' he wrote.[18] 'Without oil and asset sales, which themselves have totalled over £30bn, Britain under the Tories could not have enjoyed tax cuts, nor could the Government have funded its commitments on public spending.'

The author was one Tony Blair. He would go on to become prime minister a decade later – and custodian of a second North Sea oil mini-boom.

North Sea energy is Britain's great resource bonanza[19] of the past half-century. During the first production surge from the late 1970s to the mid-1980s, annual tax revenues reached £12bn, according to the Office for Budget Responsibility. That was more than half the value of the oil and gas drilled by the companies. The tax receipts peaked at 3.1 per cent of annual gross domestic product – a considerable sum. The same percentage take[20] in 2022 would have yielded £77bn. That would be enough to build more than 150 mid-sized hospitals, using NHS trust cost estimates.[21]

The initial North Sea tax surge was followed by more modest but still appreciable waves during the decades that followed. Revenues rose and fell, but another peak arrived as energy prices spiked after Russia's invasion of Ukraine in February 2022. The £10.6bn revenues forecast by the Office for Budget Responsibility for 2023–4 should come in handy. They are comparable with Britain's annual net contributions to the European Union, during its time as a member.

Analysis of where the money went has been sporadic – but what has been published is revealing. In 2008, John Hawksworth put out a paper entitled 'Dude, where's my oil money?' Hawksworth was no radical campaigner. He was at the time the chief economist at PwC, then the world's largest accounting and consulting firm.

The thrust of Hawksworth's argument was that the oil money appeared to have been used for tax cuts. The most notable of these was that the top rate was slashed from 60 per cent to 40 per cent by 1988. There were just under 1.2 million people who fell into the higher rate band.[22] That put them in the top 5 per cent of adult earners.

I wanted to speak to Hawksworth about his North Sea oil work, which had been picked up sporadically over the years by media including the *Guardian*. He had concluded a 33-year career[23] with PwC and its predecessor firms in 2020 and was now working as an independent economist. He had studied the subject at Oxford University in the early 1980s – the time when the promise of North Sea oil was turning into serious money.

Hawksworth said that he was inspired to write 'Dude, where's my oil money?' because he was working for a sovereign wealth fund client. These reserves are often set up by countries to save and invest the proceeds from exploiting natural resources such as hydrocarbons and minerals. The money can then be used for future emergencies, to finance capital-intensive projects, or simply invested for financial returns.

It is hardly a new idea. Many of these commodity-financed investment funds[24] pre-date or are contemporaneous with the British North Sea oil boom. Some of them were even created in UK government-controlled territories.

A pioneer sovereign wealth fund was the Kuwait Investment Authority, which was set up in 1953, eight years before the Gulf state's full independence[25] from the UK. In 1956, British imperial authorities in the Gilbert Islands (now part of Kiribati) in Micronesia taxed exports of phosphate-rich guano and banked the proceeds in a designated reserve. There are now scores of sovereign wealth funds around the world managing more than $11tn in assets, according to the Global SWF data platform.[26] Many of the biggest ones have been around more than long enough for the British to learn from them. The Abu Dhabi Investment Authority was created in 1976.[27] The Norwegians waited until 1990 to set up their fund, 19 years after production had started. Theirs is now the largest in the world, in a striking demonstration of how late can still be better than never.

These statistics are suggestive of how the UK would have fared had it set up a reserve, perhaps cannily branded the Great British Wealth Fund.

Hawksworth reckons that, even if the money had simply been invested in government bonds, the UK would now rank among the top five funds by size. 'What kind of money might we have had, had we saved at least part of the oil revenues – instead of them disappearing into the general revenue pot and being untraceable, effectively?' he asks.

The opportunity costs of failing to manage these proceeds for the long term are becoming increasingly obvious. Costs related to the aging population, such as for the National Health Service and social care, are 'really coming in with a vengeance', Hawksworth notes. The same goes for the need to upgrade UK infrastructure, from railways to water pipes. 'The fact that we haven't saved up for that as a nation is a fairly glaring omission compared with other countries,' he says.

The failure to prepare has become still more damaging since the 2008 financial crisis. That brought an era of historically high investment in public services under Labour to an abrupt end. There was no rainy day reserve to help fill the gap.

Britain's decision to throw its North Sea oil wealth into the cauldron of national revenue for immediate use has had other negative consequences. One is the lack of accountability: since the money was never officially allocated to anything, we can't judge whether it was used well. 'If you have a fund, you can have a debate,' Hawskworth says. 'It's a pot of money and you can argue how to spend it.' Instead, North Sea oil money helped stoke the 1980s consumer boom orchestrated by Thatcher and her chancellor of the exchequer, Nigel Lawson. Their vision was of a society based on ownership of assets such as property and shares in companies. It was the era of the Big Bang deregulation in the City and the privatisation of state businesses such as British Telecom and British Gas.

A signature Thatcher government policy was offering generous subsidies to aspiring houseowners. Tenants of council-owned properties were offered the right to buy their homes at a discount of up to 70 per cent.[28]

The initiative was portrayed by the Conservatives as a leg-up for ordinary working Britons. By 2022, about two million people had taken advantage of it since its launch in 1980.

The relatively narrow group who benefited did so handsomely. Right to buy was used on more than 167,000 homes[29] in the 1982–3 financial year. Sales topped 130,000 annually in the years 1988, 1989 and 1990.

It certainly worked beautifully in electoral terms, attracting working-class votes to the Conservatives that might otherwise have gone to Labour. The strategy helped deliver the Tories three successive wins between 1983 and 1992. In 1992, the preceding years' hundreds of thousands of right-to-buy deals may have been a crucial contributor to the small Conservative majority.

Right to buy was expensive. It cost the government £6bn in the years 2012–22 alone, after the discount was increased, according to the Local Government Association.[30] It is certainly arguable that North Sea oil revenues helped create the financial room to fund such a giveaway, during right to buy's 1980s peak.

Critics of right to buy say it has helped fuel the modern housing crisis[31] and a shortage of affordable homes, particularly for younger people. Hawksworth points to how both right to buy and lower taxation of the wealthy gave a big boost to property sales. North Sea oil was 'certainly one of the factors that pumped up the housing market', he says. 'So instead of getting new infrastructure, or a national pension fund, we get higher house prices.'

The decision not to earmark North Sea energy revenues helped dodge awkward debates about how the money should be distributed within Britain. The oil and gas were drilled in Scottish waters, but the proceeds went to the UK exchequer. If they had been separated from other government revenues, nationalists and others in Scotland would likely have campaigned intensely for a designated share.

The UK's North Sea oil history raises bigger questions about short-termism in national planning. The time spans of electoral cycles and political careers do not map well on to economic commitments needed in the longer run. Saving money now will not help a government in the coming election that it needs to win to carry on implementing a strategy over decades.

'This is decided on short-term political horizons rather than long time horizons,' Hawksworth says of the oil money spending. 'In a democratic system that changes over governments every few years, it's quite difficult to get that decision making for the far future.'

To which one answer might be: the Norwegians have managed it. The wealth fund has evolved over the years, in response to debates over its policies in areas from financial risk to ethical investment. Piquantly, the government has said the fund will lower its investments[32] in fossil-fuel companies.

In the late 1970s, Tony Benn and other Labour MPs made a failed push to create a UK fund for the public oil and gas revenues. Benn had noted how the audience the day he started oil flowing was 'a complete cross-section of the international capitalist and British Tory establishment'. They would end up the big winners – and those who pushed for a more strategic use of Britain's oil godsend would forever wonder what might have been.

Hawksworth has some sympathy with the UK governments that faced 'difficult economic circumstances' during the first flush of North Sea oil. The 1970s were a time of oil shocks,[33] first with the Gulf state embargo and then the 1979 Iranian revolution. Controlling high inflation[34] became a big preoccupation for successive administrations in the late 1970s and early 1980s.

But his judgement overall is unsparing. North Sea oil gave Britain a chance to prepare for foreseeable future needs – and it flunked it.

'It's easy to say now it was a missed opportunity,' he says. 'And it was.'

*

In July 2023, North Sea oil and gas hit the headlines again. Prime Minister Rishi Sunak announced that the government would grant hundreds of new licences[35] for the area. He insisted this was consistent with the UK's commitments to achieve net zero carbon emissions by 2050, although environmental groups disputed this. The prime minister attempted to project a sense of balance in his plan by unveiling new investment in carbon capture and storage. This is a technique that may help mitigate the worst impact of the climate crisis – but it will do nothing to reduce underlying emissions.

The government presented the new licences as 'part of a drive to make Britain more energy independent'. As a devotee of the 1980s Tory Chancellor Nigel Lawson, Sunak no doubt understands well the political benefits of freely flowing oil money. Both he and energy secretary Grant Shapps linked the decision to President Vladimir Putin's 2022 invasion of Ukraine, which caused a surge in gas prices.

'The North Sea is at the heart of our plan to power up Britain from Britain so that tyrants like Putin can never again use energy as a weapon to blackmail us,' said Shapps, who had days earlier vowed to 'max out'[36] the UK's remaining oil and gas reserves.

It seemed rather late to be thinking of how to insulate UK energy supplies from world political tensions. It is not as if previous eras had been characterised by global harmony. When Tony Benn had brought the North Sea online almost half a century previously, the Soviet Union was still alive under Leonid Brezhnev.[37] The 1970s were among the most turbulent years in the history of world oil and gas supply.†

The presentation of the new North Sea licences as helpful to Britain's energy needs failed to acknowledge an inconvenient truth. Much of UK

---

† Britain was, of course, hardly alone in suffering an energy hit from the Ukraine War, which upended longstanding European buys of Russian gas.

energy production is exported, with about 80 per cent of oil sold overseas. The government says most gas goes to the domestic market, although it provided no figures[38] at the time of Sunak's announcement to support this claim. Even if it is true, the prices of gas produced in the UK will still be closely linked to international market levels. Any local production discount is likely to be small.

The Sunak government's North Sea announcement seemed like yet another milestone in a history of inadequate planning for Britain's energy reserves. Energy import dependency reached 43 per cent[39] for the first quarter of 2023, up 5 percentage points year on year. This is even though renewables generation reached an all-time high of 47.8 per cent of the total.

The government had rushed out a new energy security strategy[40] in early April 2022, barely six weeks after Russia invaded Ukraine. It sought to address a wide range of concerns, including[41] the war's impact, the failure of several UK energy suppliers, and large rises in energy price caps allowed by the regulator Ofgem.

The foreword by then prime minister Boris Johnson promised to give the 'energy fields of the North Sea a new lease of life', among other proposals. He attacked the way the UK had 'drifted into dependence' on foreign energy sources. 'Sometimes this was through deliberate planning; more often it was the byproduct of policy fudges, decision-dodging and short-term thinking,' he wrote. 'For years, governments have dodged the big decisions on energy, but not this one.'

Three months later, Johnson announced his resignation. The responsibility to bring 'clean, affordable, secure power to the people for generations to come' would fall to someone else.

Britain's energy conundrum is part of a wider picture of a state that has failed to prepare adequately for shifts in circumstances domestically and internationally. This has harmed the UK's ability to respond to both foreseeable social changes and unpredictable occurrences. Brexit, the Ukraine War and other events have revealed supply weaknesses in areas from agricultural labour to gas storage.

When I started my career in the late 1990s, the international economic orthodoxy was that globalisation would help prevent supply problems. It would ensure goods flowed freely, lower costs for businesses in rich countries and bring wealth to people in poor ones. More international trade with fewer restrictions would benefit everyone.

Critics of globalisation tended to be dismissed by those in power. Warnings of the potential for multinationals and rich country governments to exploit poorer parts of the world were played down as missing the wider benefits. Insufficient attention was paid to how companies shifting production offshore to take advantage of cheaper labour would destroy sources of manual jobs in Western countries.

It is remarkable how far and fast the globalising vision of the world has collapsed in the face of pandemic, war and superpower political conflict. Now Western countries are trying to bring supply chains back onshore for security reasons. Trade curbs on key goods have been imposed by Washington, Beijing and other capitals.

The UK's pressure points are increasingly visible to me after years outside the country, including coverage of supply-chain tensions in Europe and Asia. While none of these difficulties is unique to Britain, the mix of them looks unusually tricky. In particular, the country lacks reserves of metals crucial to the electronics that make modern societies run and power new green energy technologies.

The nature of this threat is clear from a British Geological Survey report published in 2021.[42] It looks at the vulnerabilities of supplies of critical industrial minerals. The results are sobering. For a start, the UK is late in the game as an independent actor on this topic. As the report acknowledges, the

US and the European Union have been making similar assessments since 2008 (when the UK was, of course, still an EU member). Australia, Canada and Japan have also prepared similar documents in the past few years.

The British Geological Survey document was completed in 2021, the year after the 12-month post-Brexit transition period ended. It bears marks of haste. The authors refer at one point to how they narrowed the scope of their work because of 'time constraints imposed on this study'. This assessment of the strategic needs of post-EU Britain even relies partly on the bloc's research data. The EU's statistics on end-of-life recycling are 'the most complete, publicly accessible compilation for a wide range of materials', the report says.

The research is part of a rush by big Western countries and their allies to secure supplies of critical minerals. An agreement for the UK to negotiate with the US on this subject formed part of the two countries' Atlantic Declaration[43] unveiled in June 2023. The EU and US had some months earlier flagged their intent[44] to make a similar deal between themselves. The US has signalled further such pacts with Japan, Australia and India, its Quadrilateral Security Dialogue partners in Asia.

Britain's potential difficulties lie in its lack of domestic reserves or production of many metals key to modern technologies. The minerals it produces tend to be those used in areas such as construction, fertilisers and basic industries. The country's relatively small land area, island status and lack of regional trade alliances create further risks.

'Consequently the UK is potentially vulnerable to any disruption in the supply of these [new key] materials,' the British Geological Survey report says.

The research analyses in detail the supply threats facing 26 minerals.[45] It gives more than two-thirds of these – 18 – the status 'critical'. This means that there is both a high global supply risk and a high UK economic vulnerability to potential shortages of them.

China is the leading global producer of no fewer than 12 of the 18 critical minerals. These include rare-earth metals used in products at the heart of the green revolution, such as electric vehicle batteries and wind turbines. The list contains gallium, essential to the semiconductors that power the electronic devices at the heart of modern life. China announced curbs on gallium exports in July 2023; it has previously imposed rare earths supply restrictions to target the US and Japan.

Further vulnerabilities for the UK include palladium, which is key to autocatalysts used in petrol and hybrid vehicles. The leading world supplier of the metal is Russia, which the UK is pitted against over the invasion of Ukraine. Other minerals on the critical list include niobium from Brazil, tantalum from the Democratic Republic of Congo and bismuth from communist-ruled Vietnam.

These metals are part of a broader catalogue of potential strategic shortages facing the UK. The country runs a large goods trade deficit, with imports far exceeding exports. While services ran a £151bn trade surplus[46] in 2022, according to the Office for National Statistics, the deficit in goods was £219bn.

The UK is highly dependent on the EU and the ONS says it is too early to say fully what effect leaving the bloc might have on that trade. The UK's main imports[47] include machinery and transport equipment, chemical products, food, drink and tobacco, and base metals, according to EU data.

Food is a notable area where existing risks have been sharpened by Brexit, international conflict and the impact of the climate crisis on agriculture. An official report on UK food security[48] published in 2021 adopts a reassuring tone, but the underlying numbers contain grounds for concern. UK wheat yields, for example, dropped 40 per cent in 2020 because of drought and unfortunately timed rainfall.

One significant constraint on the UK is space. In 2020, an extraordinary 71 per cent of the country's land area was used for agriculture – almost three-quarters of that grassland for animal grazing. That means there is not much room for expansion – even if yields fall because of soil-quality depletion or global heating.

Even this high utilisation does not make the UK self-sufficient. Only about half of the 'actual food on plates' is produced in the country, according to the report. It could be a little higher were it not for exports.

The UK's degree of food self-sufficiency, measured by the so-called production-to-supply ratio, has declined over the past 40 years. The country met 80 per cent of its needs domestically in the mid-1980s, but that figure had fallen to around 60 per cent in 2020. About 70 per cent of imports come from the EU. The shortages are acute in some areas. Britain produces barely half the vegetables it consumes domestically and only 16 per cent of fruit. Production of strawberries and high-yielding apple varieties such as Gala and Braeburn has grown, while that of raspberries has plunged.

The UK's eating habits are as telling a symbol as any of shortfalls in both its self-sufficiency and its strategic planning. Unlike many other islands, Britain has never developed a tradition of frequent fish consumption. Fish and chips may be considered a national dish, but it is in many respects an outlier.

The surprising bottom line is that the UK does not eat much of what is caught in its waters. A country with more than 30,000km (almost 19,000 miles) of coastline[49] – equivalent to three-quarters of the Earth's circumference[50] – is a net importer of fish and seafood. 'UK consumer preference is for fish mainly caught outside UK waters, such as cod, haddock, tuna, and shrimp and prawns,' says the 2021 UK Food Security Report analysis.[51] 'Important exports include herring, mackerel, salmon and nephrops (scampi).'

Many observers have scratched their heads over why this should be. One problem may be exaggerated perceptions of the downsides of buying, preparing and consuming fish. People see the sea's bounty as 'expensive, perishable, smelly and difficult to eat', Nicholas Simpson, a cultural writer,[52] has suggested. Simpson, a Briton, highlights the contrast with the enthusiasm for seafood in his adopted homes of Spain and South Korea.

'We know British consumers are squeamish about bones in fish,' Victoria Townsend, Head of Retail at Ocean Fish, one of Cornwall's largest fish processors, has observed.[53] 'And so this will always be the stumbling block.'

An effort is underway to tackle many Britons' unhelpful marine aversion. Seafood Cornwall, an initiative of the Cornish Fish Producers' Organisation, is trying to promote the consumption of megrim sole and spider crab. Most of each has historically been exported to other European countries. Spider crab is considered a premium product in France.

Not for nothing does Seafood Cornwall style the situation 'The Great British seafood dilemma'. It says up to 40 per cent of whitefish eaten in the UK has come from Russia, which seems a clear vulnerability given current bilateral relations.

As in other parts of everyday British life, a little-commented-on historical supply and consumption trend could be about to catch up with the country. Just as with the North Sea oil reserves, the UK is failing to make the most of what is right on its doorstep.

'As a nation, we export most of the seafood we catch, and import most of the fish we eat,' Seafood Cornwall laments.[54] 'It's clearly counterintuitive.'

6

The Empire Strikes Back

A Nigerian royal flew to London in 2016 with four bottles of water – and a goal to confront a famous company on its home ground. His Royal Highness Emere Godwin Bebe Okpabi had travelled from the Niger Delta's swamps to the Royal Courts of Justice buildings on Strand. His aim: to hold Shell responsible for oil pollution in the land of his Ogoni people.

Okpabi claimed oil leaks had discharged dangerous chemicals into the Niger Delta tap water he had poured into his quartet of containers. 'If you open it and smell it, you see,'[1] he said, brandishing one of the bottles marked with the name of his Ogale community. 'It's crude – that's what we're drinking.'

Okpabi is among more than 13,000 legal claimants from Ogale and its fellow Niger Delta community Bille. They are suing Shell, which is listed on the UK stock market, and its Nigerian subsidiary in an epic litigation in the High Court in London. By late 2023, the case was still at a preliminary stage and no trial date had been set.

Shell has been active in Ogoniland since the days when Nigeria was occupied by Britain. Now Okpabi, like other citizens of countries once under the imperial yoke, was turning to the institutions of the former coloniser to fight back.

The case brought the troubles of resource-rich southern Nigeria to the centre of London's legal establishment. The king posed for pictures outside the Royal Courts of Justice, his dark traditional robes and black top hat congruent with the Victorian Gothic building. His orange-beaded necklace provided a splash of colour on an English November day.

'What we are asking for now is justice, when you look at the whole history,' Okpabi tells me, almost seven years on from that day. 'And I think the onus is on the British system to give us justice.'

The lawsuit is one of a growing number in which claimants are seeking to hold British authorities or businesses to account over alleged actions overseas. The facts of each case vary, but each brings seemingly distant events to the heart of arguments in the UK. The movement is forcing the government and companies to take it seriously, whether or not they contest the underlying claims. It is a sign that many people outside Britain feel they have unfinished business the country is yet to fully acknowledge.

The Shell companies strongly dispute the allegations against them in the Ogale/Bille case. Shell's Nigerian subsidiary, the Shell Petroleum Development Company of Nigeria (SPDC), says it has remediated oil spills according to its responsibilities and that the vast majority of the incidents were caused by sabotage that was not its fault. Other spills cited in the lawsuit were small and had no impact on third parties, or happened so long ago that they should be time-barred.

Shell plc, the parent company, argues that it doesn't have operational responsibility for SPDC. It says any legal claims should in any case be dealt with in Nigeria.[†]

The sight of litigants from former parts of the British Empire seeking redress in the country of their ex-rulers is becoming increasingly common.

---

† SPDC works in Nigeria as the operator of a joint venture, in which the country's state oil company owns a majority stake.

In a landmark 2009 case in London, a group of elderly Kenyans alleged colonial authorities tortured them during the 1950s Mau Mau rebellion. The claimed abuses included rape, castration and severe beatings.

In 2013, the British government admitted that Kenyans were 'subject to torture and other forms of ill treatment at the hands of the colonial administration'. [2] It continued to deny liability for the past abuses but agreed to pay almost £20m to more than 5,000 victims – an average of about £4,000 each. Foreign Secretary William Hague expressed 'sincere regret' over the 'pain and grievance felt by those who were involved in events of the emergency in Kenya'.

Another big case[3] is the long-running campaign by Chagos Islanders to return to their Indian Ocean archipelago after being evicted by the British government. They were removed in the 1960s and 1970s to allow the US to set up a military base on strategically located Diego Garcia. Islanders won a partial victory at the High Court in 2000, but the Supreme Court denied them the right to return in 2016. In 2019, the UN International Court of Justice issued an advisory opinion that the UK should cede control of the Chagos Islands as soon as possible. In November 2022, the British government said it had begun talks with Mauritius over the islands' sovereignty and the islanders' return.

The history of the Mau Mau and Chagos cases shows how the English court route to restitution is inadequate – as well as prolonged, costly and stressful. In 2018, the High Court ruled that a second lawsuit launched on behalf of 20,000 further Kenyan alleged torture victims was time-barred. Bryan Cox, a claimant lawyer in the case, argued later[4] that this showed the system to be unsystematic and unsatisfactory. 'The fact is Britain has not fully faced up to its colonial past and no proper mechanism has been devised to compensate those who suffered,' he wrote.

An even wider-ranging battle for historical accountability is taking place over the UK's history in the slave trade. Ground-breaking research including by University College London has revealed more about who owned thousands of slave estates and the British official pay-outs they received. In tandem with the emancipation act of 1833, the Bank of England administered pay-offs[5] totalling £20m to slaveholders for loss of their 'property'.

Some descendants of slaveowners have started to try to make amends. A group called Heirs of Slavery[6] now brings together people who want to acknowledge their ancestors' crimes. They include Charles Gladstone, whose three times great-grandfather John owned sugar plantations in Jamaica and what is now Guyana.[†]

Another heir – David Lascelles, Earl of Harewood – has launched a project called Missing Portraits[7] to depict people of African-Caribbean heritage linked to the family. One is of the actor David Harewood, whose ancestors were enslaved in the 18th century by a previous Earl of Harewood. David Harewood has said the portrait is a 'fine example of the resilience of my people; that not only did we endure and survive, but we have also managed to thrive'.

Other descendants of slaveowners remain in varying degrees of denial about their responsibilities. The Conservative MP[8] Richard Drax has said his family's past in the Caribbean slave trade is 'deeply, deeply regrettable'. But he has insisted that 'no one can be held responsible today for what happened many hundreds of years ago'.

Britain's failure to fully reckon with its previous actions is a 'national affliction',[9] Alex Renton, an Heirs of Slavery co-founder, wrote in the *Guardian* in 2023. The UK is 'viciously in conflict with its colonial history' and 'pathologically unable to come to terms with the less comfortable aspects of the past', he said. This included the enslavement of more than three million Africans and their descendants, as well as

---

† John's son, William, was a British prime minister.

centuries of looting of Asian and African states. 'Even if these histories are accepted – and that is not happening – we cannot reach any consensus on how, or whether, to address their continuing consequences,' he said. 'Other nations have done better.'

British official attitudes to slavery remain circumspect, perhaps in part because of the fear that full acknowledgement would prompt more litigation. In 2007, on the 200th anniversary of the UK law that finally prohibited slave trading, Prime Minister Tony Blair stopped well short of an apology. He instead expressed 'deep sorrow and regret'[10] for Britain's role in the 'unbearable suffering, individually and collectively, it caused'. (Some cite the 1807 law as evidence that Britain was 'first out' of the trade, although it took more than 25 years and further legislation to end slavery in practice.)

Other establishment observers have come closer to recognising the uncomfortable fact that Britain's contemporary rich-nation status owes a good deal to slavery. At a 2007 commemoration in Westminster Abbey attended by Queen Elizabeth II, Archbishop of Canterbury Rowan Williams spoke of slavery's 'hideously persistent' legacies. 'We, who are the heirs of the slave-owning and slave-trading nations of the past, have to face the fact that our historic prosperity was built in large part on this atrocity,' he said.

In 2023, Buckingham Palace said it was cooperating with a study into the British monarchy's links with slavery.[11] The research is being done by the University of Manchester and Historic Royal Palaces, which manages six regal properties. The palace's pledge came after the *Guardian* discovered a previously unreported document showing a 1689 allocation of shares in the Royal African Company to King William III. The shares were transferred from Edward Colston, a slave trader and Royal African Company deputy governor.

The idea that the UK's modern wealth is partly rooted in slavery threatens cherished national myths. The 2023 book *Slavery, Capitalism and the Industrial Revolution* charts how some histories seek to minimise the importance of slave profits to industrial revolutionary Britain. That link has been 'obscured in favour of a more heroic island story of early economic improvement and cultural benevolence', authors Maxine Berg and Pat Hudson write.

The 2020 toppling of Edward Colston's statue in Bristol offered a litmus test of British attitudes to accounting for the past. The action – part of a surge of protests for racial justice after the murder of the Black Minnesotan George Floyd by US police – drew condemnation from some senior politicians. Prosecutors charged four people with criminal damage. (They were acquitted in 2022.)

What was striking was the defence of the statue on the grounds that it was a part of history and thus shouldn't be erased. It seemed to miss the point that Colston was not an ambivalent figure, like Churchill, with both achievements and flaws. Colston was immortalised only because of the money he derived from slavery, some of which he then used for philanthropy in Bristol. Without his crime, he would have no fame.

The historian David Olusoga pointed out how the outcry ignored previous attempts[12] to have the statue removed peacefully. Colston's defenders had obstructed efforts[13] to change a plaque that lauded him as 'one of the most virtuous and wise sons of [the] city'. The statue removal was not an 'attack on history', Olusoga wrote. On the contrary, he argued, 'This is history.'

Olusoga is one a group of authors who have been targeted for harassment over their work on colonialism and its aftermath. Sathnam Sanghera, author of the best-selling *Empireland*, said in 2023[14] that he had 'more or less stopped doing events in Britain' because of verbal abuse. He was worried about US-style culture wars coming to Britain, he added.

'There was a survey out a few months ago showing that people going to libraries are saying, "Why are you even stocking this book? It's woke nonsense." And in Florida, you've got books being banned,' he said. 'And I feel like whatever happens with the culture wars over there, eventually comes over here. I feel like that is the next step.'

The strength of hostility in some quarters to even measured explorations of Britain's darker past is in itself revealing. It seems possible that it is a subconscious reflection of unease at the scale of the review and restitution needed. If you start to think about the magnitude of the impact of slavery and colonialism on modern British life, where do you stop?

The UK imperial legacy flows in many striking ways into the channels and crevices of modern societies at home and abroad. It is in anti-gay laws in some African countries and rules restricting public protest in places such as Hong Kong. Laws allowing caning of criminals in Singapore and Malaysia have their roots in British rule in the 19th century.

Some British observers who travelled within the empire recognised these dynamics long ago. A century back, George Orwell was examining the British imperial record in the country then known as Burma. His spell as a 1920s colonial police officer in the country now officially called Myanmar spawned the classic essays 'Shooting an Elephant' and 'A Hanging'. It powered his first novel *Burmese Days*, an excoriation of British imperialism.

Orwell spent five years in Myanmar and saw quite a bit of the country that Britain had occupied. His stay included time in the cool comfort of the Maymyo summer hill station (Pyin Oo Lwin today) and the haunting mists of Moulmein (now Mawlamyine). The experiences made a deep impression on him and how he was viewed as an agent of his empire. His essay 'Shooting an Elephant' begins, 'In Moulmein, in Lower Burma, I was hated by large numbers of people – the only time in my life that I have been important enough for this to happen to me.'

Fast-forward a hundred years and the author would doubtless be astonished to see how his position has changed. Street sellers in downtown Yangon display his books on blankets on the pavements – or at least they did before the 2021 military coup. Orwell's work had enjoyed a revival from the early days of Myanmar's – sadly ephemeral – political reopening. The author of a 2012 piece on the Orwell Society's website reported that a 'smiling woman brandished a copy of *Burmese Days*'[15] at the foot of a Mandalay pagoda. The book was 'one of a pile' available now censorship had been eased. 'Evidently Orwell now represents something of a hot ticket of opportunity in Burma,' the piece noted.

Orwell's Myanmar journey from colonial hate figure to modern cash cow would doubtless have prompted a pithily arch observation from the man himself, were he still alive. He would probably have noted, too, how *Burmese Days* was prescient in its anticipation of later attempts to airbrush empire. The character Dr Veraswami serves as a devil's advocate by listing supposed compensatory merits of British occupation,[16] much as some UK newspaper columnists do today.

Orwell, the agent turned sceptic of British domination, had little time for the blind loyalty of 'my country right or wrong' supporters of colonialism. In his essay 'My Country Right or Left', he played on the phrase to try to reclaim the idea of patriotism from imperialist conservatives.

He hardly succeeded. The idea of 'my country right or wrong' has become one of the most powerful transatlantic nationalistic tropes. Originally coined by Stephen Decatur, an early 19th-century US naval officer, it has long since reproduced around the world. It provides the title in translation of the book *Leur Patrie* by Gustave Hervé,[17] the French socialist turned fascist sympathiser who died in 1944. It was the headline for a 2022 obituary of Hideaki Kase,[18] a Japanese ultranationalist who was Yoko Ono's cousin and who wrote a book about John Lennon and Shintoism.

The concept of unwavering support for the UK's past and traditions has become a touchstone for a certain kind of historically unapologetic English nationalism and the array of views it represents. In 2021, the thriller writer Frederick Forsyth deployed it to decry how Britain had allegedly ditched[19] all kinds of important truths about how to live. He claimed the modern nation had no time for invocations like 'don't make a fuss' and 'keep a stiff upper lip'. Apparently anyone telling someone to 'pull yourself together' could be 'heading for Belmarsh [maximum security] prison draped in chains'.

Forsyth concluded with an attack on what he saw as the 'seriously nasty' contemporary repudiation of the idea of 'my country right or wrong'. He scorned efforts to acknowledge the UK's history in full. 'Everyone knows that we are horrible people in a horrible country whose horrible ancestors spent centuries doing horrible things,' he mocked. 'Any statues to those people must be torn down and replaced by glorious images of vastly overpaid footballers genuflecting to highlight inequality.'

The author's spleen unintentionally illuminates the heart of the matter. His grotesque characterisation of efforts to force Britain to deal with its history shows exactly why they are necessary. To dismiss past actions of your nation makes as little sense as ignoring your family history. You may have had nothing directly to do with your ancestors' actions. But they have shaped how your country is today – and how it interacts with others.

Forsyth's bile is the more striking given his experience of observing – and sometimes criticising – Britain in the world. He has long been a Eurosceptic conservative, but his career is not that of a stereotypical little Englander. He has enjoyed great success from writing thrillers with an international dimension, from mercenaries in Africa to the Cold War.

Forsyth even wrote a non-fiction book about Nigeria. As a journalist, he had covered the civil war of 1967–70 and his work was very far from an apologia for the former colonial power. Instead, he condemned the UK support for the Nigerian government against the breakaway republic of Biafra. Forsyth saw first-hand how the British occupation of Nigeria had stoked the deadly conflict that followed less than a decade after independence.

The Nigeria pollution lawsuit against Shell in London has its own origins in the power relationships of the British Empire. The company has built its status as the largest oil-producer in Nigeria today on the position it established before the UK left. Shell created a corporate presence[20] in Nigeria in 1936 and shipped its first oil in 1958 – two years before independence.

The case took me back to the many times I had visited the oil-producing Niger Delta. I had been the *Financial Times* Nigeria correspondent between 2002 and 2005, returning over the following years for research for a book. The Delta is a region of evocative and at times heart-breaking beauty, but it has been plagued by pollution, corruption and violence related to oil.

When I speak to King Okpabi in August 2023, it is early morning in Nigeria and he tells me he is still at his home in Ogale. He listens attentively to my introduction and then begins to reminisce about growing up in the area. His account overflows with a sense of natural abundance. He rolls his 'r's with relish as he recounts wrapping leaves around bushmeat – wild animals he and others had hunted. He recalls his grandmother preparing a 'concoction' of medicinal roots in an attempt to ease his suffering from typhoid.

Shell is part of those childhood memories. Okpabi recalls seeing the company's Land Rovers and trucks when he was a little boy in the 1960s, soon after oil production had started. He and his friends used to think the vehicles carrying pipes were called 'danger wide loads' because that was the written warning they all displayed.

The company was doing something entirely new in Ogale. It had to carve roads out of the jungle to access its well locations. While villagers lived in houses made of mud, with zinc roofs for a few higher-status residents, the Shell accommodation had electric light.

Okpabi described a communal sense of wonder at the foreign incomers. When the Shell employees sat outside and drank beer, it was a 'sight to behold just to surround white people', he says. 'Even the little [kids], five, six, seven, eight years old, we derived a lot of pleasure just being around them. If their Land Rover got a puncture and we had the opportunity to push it, we would be so happy to do it for free.'

The young Okpabi eventually left Nigeria for a while to study in Texas – another place at the heart of the 20th-century oil industry. He graduated in criminal justice and political science, staying on in the US to work. He didn't return to Nigeria until the early 1990s, where he confronted a very different scene from the idyll of first oil he had described.

Crude was no longer a curiosity but a point of conflict, Okpabi says. Pollution had damaged the community's ecosystem. Fish seemed scarcer in the streams, crop yields lower and vegetation thinner. Fruits that he used to enjoy as a child were sourer. 'The pawpaws here are uneatable,' he adds. 'The taste has changed.'

As Okpabi tells it, the community had learned bitterly of the impact of the oil industry that now enveloped it. Whatever consent it had given and whatever hospitality it had offered had been without full knowledge of the consequences.

'I don't think the elders then knew the economic value of what [the company] were taking from our land,' Okpabi said. 'Looking back, I think that is what I would call a betrayal of trust.'

The British had taken firm control of the Delta in the late 19th century. It was the era of the 1884–5 Berlin Conference at which European powers divided up the African continent between them. The Royal Niger Company, the West African equivalent of the East India Company, was key to imposing Britain's authority. It even had an official charter from the government in London. Various traditional rulers in the Delta and its hinterland signed treaties of protection with the British. These contained onerous restrictions on trade. Some chiefs who protested were sent into exile[21] by the British for their effrontery.

Okpabi says he believes that his great-grandfather signed an agreement with the British on behalf of Ogale, though he doesn't have a copy. He asks me if I can get it for him from the UK National Archives, if it is available.

When I visit the archives some weeks later, I find a file that indexes British treaties in the Niger Delta. There is a reference to agreements with 'Ogalay (Great)' and 'Ogalay (Small)', but it is unclear if this is the same place. In any case, the document itself isn't in the file.

What the file does contain is sample language from the treaties that shows how much authority the British took to exploit Delta land. It opens with a bald declaration that the signatory chiefs cede all their territory 'for ever' to the Royal Niger Company. The British business has 'full power to mine, farm and build' anywhere, with an obligation only to 'pay native owners of land a reasonable amount'. Who decides what is a 'reasonable amount' is not specified. It does, however, seem unlikely that community petitions on this point would have been entertained at the Royal Courts of Justice in London.

Okpabi sees a clear link between the treaty establishing British hegemony and the arrival of the energy industry more than half a century later. The UK was the ultimate power in Nigeria at the time it was starting up oil exploration and production. 'That opened the way for the British, and for Royal Dutch Shell to go into the area,' he says. 'I am sure that if my great-grandfather knew what his descendants would be facing, he would not have signed that treaty.'

Okpabi's career has taken in various jobs in the Rivers State government in the Delta, which takes a portion of the country's oil revenues. He has been chairman of the broadcasting corporation and the road regulatory authority. He was first inducted into chieftaincy in 1997 and has risen since to become ruler of Ogale and five other communities in the wider area. He may be the lead petitioner to the UK High Court, but he sits on the other side of the legal process in Nigeria. As a regional ruler, he says he is the appellate authority for disputes that the communities he oversees can't resolve themselves. The matters he rules on range from divorces to land rights.

Okpabi commends the British judicial system for agreeing to hear his community's case, but derides Shell's decision to fight it. He gives short shrift to the company's claims that it has remediated pollution as required. He characterises Shell's position instead as 'we are going to pay lawyers to drag you through the courts'.

'Why don't you sit down with us, see how you can clean our environment that you know you have destroyed?' he asks Shell rhetorically. 'Why don't you pay us some compensation?'

Ogoni communities tried to bring a case over pollution in Nigeria some years ago, but it went nowhere, Okpabi says, before adding that he has no faith in the country's judicial system. 'Nobody defeats Shell in Nigeria. If the British courts and judicial system fail us, we are finished.'

He dismisses as 'very stupid logic' Shell's arguments that it is not liable for the pollution. He says there were no illegal refineries in Ogale used to process oil taken from pipelines. Besides, whatever the cause of the spills, Shell is responsible for ensuring the integrity of its infrastructure. He frames his point as if he were a lawyer accusing the company in a courtroom. 'You are the one transporting [the oil],' he says. 'You are the one laying the pipe. Why don't you look for a technology that people can't tamper with? How come people don't tamper with the crude in Texas?'

Okpabi says he tries not to get emotional telling his story, but it is hard not to do so. It is 'mind boggling' that people can 'come in, make money' and then 'not pay compensation for what they have destroyed'. 'It is devastating,' he sums up. 'Our story is pathetic. It is catastrophic.'

An overseas resource discovered under British imperial rule has been exploited to the benefit of that country's businesses and people, Okpabi notes. Now, more than half a century on from first oil in Nigeria, he sees the events in a London court as a reckoning.

'It is sad that this is where we are in the very painful colonial story that started in the 1950s here in Ogale,' he says. 'When you talk about the history, it's a very big case.'

Shell insists that is has acted responsibly in the way it has handled pollution in Ogoniland. It says its Nigerian subsidiary SPDC cleans up and remediates areas affected by spills from its facilities or pipeline network, irrespective of their cause. It works to do this with 'regulators, local communities, and other stakeholders'.

Shell argues that the main source of the problem is that 'oil is being stolen on an industrial scale in the Niger Delta'. This 'criminality' is the cause of the majority of spills in the Ogale and Bille claims, the company says. It adds that lawsuits like this one are not the answer to the manifest pollution problems in Nigeria's oilfields.

'We believe litigation does little to address the real problem in the Niger Delta: oil spills due to theft, illegal refining and sabotage, with which SPDC is constantly faced and which cause the most environmental damage,' it says.

Shell's history intertwines like a Niger Delta mangrove with the British Empire. The company's origins lie in a 19th-century London antiques business run by Marcus Samuel, who decided to branch out into importing sea shells from Asia. Samuel's sons expanded further into oil shipping: their company, Shell Transport and Trading, and its distinctive insignia honoured their father's business. In 1907, Shell Transport and Trading merged with its rival, Royal Dutch of the Netherlands.[22] A telegram announcing the merger to create Royal Dutch Shell was received on 23 April. That date – marked in the UK as St George's Day – is now celebrated by Shell as its birthday.

Nigeria became important to Shell after the Second World War. The company has described the years that followed as 'some of the toughest' it has ever faced, due to reconstruction costs and shifts in the oil market.

Shell started operating in Ogoniland[23] in the 1950s. The oil flowed over the following decades – but at the cost of growing opposition. By the early 1990s, around the time Okpabi returned to Ogoniland from the US, an uprising had begun. Ken Saro-Wiwa, a writer and environmental activist, had co-founded the Movement for the Survival of the Ogoni People. It campaigned against pollution and for a greater share of oil revenues for Ogoniland. By 1993, Shell had stopped operating in the area. It has never restarted.

In 1995, Saro-Wiwa and eight other Ogoni activists were arrested and sentenced to death, their alleged crime organising the murder of four political rivals. Saro-Wiwa and his supporters denounced the charges as trumped up by the military dictatorship of General Sani Abacha.

The case went global. I remember being transfixed by it as a student. Public figures from around the world pleaded with Nigerian authorities not to carry out the sentences. Critics pointed to huge flaws in the legal process, which was conducted by a secretive military tribunal.

The Nigerian dictatorship ignored the outcry. The 'Ogoni Nine' were hanged on 10 November 1995, triggering intense international condemnation. Nelson Mandela, South Africa's president, decried the 'heinous act'. He called for Nigeria to be expelled from the Commonwealth pending its return to democracy. The country was suspended the next day, returning only after Abacha's death opened the way to the restoration of civilian rule in 1999.

The Saro-Wiwa case triggered criticism of Shell and questions over its role in events. The company insisted it bore no responsibility for the hangings of its high-profile opponents, saying later that it had 'attempted to persuade the government of the day to grant clemency'.

Saro-Wiwa's execution took place at the prison in Port Harcourt in the Niger Delta. The city was named by Nigeria's British occupiers for an old Etonian secretary of state for the colonies, Lewis Harcourt, who opposed women's suffrage[24] and had a reputation as a sexual predator.[25] Nowadays, this memorial to British depravity is the oil industry's nerve centre. Its traffic-choked streets lead to a web of jetties from where boats venture into the swamps beyond.

One detail that stayed with me was of Saro-Wiwa's last moments between several botched attempts to hang him. It took five tries, according to contemporaneous reports.[26] Versions differ on the exact wording of what Saro-Wiwa said, but the most common rendering of how he began is, 'What kind of country is this?'

The condemned man's horrified incredulity as his executioners fumbled with the scaffold did not catch only my imagination. Saro-Wiwa's six words have often since been cited by Nigerian commentators in writings on other national iniquities. His statement burns with righteous outrage and scorn for the oppressor, even with death imminent. It summons past ghosts of the Port Harcourt gallows, where the country's previous British rulers[27] disposed of their own irritants.

The Ogoni Nine executions marked the start of a long posthumous campaign for justice. Plaintiffs including relatives of the hanged men took Shell to court in the US. They accused the company of conspiring with the Nigerian authorities to arrest and execute the men – allegations that Shell denied. In 2009, the two sides announced a settlement just as the case was about to go to trial. Under the deal, Shell paid $15.5m[28] but did not admit liability. It said instead that it was making the payment in recognition of the 'tragic events' and to 'focus on the future for Ogoni people'.

It is one of a lengthening series of Nigeria-related lawsuits Shell has faced in courts in Western countries. The company's hybrid Anglo-Dutch status has opened the way to legal claims against it in the Netherlands as well as the UK.

In 2022, four widows of men who were executed alongside Saro-Wiwa lost a Dutch case[29] seeking compensation from Shell. The court said Esther Kiobel, Victoria Bera, Blessing Eawo and Charity Levula had not proved claims that Shell representatives paid witnesses to testify against their late husbands. The company had denied the allegations. It added that the ruling did not 'diminish the tragic nature of the events of 1995'.

Community members and activists have fared better in actions launched over alleged pollution. In December 2022, Shell agreed to pay €15m[30] in the Netherlands to compensate three Niger Delta communities affected by four oil spills between 2004 and 2007. The lawsuit, initially brought in 2008 by four Nigerian farmers and the Friends of the Earth campaign group, took almost 15 years to conclude. Shell claimed the spills were caused by sabotage, although a Dutch appeals court said it had not proved this 'beyond reasonable doubt'.

The sums may appear large, but they are still modest compared with Shell's income. In 2022, its annual profits more than doubled to $39.9bn[31] after Russia's invasion of Ukraine drove energy prices up. The company did not reveal its earnings from its Nigeria operations, but it did say that it paid $1.36bn to the government[32] in taxes and royalties.

The UK case brought by Okpabi and the other Ogoniland residents is the latest clash between Shell and the British law firm Leigh Day. Leigh Day has carved out a specialism representing group claimants against the British government and companies over alleged abuses from Iraq to Ivory Coast. Martyn Day, the firm's co-founder, has argued that the law should treat 'people in places like Bodo in Nigeria in the same way as they would people in Birmingham.'

In 2011, claimants represented by Leigh Day sued Shell and the Nigerian subsidiary SPDC[33] in the first UK case seeking damages from a company over alleged pollution overseas. The action on behalf of thousands of residents of the Bodo fishing community, south-east of Port Harcourt, related to two 2008 oil spills. SPDC admitted liability, but settlement talks dragged on for years over disputes about the scale of the leak and the compensation payable. In 2015, the two sides finally agreed a deal for Shell to pay a total of £55m.[34] More than half the amount went to 15,600 claimants, including 2,000 children, who received average payments of £2,200 each. The remainder of the money went to the community.

While out-of-court settlements like this bank cash and save the cost, time and stress of a trial, they are double-edged. They mean a judge never has the chance to rule on points of fact and law that could be crucial to similar lawsuits. The money is significant for the companies, but the case becomes an operating expense rather than a wider threat to the way they do business.

The Bodo case concluded without a ruling on big discrepancies over the alleged size of the spills. SPDC initially said it was responsible for a total leakage of just 4,000 barrels, although it later admitted this was an underestimate. By contrast, Leigh Day said expert evidence suggested the leaks totalled 500,000 barrels. These were said to have damaged 600,000 hectares (2,300 square miles) of mangrove swamp – an area more than ten times larger than the Isle of Man.[35]

In 2023, Shell saw off a separate Nigeria pollution-related action at the UK's Supreme Court. The court threw out[36] a claim by more than 27,000 Nigerians against two Shell subsidiaries over a 2011 oil spill in the giant Bonga offshore field. The judges said the plaintiffs, who were not represented by Leigh Day, had missed the deadline for taking legal action. The court didn't rule on the substance of the lawsuit, which alleged the incident had polluted onshore farms, forests, waterways and shrines.

Shell argued the claims were unfounded. It attacked the claimants' lawyers for 'disregarding the court's time and costs'. It added, 'While the 2011 Bonga spill was highly regrettable, it was swiftly contained and cleaned up offshore.'

It is a long arc from Britain's colonial domination of Nigeria to the judicial grandeur of establishment London. This gives the Ogale case a wider significance that is not lost on King Okpabi.

'What a story,' he says. 'I am sure if my great-grandfather could look into the seeds of time, he would not believe his eyes.'

He is aware, too, of a warped historical irony. A case involving an industry that began to prosper under imperial rule will now be decided in the capital city of the former oppressor.

'It's funny, isn't it?' Chief Okpabi says. 'To get justice, we have to go back to them.'

7

Tinder Britain

Mu Sochua has been forced into exile from her native Cambodia twice during her life. The first time was in 1975, when the genocidal Khmer Rouge seized power while she was studying abroad. The second was more than 40 years later, when authoritarian Prime Minister Hun Sen cracked down on resistance to his decades-long rule.

Now Mu Sochua lives in the US and organises opposition to the regime in Phnom Penh from there. She is dismayed that foreign countries have had little to say about the political oppression – and the UK is high among her disappointments. Britain had been a leading supporter of the 1991 Paris Peace Agreements to restore democracy in Cambodia. Now it seems more concerned with boosting trade as part of a post-Brexit commercial tilt towards doing more business in Asia.

'Britain is forgetting its obligations as a signatory to the Paris Peace Agreements, which stipulate that Cambodia must be neutral, and must have regular free and fair elections,' Mu Sochua tells me. 'There is no rationale in trading policy for this. Cambodia is far too small and far too poor to ever become a significant trading partner for Britain.'

The UK is focusing on Cambodia and other South-East Asian countries in an effort to reassert itself and boost commerce in the world beyond Europe. A stream of ministers have paid court to nations in the region, trying to drum up business as part of the campaign to create a so-called 'Global Britain'. In doing so, they have highlighted profound differences between how the UK views its international heft and how it appears to others.

Since its divorce from its European partners, Britain has spruced itself up for attractive new dates. It has touted its attributes in an international outreach that is the diplomatic equivalent of signing up on Tinder. But in geopolitics, as in romance, potential partners can smell desperation – and exploit it if they wish. Britain's craving for commerce risks leading it to ignore other important needs, such as honouring values it claims to hold dear.

It is not that the idea of improving ties with countries in South-East Asia is bad in itself. It is that the energy, resources and rhetoric Britain is throwing at it seem out of proportion to the possibilities – and heedless of the downsides. The potential returns are modest, while cultivating autocratic governments such as Cambodia's risks undercutting those who campaign for the democratic principles Britain claims to support.

Most of all, there is a big question of how realistic Britain is about its influence and appeal. I lived in Thailand and travelled extensively in South-East Asia between 2013 and 2017. It was evident then that the UK was a relatively minor presence there – and logically will continue to be. China and the US are the great political powers, while big business is dominated by companies from Japan, Korea and the region itself.

Britain's anxiety to impose itself in the world has been palpable since it left the EU in 2020. The then Foreign Secretary Liz Truss's Conservative Party Conference speech[1] in September 2021 highlighted the neuralgia plainly. Its thrust was that the UK would become the centre of what she dubbed a worldwide 'network of liberty'. Truss's choice of ideal partners was revealing. She did not mention the EU or big member states such as France, Germany, Italy and Spain. Instead, the few European countries she name-checked included the so-called Visegrád Four of Hungary, Poland, the Czech Republic and Slovakia. Hungary and Poland in particular are eye-catching choices for a supposed campaign for freedom. Both have become increasingly repressive as ruling parties have tightened their grip on national institutions. (As of November 2023, a rival coalition was attempting to oust Poland's governing Law and Justice Party after elections the previous month.)

Even more strikingly, Truss included the Gulf states on her list of freedom-loving nations. These countries are ruled by monarchies. None have meaningful elections and dissent is suppressed in all of them to varying – and sometimes draconian – degrees.

The policy Truss launched has been tweaked since she left the Foreign Office and, after her blink-and-you-miss-it premiership, Downing Street. The 'network of liberty' branding appears to have been quietly dropped – but the push to deepen partnerships with autocracies as well as democracies remains.

In December 2022, Truss's successor as foreign secretary, James Cleverly, announced the outcome of an internal review on his department's direction for the next three decades. He said the Foreign Office needed to respond better to the way the 'geopolitical centre of gravity' was 'moving south and east'.[2] Britain could not 'hang on to the comfort blanket of our pre-existing friends'.[3] It must 'have conversations in diverse countries that are moved by different philosophies', he said.

Cleverly's criteria for potential partner countries was that they should honour the international rule of law, free trade and national sovereignty. These are specific enough that many authoritarian states would comply with them (although Cleverly skirted round the fact that Britain itself, because of the Iraq invasion, might not). Democracy and human rights were notably absent from the foreign secretary's checklist of desired qualities.

Aiming to make diplomacy as wide-ranging as possible is reasonable and sensible in principle – but the test is what that means in practice. If it leads to an indiscriminate cultivation of relationships with countries simply because they are not China or Russia (or the EU), then that carries dangers of its own. It could lead to Britain being seen to tacitly condone political repression and other abuses by its new allies.

The UK's post-Brexit interest in South-East Asia is hardly surprising. While global attention on Asia understandably focuses on the giants China and India, the ten Association of South-East Asian Nations (Asean) members are substantial in themselves. The member countries are Indonesia, Malaysia, Singapore, the Philippines, Brunei, Cambodia, Thailand, Laos, Vietnam and Myanmar. Their population, estimated to total more than 650 million, is around 50 per cent higher[4] than that of the EU's 27 countries.

The UK inevitably has a colonial history in the region. It once ruled four Asean member states – Singapore, Malaysia, Myanmar and Brunei – and it retains a popularity with elites in those countries as a place for education, shopping and property. In a neat reversal of imperial power balances, South-East Asian investors have bought iconic London real estate, such as Battersea Power Station.

The UK engagement with South-East Asia ticked up sharply once Boris Johnson took over as prime minister and Brexit became inevitable. In July 2019, just after Johnson arrived in office, Dominic Raab visited Thailand in his capacity as foreign secretary. While he was there, he met Abhisit Vejjajiva, a former prime minister.

It seemed a strange choice to pay court to a man who had left power eight years previously – and whose premiership had been contentious. Abhisit was parachuted into government in 2008, when the country was ruled by a military junta. He oversaw a deadly army crackdown on anti-government protests in 2010 and was trounced in an election the following year. He had been a marginal political figure ever since.

There is one more relevant fact about Abhisit. He was a classmate and friend of Boris Johnson at Eton. They spent time together in Thailand in a gap year before they went to university and have kept in touch[5] since. Abhisit even said Johnson had told him in 2018, when he visited Bangkok as foreign secretary, that he would go for the British premiership.

In late 2021, it was new foreign secretary Liz Truss's turn to visit Thailand. She posed for a photo astride a Triumph motorbike made there. It was quite an image, given that the company had announced plans the previous year to stop mass-producing bikes in Leicestershire and to raise its Thailand output instead. Truss characteristically bulldozed past the apparent contradiction to insist she was doing the right thing. She asserted that improving ties with South-East Asian countries would create 'jobs and opportunities for British people'.

On the same trip, Truss tweeted about meeting Thailand's prime and foreign ministers. Only her encounter with the foreign minister was pictured, which seemed unusual in protocol terms. The absence of the premier, Prayuth Chan-ocha, might have been because he was a former head of the army who took power in a 2014 coup. Truss did not tweet about this, nor of human rights concerns such as the detention of protesters by the military.

The foreign secretary likewise didn't appear to have published any photos of visits to the British embassy in Bangkok. This was probably just as well. It had been sold off to a retail company which had plans to make it into a shopping mall. Photos and video posted online showed the old building being demolished, a symbol of crumbling British influence. Only the statue of Queen Victoria remained, half hidden by jungle plants.

Truss did take the chance to pen an opinion piece in which she extolled the economic opportunities she saw for Britain in South-East Asia. 'Indonesia, like Thailand and Malaysia, has a booming middle-class craving the best of British, from our world-class food and drink like Welsh lamb [to] best-selling computer games such as Minecraft,' she wrote[6]. It was quite an achievement to raise so many contentious points in a single sentence. Most egregiously, Minecraft was developed by Swedish entrepreneurs. The rights to it were then bought by Microsoft of the US in 2014.

The reference to Welsh lamb was also telling. Just days before Truss's trip, the UK government announced an agreement in principle over a trade deal with New Zealand. According to the government's own figures, the agreement would bring negligible to no benefit to Britain. But one of the consequences would be to remove tariffs from New Zealand lamb and other animal products, making it easier for them to undercut UK producers. It will no doubt be a great consolation to Welsh farmers to think that they can export their unsold produce 10,000-plus kilometres (well over 6,000 miles) to South-East Asia.

There is likewise scant evidence of an economically transformative 'craving' by these South-East Asian 'middle classes' – read elites – for British products. In 2022, the UK exported just over $23bn of goods and services to Indonesia, Thailand, Malaysia and Asean's other seven members. That trade is less than UK annual exports to the Netherlands (population 18 million).

The British government's styling of these countries as significant future trade partners because their economies are growing fast ignores a basic mathematical truism. It's easier for poorer and middle-income countries to register high growth rates than it is for rich ones because they are coming from a lower base. But that does not mean they offer more business in absolute terms. Ten per cent growth from a base of 10 is no more of a gain than 1 per cent growth from a base of 100.

In a video to accompany her South-East Asia trip, Truss reeled off more British industries she wanted to promote in 'fast-growing parts of the world'. The first she mentioned was whisky. It was a strange choice, given that two of the three countries she was visiting were majority Muslim. It felt like an unintended signal of the clumsy over-eagerness of the Global Britain strategy.

In August 2023, Britain set out to woo another of South-East Asia's big players. The government announced that trade minister Nigel Huddleston would visit Vietnam as well as Indonesia to 'turbocharge trade' in the region.[7] There were 'big opportunities for British businesses' and the UK was 'working hard' to remove barriers and 'help companies sell even more', he added. The press release enthused that Huddleston's trip came just weeks after Britain had joined the Comprehensive and Progressive Agreement for Trans-Pacific Partnership (CPTPP) trade group.

The CPTPP is an example of the government's habit of exaggerating trade benefits that are marginal – and far smaller than the damage Brexit has caused. There are, it turns out, reasons why Britain is the only non-Pacific country to join the CPTPP. Distance counts in world commerce. The CPTPP would increase long-term UK gross domestic product by just 0.08 per cent,[8] according to the government's own estimates. By contrast, the UK Office for Budget Responsibility has estimated that Brexit will depress productivity[9] by 4 per cent in the long run. (In November 2023, the Office for Budget Responsibility forecast the CPTPP would deliver a GDP boost of just 0.04 per cent after 15 years of membership.[10])

During Huddleston's ministerial visit, he posted a series of messages and videos hailing Britain's relationship with Vietnam. The country was described as 'a key trade partner for the UK'. Commerce between the two countries was 'flourishing' and rose 29 per cent to £6.9bn in 2022, the minister enthused.

That £6.9bn is barely one-tenth[11] of the £59.1bn of trade the UK did with Belgium alone in the year to the end of March 2023. Belgium has less than 15 per cent of Vietnam's near 100 million population, so the relative difference per capita is even starker. Yet it is hard to recall the last time a British government minister hailed Belgium as a 'key trade partner'.

There was another telling omission in the UK government public relations around Huddleston's visit. In the four quarters to March 2023, the biggest British export[12] to Vietnam by value was pulp and waste paper. In other words, the largest contributor to the supposedly booming commercial relationship appears to have been the UK sending rubbish to South-East Asia.

Huddleston went further with his warm words for Vietnam in a video shot by the waterside[13] in the capital Hanoi. He highlighted a bilateral 'history of cooperation and friendship that spans five decades'. 'Let's seize the opportunities, break down barriers and pave the way for a future of shared prosperity between the UK and Vietnam,' he concluded.

The praise contained no hint of how Vietnam is an authoritarian communist one-party state that routinely persecutes dissidents. Vietnam has a difficult relationship with China for historical reasons, but the two have strong political affinities. If London's position is that human rights count for something in international relations, they cannot be relegated just to sell a few more medicines in Vietnam.

There are good reasons for Britain not to be seen to lecture other countries on human rights, particularly outside the Western world. It looks hypocritical given the UK's historical record and its harsh modern-day policies in areas such as immigration. Its impact can be limited or even counterproductive, especially if autocratic regimes portray it as foreign meddling. But there is surely a middle ground between preaching and ignoring. It is legitimate for concerns about human rights to limit how close bilateral relations can become. Britain must not be seen to condone abuses or corruption, which its financial institutions have helped facilitate all too often in the past.

Which brings us back to Cambodia, where the UK has been busy rekindling relations for a while. In 2021, Dominic Raab tweeted an early-morning view of the Mekong River in the capital Phnom Penh. The panorama was, he boasted, 'the first, I'm told, for a British foreign secretary since 1953'.[14] He said he was in the country to 'boost trade, support Cambodia's energy transition, expand UK Asean cooperation – and as a force for good in the Indo-Pacific'.

What he left out was striking. He didn't point out that Cambodia has been dominated by one man since the days when Margaret Thatcher was UK prime minister. It was 'almost as if the Foreign Secretary is not on a trade mission to an authoritarian, one-party state', a journalist with long experience of Cambodia tweeted drily in response.

The deterioration of democracy in Cambodia was pronounced even during my four years of visiting the country. In parliamentary elections in July 2013, just before I arrived in South-East Asia, Prime Minister Hun Sen had received a political fright. Official results gave his Cambodian People's Party 48.8 per cent of the vote, not far ahead of the opposition Cambodia National Rescue Party's 44.5 per cent. The CNRP alleged ballot fraud. The US, EU and international groups such as Human Rights Watch called for an inquiry into the claimed irregularities.

Hun Sen, a former Khmer Rouge commander who had ruled the country since 1985, responded instead by tightening his grip. Opposition activists and rights groups were harassed. Sam Rainsy, the CNRP president, left the country in 2016 after being charged with incitement and defamation.

Mu Sochua was another leading figure in the CNRP at that time. I first saw her at a demonstration in Phnom Penh in July 2014. She and fellow campaigners rallied at Naga Bridge, with its eponymous ornamentation of seven-headed cobras. They were calling for the reopening of nearby 'Freedom Park', which the government had shut down after protests there over the previous year's elections. Mu Sochua and other opposition MPs were arrested and charged with insurrection for their pains. They were released about a week later after the CNRP agreed to end a boycott of parliament.[15]

I saw Mu Sochua again on the 40th anniversary of the Khmer Rouge's 1975 takeover of Phnom Penh. She was commemorating the event at the former Choeung Ek extermination camp run by Pol Pot's genocidal regime. It was one of the so-called 'killing fields', where thousands were slaughtered and children were battered to death by having their heads smashed against a tree. Fragments of human bone still sometimes surfaced decades later, especially after the monsoon rains.

Mu Sochua's parents disappeared during this reign of terror, when she was studying in the US. Altogether an estimated quarter of the population were killed before a Vietnamese invasion ousted the Khmer Rouge in 1979. Years of instability followed, until the 1991 international deal struck in Paris gave the UN a mandate to govern Cambodia and deploy a peacekeeping mission there. Hun Sen lost UN-organised elections in 1993, but did a coalition deal with the winning party – and then ousted it in a 1997 coup.

Mu Sochua, who had become a women's rights activist, finally returned to Cambodia in 1989. She became an MP and then the country's women's minister. During her time in office, she helped force the deportation in 2003 of the British paedophile pop star Paul Gadd, better known as Gary Glitter. She resigned in 2004, dismayed by official corruption, and threw herself into opposition to Hun Sen's increasingly repressive rule.

I last saw Mu Sochua in person for lunch in Phnom Penh in July 2017, during my last weeks based in South-East Asia. It was clear the political pressure was growing intolerable. Less than three months later, she fled the country, citing a warning[16] from an official that she was about to be detained.

The previous day, Hun Sen had claimed 'rebels' and 'foreign slaves' were vying to 'betray and destroy the nation and peace'. He warned that the arrest of opposition leader Kem Sokha in September 2017 on treason charges would be followed by others. In March 2023, Kem Sokha was sentenced to 27 years of house arrest.

Two months after Kem Sokha was jailed, the UK and Cambodia held their first joint trade and investment forum. UK ambassador Dominic Williams and Pan Sorasak, Cambodia's commerce minister, signed a memorandum of understanding. This would 'provide an opportunity to shape & strengthen the trade & investment relationship', the British embassy in Phnom Penh tweeted.

The publicity gave no sense of how modest the UK economic relationship with Cambodia is. Total trade between the two countries was less than £1bn[17] in 2023. Most of this was imports of clothing and footwear from Cambodian factories. Sales by UK businesses in Cambodia accounted for just £217m of trade – less than a quarter of the total. Cars were the largest component at £17.4m, followed by metalworking machinery and animal feed.

In all, Cambodia was the UK's 101st largest export partner worldwide. It accounted for just 0.1 per cent of UK trade. That figure is unlikely to change dramatically, since Cambodia is a poor country of only about 17 million people.

In July 2023, ten years after Hun Sen had nearly lost power, parliamentary elections showed how effectively he had crushed opposition to him. The Cambodia National Rescue Party and its successor the Candlelight Party had both been dissolved on technical grounds. Hun Sen won 96 per cent of the seats in a poll that was, as a BBC piece put it, 'more of a coronation than an election'.[18] The British government acknowledged the vote was 'neither free nor fair', but concluded mildly that it was merely a 'missed opportunity to strengthen Cambodia's democracy'.[19]

A few weeks later, Hun Sen stepped down as premier after 38 years. He handed the role to his son Hun Manet, a four-star general and former Cambodian army chief. Hun Manet had benefited from multiple foreign educational opportunities, including an economics PhD from the UK's

Bristol University. The new leader told Parliament that his cabinet would follow the 'heroic example'[20] of its forebears. His father made it clear that he would continue to exert influence in the background.

The Bristol degree was not Hun Manet's only connection with the UK. He had a military link, too. In February 2023, the offshore patrol vessel HMS *Spey* became the first British navy warship to visit Cambodia[21] in 65 years. The following month, UK ambassador Williams met Hun Manet and welcomed the growing military-to-military ties[22] between the two countries. Hun Manet in turn spoke warmly[23] of Cambodia's relationship with the UK, particularly armed forces cooperation.

Mu Sochua is aghast at Britain's decision to embrace Cambodia's father and son regime. Cambodia under Hun Sen has built a close alliance with Beijing and a dependence on its money, despite efforts by Western powers to increase influence. China has been building an extensive naval base[24] on Cambodia's Gulf of Thailand coast, although it denies the People's Liberation Army will have access.

Mu Sochua argues that, far from wooing Hun Sen and Hun Manet, Britain should be repudiating them. She suggests they deserve the kind of punishment aimed at governments, such as Russia's, that are accused of persecuting political opponents and other rights abuses.

'Accepting the Hun Manet regime as a legitimate partner allows regional security risks to continue to develop,' she says. 'Targeted sanctions against the regime, which are coordinated with those taken by other democratic countries, is the best way forward.'

Britain's uncomfortable bear-hug with countries such as Cambodia has clear origins in the urgent need created by Brexit for new relationships. I was living in South-East Asia at the time of the 2016 referendum and saw how odd the result looked[25] to many in the region. This certainly didn't reflect sentimental affection for the EU, which has frequently clashed with various countries over human rights and environmental policies. Rather, the puzzlement was pragmatic: why had the UK chosen to disregard and discard the benefits of being part of its main regional organisation?

The comparison with South-East Asia's own main intergovernmental grouping is instructive. Asean was founded on 8 August 1967 by Indonesia, Malaysia, the Philippines, Singapore and Thailand. This was just weeks after the UK had caused alarm in the region by announcing it would withdraw troops from its bases in Malaysia and Singapore.[26]

The creation of Asean was in part an attempt to stop the spread of communism in the region, where the Vietnam War was raging. Asean's founding declaration laid out a wide spectrum of goals, which included promoting economic growth, social progress and wider regional collaboration. The ambitions echoed those of counterparts in Europe, where the European Commission had come into being barely a month earlier. [27]

As political circumstances in South-East Asia changed, Brunei, Vietnam, Laos, Myanmar and Cambodia swelled Asean's membership to ten countries. It is a much looser organisation than the EU: it offers some travel privileges, but it doesn't have trade arrangements anything like the European bloc's customs union or single market.

Asean is no subject for romanticisation. Like the EU, it is frequently criticised for its ineffectiveness and its shortcomings in policing its own members, such as Myanmar's military regime. In an August 2023 commentary[28] headlined 'Asean is quietly coming apart at the seams', analyst Michael Vatikiotis laid out the problems the organisation faced. These included the US–China power struggle, internal political tensions and the disintegration of Myanmar. 'All this has made Southeast Asia more fragile and isolated than it appears,' the author said.

For all the truths in these arguments, it remains a significant point that Asean exists and has a stable membership. This is the more remarkable given the differences – and at times antagonisms – between its countries. The organisation's emblem, a sheaf of ten rice stalks, represents the utility its members hope to find in bundling themselves together.

The countries of South-East Asia are no less nationalistic than their European counterparts. In many ways, they are more culturally diverse. There are few linguistic overlaps in a region that includes Myanmar's many tongues, Thai, Khmer, Vietnamese, Malay and Tagalog: for this reason, Asean's official working language is English. Its population includes adherents of many religions. Indonesia is the world's largest Muslim majority nation. Buddhism predominates in Thailand and Christianity in the Philippines.

The span of incomes across Asean is far greater than it is in the EU. Oil-rich Brunei and the highly developed city state of Singapore are among the richest countries in the world per capita. At the other end of the scale lies the mass rural poverty of Myanmar and Cambodia. Asean's membership also covers a broad range of political systems. They include military dictatorship, single party rule and democracies offering varying degrees of freedom.

All this means Asean is riddled with contradictions. Its most high-profile rift is over its response to the February 2021 military coup in Myanmar. 'Asean prides itself as a "rules-based organisation",' a veteran South-East Asian diplomat[29] reflected ruefully to Nikkei Asia later that year. '[But] the truth is, there are no real rules. We make them up as we go along.'

Yet, despite everything, the organisation still hangs together. That is because, on some fundamental level, all its members see the self-interest of being part of the main regional grouping with their neighbours. They know they need as many levers as possible to deal with a world of political conflict between powerful countries, primarily China and the US.

South-East Asian nations certainly took lessons from Brexit. They saw it as a warning against integrating too far and too fast. Asean members had signed a charter in 2007 pledging to move towards an 'EU-style community', but the 2008 financial crisis had already put that in question.

Asean is very far from being a model international organisation. But the point is that no one has left and no one is seriously threatening to do so, despite episodes of severe friction. In a troubled world, it pays not to be alone – nor be seen as pressingly in need of friends.

Veteran Singaporean diplomat Chan Heng Chee came into the world in 1942 at a moment that symbolised the UK's shrinking international power. She was born barely two months after imperial Japanese troops captured her home country, then under British rule. The fall of the strategically located South-East Asian island shocked both London and international capitals used to the idea of British naval capabilities. Japanese bombers sank the British battleship[30] *Prince of Wales*, along with the battlecruiser *Repulse*.

'People were alarmed when British forces surrendered to the Japanese and so on,' Chan tells me. 'The *Prince of Wales* was invincible, and suddenly bang, it was sunk. Our idea of trust and belief that the British Empire was invincible – that was shaken.'

Chan's background and long career have given her a sharp perspective on Britain's changing international status and ambitions over the decades. She grew up in a colony that London quit in the 1960s, part of a dramatic wider pullback from South-East Asia. More than 50 years later, the British state would turn to her for advice on defining the country's role post-Brexit.

I wanted to explore the meaning of all this. Chan speaks to me from her home in Singapore, a 15-minute journey from her professional base at the Foreign Ministry. The white walls and black beams of her study, designed by her architect ex-husband Tay Kheng Soon, give it something of a modernist Tudor feel. The wall behind her is dominated by a shelf of books and a wooden puppet visible over her left shoulder.

Chan's black-framed glasses and the soft undulations of her parted hair frame her forehead as if to emphasise the brainpower beneath. At 81, she remains as precise as you would expect from someone who still represents her country as an ambassador at large. Her career has included postings at the United Nations and more than 15 years as Singapore's envoy to Washington. She is on the governing board of the Stockholm International Peace Research Institute and has honorary degrees from universities including Warwick and Buckingham in the UK.

Chan's parents were Cantonese speakers who were born in Singapore and had family roots in Hong Kong. After Britain's defeat by Japan, they moved to the countryside in what is now the Malaysian region of Malacca. They started a business rolling cigarettes and sold them to Japanese troops, so they were 'not down and out', Chan says. After the war they were part of what she calls the 'merchant class'. They ran an import-export company in Singapore's Chinatown, where their business included selling canvas sailcloth to Indonesia.

'I grew up that way, so one foot nearer Chinese culture, though I speak English and in many ways my background in literature and learning is very much Western – British, actually,' Chan says. 'I've never read American literature. It was pure British literature in school and the university.'

Given that history, it's perhaps no surprise that Chan names Jane Austen first when asked for her favourite authors. She likes novelists who write sparely, like Graham Greene. Among more recent writers, she cites Anita Brookner and Alan Hollinghurst.

Chan's exact delivery and her account of her literary influences remind me a bit of Myanmar's Aung San Suu Kyi. The two women are from opposite ends of South-East Asia, but they were both born under colonial rule and grew up with British-inflected education. They attended convent high schools and were fed a good part of the English literary canon.

'I was taught by Irish nuns, and teachers who spoke very good English – and I'm a product,' Chan says. 'That's why I speak like this. They emphasised speaking, poetry, enunciation, acting in plays and so on.'

Chan's experiences left her with an ambivalent view of UK occupation. The British 'weren't really hated' in the way French and Dutch invaders were elsewhere in South-East Asia, she says. People remembered the imperial period for 'good education, good civil service, and good hospitals'. 'It was seen to be a gentler kind of colonialism,' she adds. 'But it had its hard bits.'

Those hard bits included routine discrimination against Chinese speakers. Chan's own mother spoke about how the British created an environment that disdained those who couldn't speak English, like her. They were made to feel as if there was 'something missing' and that they were 'not the same class', Chan says.

Chan says she agreed with the psychiatrist and Marxist intellectual Frantz Fanon's view on the imperialism of language, if not with his overall politics. Fanon pointed to how people who can speak the coloniser's language become culturally distanced from those who cannot. Chan describes the discomfort she and her English-educated peers felt about this linguistic alienation from their parents. 'We felt more modern and they were not modern,' Chan says. 'Because the language of English became the language of modernity.'

Chan's equivocal take on the British imperial era reflects a wider ambiguity in Singapore. She points out how the country has kept many English street names, such as Cotswold Close and Lyndhurst Road. It has retained the bronze statue[31] of Sir Stamford Raffles, the British official who took control of the city state in 1819. Lee Kuan Yew, the founding leader of independent Singapore, said the memorial was a 'symbol of public acceptance of the legacy of the British'. 'It could have a positive effect on Singapore's future development,' he added.

'It was a signal to the world that we are open,' Chan says of the way Singapore has dealt with its British colonial history. 'We are not anti-anything. And for a small state, you have to accept everybody.'

There are other reasons why Singapore may have less negative feelings towards UK rule than other colonised countries. There were few resources for the occupiers to plunder, unlike in other nations that were rich in timber, metals or oil. London did not lethally suppress independence campaigners; nor did Singapore suffer massive bloodshed like that triggered by the partition of India and Pakistan. Many of Singapore's independence-era leaders, including Lee Kuan Yew himself, had been educated in Oxford, Cambridge or London.

Chan laughs when I say that it is perhaps easier for Singapore to be magnanimous, given it is now significantly wealthier than its former ruler. In 2022, the city state's gross domestic product per capita on a purchasing power parity basis was $127,565, according to the World Bank.[32] This figure, which is controlled[33] to take into account price differences between countries, was comfortably more than double the UK's $54,603. On unadjusted GDP numbers, Singapore is still well ahead,[34] with $82,807 to the UK's $45,850.

'We are an entrepot economy – there are hardly any riches,' Chan says. 'We have a strategic position. Our selling point for Britain was the strategic location, the security angle. And we happen to be good at trading.'

Modern Singapore may be rich, but it is realistic, too. It knows it is a small country in a region shaped by battles between great powers. It always needed allies and so switched to the US once it became clear Britain was pulling back from South-East Asia.

'Lee Kuan Yew said, "I do need to have a major defence partner, someone with an umbrella to protect us,"' Chan says. 'And then he turned to the United States.'

Chan's point about the centrality of international alliances ran through an appearance she made in 2020[35] before the UK House of Commons Foreign Affairs Committee. The hearing was to gather evidence for the Integrated Review on the UK's international strategy that would be published in 2021.

Chan appeared remotely at the event after Koji Tsuruoka, who was formerly Japan's ambassador to the UK and deputy foreign minister.

Chan began with a polite statement saying that Britain had 'plenty' of capabilities and qualities to offer South-East Asian countries. She said it was a military and nuclear power, with a commitment to multilateralism. She cited its status as a permanent member of the UN Security Council and member of the G7 and G20. 'Those are very important forums, so when you come to the region, you come as a member that has a voice that will reach out to many, and you impact on policies,' she said.

The conversation became more pointed when Labour MP Chris Bryant asked about the importance of the Commonwealth, which comprises the UK and its former colonies. Chan said it would be 'difficult' to build on that, in part because of competition from other international gatherings. But it was worth trying to do so, she added. 'We are in a world of interlocking groupings and networks,' she said. 'No one gives up a grouping. You should keep groupings and enlarge them.'

I ask Chan what she meant by that. Part of it is about security, she says, but it also reflects that Singapore sees economic alliances as crucial. It has bilateral and regional trade agreements. It seeks to be part of gatherings within Asia, with other regions and on a global level.

'Singapore believes in groupings,' Chan says. 'And we could not understand why Britain, when you are ensconced in such a well-established European Union grouping, that you would want to voluntarily pull out.'

Brexit had lurked in the shadows of the UK parliamentary committee hearing until a revealingly comic moment illuminated it. The Tory MP Royston Smith appeared to misread Chan's comments as an endorsement of his pro-Brexit views. Smith is a long-time Eurosceptic who supported Sir James Goldsmith's Referendum Party in the 1990s. He seized on Chan's description of Britain as a 'pragmatic country' and 'much easier to work with' than those that aren't.

'That is very helpful, thank you,' he said. 'Some of the people like me who wanted to leave the European Union always felt that it hamstrung us, and the more conversations like this we have, the more I feel that is, in fact, the case.'

Chan fired back that she 'really regretted hearing that Brexit did happen, but there you are'. Smith interjected hurriedly to conclude the exchange. 'And I know you were not alone in that,' he said.

It was unsurprising to see Smith shut down a conversation that did not go in the direction he had hoped. The back and forth reads like a clash of ideologies between the internationalist realist and the little Englander. I ask Chan to expand on why she thought Brexit a mistake.

Britain had a 'bigger voice' when it was in the European Union, she says. It was valued by Singapore as an advocate of free trade, although she acknowledges these have become 'dirty words' given the world's tilt towards protectionism. The UK was also able to 'counsel the US' about Europe.

'So we thought your voice was very important,' Chan says. 'When Britain spoke when you were in Europe, you spoke with the voice of the United Kingdom, but also you could claim to speak for the EU as well. And we thought your influence in the EU could have mitigated some of the protectionist tendencies of other European countries. That's why I think we regret it in Singapore.'

Of course what is good for Singapore is not necessarily good for the UK. Chan is far from starry-eyed about the EU and its shortcomings, particularly on foreign policy. As a former diplomatic correspondent in Brussels, I too recognised well the bloc's many hypocrisies, its big internal tensions and its struggles for external influence.

But Chan's fundamental point is persuasive. Any country probably has to be part of a body to which most of its neighbours belong, whatever the frustrations. The logic is blunt: you cannot afford not to be. Whether it is an

apartment tenants' association or an intergovernmental organisation, you
have to be there to guard your interests.

'Otherwise if you are not in the grouping and not in a loose alignment
with them, they will align against *you*,' Chan says.

I ask Chan about another aspect of the post-EU debate in the UK
that has bugged me for a long time. It has become commonplace to refer
to some Brexiters' ambitions to introduce a 'Singapore-on-Thames'
model to the UK. This refers, often pejoratively, to making the country
a deregulated free-for-all. The phrase is so widely used it even has its own
Wikipedia page.[36]

One reason why I dislike the term is that it seems dismissive and
stereotypical. Another is that it seems to be based on a mistaken idea of
what contemporary Singapore is and how it has developed. It appears
to ignore the way the modern state is the product of decades of national
planning, government intervention and state subsidisation. It also skirts
over the fact that the autocratic foundation of Singapore's political
system jars with Britain's proclaimed ideas about democracy and popular
representation.

Chan agrees the 'Singapore-on-Thames' rhetoric is flawed and outlines
another reason why. Her country has distinctive features that make it hard
to use as a model. It is tiny, it has an extraordinarily strategic location, and
its history gives it an unusual openness to ideas from elsewhere. These are
not characteristics shared by many other countries – and certainly not the
UK. Chan points finally to Singapore's willingness to learn from others.
This, again, is not necessarily a quality for which the UK has traditionally
been renowned.

'How you create your own model is up to the country,' Chan says. 'You've
got to figure out what it is and that's what Singapore did. We figured it out
and even today, we still figure it out by going to other countries to learn. And
we come back and say, "This is what we want. This will work."'

Singapore is providing a niche but growing subculture of critiques of the modern UK. George Yeo, the country's former foreign minister, wrote one in *The Economist* in 2022.[37] He described how his old Cambridge college looked 'better than ever' when he visited for lunch. But when he went to the coastal town of Great Yarmouth to see his son, it required a 'slow rickety train ride'.

'My day there made me nostalgic for the Britain I left in the 1970s (former prime minister Edward Heath's three-day week notwithstanding),' Yeo wrote. 'But it also bothered me that too little had changed. I wondered how long it would take for Chinese companies to revamp the country's creaking infrastructure.'

Yeo's piece is revealing for several reasons, even if his prescription of more Chinese infrastructure raises its own questions. He highlights the contrast between the impression of prestige that Britain's famous institutions still present to the world, and a wider sense of public dilapidation. His piece contains an undertow of pity, like that for a friend who has gone off the rails.

Yeo did throw out a line of hope, like the crab fishers he describes on the Great Yarmouth waterfront. 'With its bruised economy and disruptive politics, there is no shortcut to recovering Britain's standing in the world,' he wrote. 'The country's recent political crises have hardly helped. The new prime minister, Rishi Sunak, should appreciate that the journey to recovery will be arduous. Fortunately, there are many old friends too-long forgotten or underrated, particularly in Asia, who can be willing travel companions.'

I ask Chan if she agrees with Yeo's diagnosis. She says that political instability has certainly become a problem in the UK – including whether Scotland ends up leaving the union. 'Britain has to try to get stronger leadership and come through,' she adds. 'It's harder with Brexit. It's about keeping Great Britain – not Little Britain. So people wonder.'

Chan has seen British foreign policy crises before – including a much more deadly one. She was in Washington during the era of the Iraq War. The

UK's enthusiastic support for the US in that invasion damaged relations with many countries in Europe and beyond.

Now Britain is trying to rebuild its international stature again after the shock of Brexit. Chan says she does not think Britain seems lost exactly in its foreign policy, but it does need to 'make more friends'. This applies particularly with the countries of the so-called global south, generally understood to mean nations outside of the West and not closely allied to it.

The unspoken coda is that London has put itself in a position where it can't be picky about who those new friends are. Otherwise, the future may be one of unquestioning alignment with Washington of the kind that spawned the Iraq catastrophe. It is an especially troubling prospect given the possibility that Donald Trump could return as president.

'Right now, post-Brexit, you are trying even harder to prove you are relevant,' Chan says. 'But on the other hand, if I'm being very cold and calculating on this, I don't think Britain has much of a choice except to be on the right side of the US. Because what [other] path would you cut?'

Britain's new direction in the world seems increasingly clear from its South-East Asia policy, encapsulated in its dealings with Cambodia. In 2023, as Hun Sen prepared to pass power to his son, Mu Sochua and fellow opposition leaders lobbied the UK to take a tougher line. They pressed for action in an April 2023 letter sent to UK Foreign Secretary James Cleverly and seen by me. The document, signed by long-time opposition leader Sam Rainsy, points to claims that Cambodia's national police chief Neth Savoeun has overseen serious human rights abuses by the force. The letter highlights further allegations[38] that relatives of Neth Savoeun have bought property worth millions of pounds in central London. (Neth Savoeun didn't respond to requests for comment submitted via his Facebook page, a WhatsApp account bearing his photo, and a close aide. Cambodia's defence ministry has previously denounced the allegations of rights abuses as 'fabricated'.)

The UK has 'allowed the family to continue to use London as their playground', the letter claims. 'Neth Savoeun and his family members should be barred from entering or living in the UK, and their property in the country should be confiscated.'

The Foreign Office gave the letter short shrift. A reply sent in May by its Cambodia desk – again seen by me – says Britain does not comment on future or individual sanctions designations. 'The UK established a human rights dialogue with Cambodia to make our concerns about human rights clear,' the reply says. 'We will continue to engage with Cambodia on human rights and raise our concerns where appropriate.'

I wrote to the Foreign Office seeking more information about the Neth Savoeun case. I inquired whether any investigation was being conducted into the claims of the family's London property ownership. I also addressed the UK's political position in Cambodia. I asked for comment on the allegation that Britain has focused on commercial ties with Cambodia, while paying little attention to alleged government abuses. The department did not respond.

In August 2023, Neth Savoeun was made deputy prime minister by new premier Hun Manet. It was another manifestation of how government is often a family affair in Cambodia. Hun Manet had inherited power from his father; his new deputy's wife Hun Kimleng is his cousin.

Cambodia is hardly alone in its dynastic politics, but the combination with the harsh repression of any alternative is particularly insidious. The UK's near-silence on this is not unique, but it sits uncomfortably with claims that Britain cares about promoting human rights and democracy.

Mu Sochua, a dissenter once again unable to return home, protested at the United Nations General Assembly in September 2023 over Hun Manet's appearance there. The new prime minister told his fellow world leaders that Cambodia's polls two months previously had been 'free and fair...credible and just'.[39] The demonstrators outside chanted, 'Change, or no change?' – a cry heard from the Cambodian opposition during its rallies against the 2013 election irregularities.

Mu Sochua is dismayed at what she sees as Britain's help for the self-perpetuation of Cambodia's rulers. She says the regime uses the UK's willingness to work with it to bolster its internal legitimacy. 'A "business as usual" approach to dealing with such a government is not a neutral position,' she adds. 'Hun Sen has repeatedly used international endorsements to underwrite his domestic tactics of repression.'

If this is how 'Global Britain' projects itself, it is far from clear to Mu Sochua how it is contributing to a better world. Most grievously, the UK's approach allows Cambodia's regime to give its people the message that there is no point protesting. After all, no one in London seems to be listening.

'This effect may well be invisible to British policymakers,' Mu Sochua says. 'It is keenly felt and resented by Cambodians who demand democracy and who expect more from countries who claim to stand for democratic values.'

8

The Wizard Behind the Curtain

The rescue of the Sultan of Brunei by British troops led by Digby Willoughby was an unlikely collision of worlds. The repercussions of the encounter would shape UK global military ambitions more than half a century later.

The year was 1962 and Sultan Omar Ali Saifuddien III was holed up with his entourage in his palace in the Borneo island territorial enclave. A rebellion had erupted in Brunei, which had become a site of both internal and external power struggles as European empires retreated from South-East Asia. Omar had called for help from Britain, which had taken over the country as a protectorate in Victorian times.

The UK responded quickly and sent a contingent of Gurkha troops from Singapore. One group of soldiers, commanded by Willoughby, was to protect the sultan and his associates. The deployment in the tropical jungle zone of South-East Asia was quite the change of scene for Willoughby. Months before, he had represented Great Britain in bobsleigh[1] at the World Championships, having broken a course record at St Moritz the previous year.

Willoughby and his men extracted the royal party and took them to the safety of the police station in the capital, then called Brunei Town (now Bandar Seri Begawan). Shortly afterwards, the sultan addressed the country's people on state radio. He was not in a forgiving mood about the revolt, which was now destined for failure because of the British forces' arrival.

'The specific aim of these rebels was to overthrow my government,' he declared.[2] 'This action was not only prohibited by the laws of the country but [was] also condemned by God.'

Omar's deliverance represented a decisive intervention by the UK in his favour and against opponents of his authoritarian rule. It was the first embrace of a military bear hug that led the UK to station a Gurkha battalion in Brunei – paid for by the sultan. The soldiers remain there to this day, funded by Omar's son and successor Hassanal Bolkiah. They are the only British fighting unit in an Indo-Pacific region in which security tensions have risen in the past few years.

The tale of the Brunei battalion highlights the precariousness of modern Britain's place in the world. The presence of the Gurkhas, who are mostly recruited from Nepal, is both a colonial relic and a modern-day political risk. The Borneo unit occupies an isolated outpost in a dangerous region. It is financed by a repressive regime that may one day pull its funding.

The battalion is part of a wider struggle about what kind of security power the UK should be now Britannia no longer rules the waves. Britain is trying to project itself as a world player, even amid growing domestic difficulties and heavy commitments to Ukraine's defence against Russian invasion. The tension reflects a conflict in Britain between an assertive nationalism and those who think the country should play a more circumspect role.

The strange history of Britain's Borneo contingent is an indicator of the stretches the country is making as it seeks a global military presence. The strategy has a Wizard of Oz quality, with the UK behind the curtain attempting to portray itself as more imposing than it is. Britain has talked of opening more bases in Asia and it is deploying more ships there. This is almost the opposite of the conclusion reached after a similar domestic debate more than 50 years ago. Then, Britain decided for resource reasons to exit facilities east of the Suez Canal.

Now the UK risks being caught up in conflicts in Asia over which it has little sway. The South China Sea around Brunei includes some of the world's most contested waters. They are a spider's web of competing maritime territorial claims.

The situation onshore in Brunei could be equally delicate. There is the perpetual possibility that the sultan could demand payback from Britain for his years of financing its military.

'It would become extremely uncomfortable for us if there is serious trouble in Brunei,' says Francis Cornish, who was British high commissioner to the country when it became independent in 1984. 'Because the sultan will certainly turn around and say, "Gurkhas, please put it down, please sort it out." And that will cause us all manner of angst.'

The sense that the UK is in danger of overextending its international ambitions runs through the government's latest review of foreign policy. The document, entitled *Global Britain in a Competitive Age,* first came out in 2021. A 'refresh' was unveiled[3] in March 2023, along with £5bn more military spending, mainly on the UK's nuclear submarine capability and weapons for Ukraine.

In the original *Global Britain* paper, you can almost feel the authors' desperation to avoid citing the European Union. The bloc is barely mentioned. There is simply a wish for 'constructive and productive relationships' with member states – and a counterpoint about the UK's 'freedom to do things differently'.

The document makes a string of questionable exceptionalist assertions, including that Britain has 'uniquely global interests, partnerships and capabilities' – a claim that might surprise other countries with similar feelings. The idea that Britain has a 'global perspective and global responsibilities' sounds like a gentler rewrite of the imperialist idea of the 'white man's burden'.

The strategy makes a 'tilt' towards Asia a central plank of Britain's diplomatic and security policy. It echoes former US President Barack Obama's declaration almost a decade previously of a 'pivot' to Asia, even if this proved more principle than practice.

Britain had already strengthened its military presence in the Gulf states of Bahrain and Oman in the 2010s and announced it was considering new bases in South-East Asia. The integrated review went further still. It said the UK would 'pursue deeper engagement in the Indo-Pacific in support of shared prosperity and regional stability, with stronger diplomatic and trading ties'.

The central idea of a Britain unfettered by the destiny of its European geography has long been enthusiastically promoted by Brexiters, including Boris Johnson. In 2016, when he was foreign secretary, he gave an address in Bahrain entitled 'Britain is back east of Suez'. That was a reference to the Labour government's move in the 1960s to slim down Britain's overseas military presence for both financial and political reasons. One academic has even dubbed that move 'Brexit 1967',[4] part of 'Britain's retreat from empire and Cold War Southeast Asia'.

The Bahrain speech was classic Johnson. One of his rhetorical tricks is to use bombastic language to evoke an era when Britain basked in global power. It is a linguistic dog whistle to feelings that some in Britain wish could be recreated today.

Johnson cast Britain's withdrawal of military installations east of Suez almost half a century previously as a mistake. He wanted to reverse course, he told his audience in the Bahraini capital Manama – a city where authorities had cracked down with deadly effect on protests during the 'Arab Spring' uprisings. That repression was not on his agenda, however: he wanted to talk only about closer security ties. 'We recognise the wisdom of those who campaigned for a policy of engagement east of Suez. That your interests – military, economic, political – are intertwined with our own,' he said.

Johnson's grandstanding was a striking example of a stubborn refusal at the top of British politics to adapt to changed international power dynamics. The east of Suez policy acknowledged the UK was living beyond its international means. It meant the closure of military bases across the Middle East and Asia, in favour of a Euro-Atlantic focus. The point was made plain by then prime minister Harold Wilson, who outlined how the east of Suez policy was a response to a realistic assessment of Britain's place in the world. It prioritised 'our ability to get to places where we were needed rather than reliance on vast, costly and sometimes indefensible bases in those areas', Wilson said.

Fast-forward more than 50 years and that logic seems to have been abandoned. Instead, deployments are planned that increase the UK's exposure but lack the necessary support. Those could prove to be 'large enough to "get us into trouble" but too small to get us out of trouble once it starts', as one analyst has put it pithily.[5]

Britain's efforts to project power internationally have provoked some domestic unease. In 2023, Simon McDonald, a former top official in the Foreign Office, made waves with an interview on the subject. His talk with the *New Statesman*[6] was most revealing for how many nerves it touched.

McDonald was already despised by a faction of the Conservative Party over his role in bringing down Boris Johnson's premiership, by releasing a public letter. It concerned accusations that the MP Chris Pincher, who had been a Foreign Office minister, had drunkenly groped two men in a London club. McDonald claimed Johnson knew much more than he had admitted about the allegations when he appointed Pincher deputy chief whip. (In July 2023, Pincher was suspended from the Commons[7] for eight weeks over the allegations. He subsequently announced he would resign as an MP.)

Some of McDonald's foreign policy criticisms seemed obvious. He censured the fast-tracking of people with little or no ministerial experience into top jobs. He noted pointedly that Boris Johnson's first job in government had been as foreign secretary.

McDonald went on to highlight the inevitability of the UK's relative decline as countries such as India, China and Brazil have grown in power. He cited Brexit as another factor in the UK's changed position, depriving it of its natural regional alliance and increasing its reliance on the US. Washington was less interested in Europe anyway and much more preoccupied with China and the rest of Asia, McDonald argued. He referred regretfully to past British foreign policy disasters, noting that the Iraq War had caused a huge number of deaths and brought 'no benefit'.

The part that appeared to annoy McDonald's critics most was when he suggested Britain should adjust to being less influential. Asked by the interviewer if it was the end of the 'great game' for the UK, he replied, 'Yes.' He thought Britain shouldn't be sending aircraft carriers to the Indo-Pacific. The UK was 'still trying to play a hard power game, but we don't have the resources to back that up any more', he said.

The interview provoked a strong reaction both inside and outside the country. Nick Timothy, the adviser to former Premier Theresa May who quit after her botched 2017 election campaign, tweeted: 'The civil service is its own worst enemy.' Philip Cowley, professor of politics at Queen Mary University of London, sniffed, 'Someone comes out of this interview quite badly, and I'm not sure it's Boris Johnson.'

Ulrike Franke, a German senior fellow at the European Council on Foreign Relations, wrote, 'That is quite the read! I am used to Germany saying they have no power in the world, but hearing this from Britain, from a former senior foreign policy official is quite something.' [8]

There were certainly points to quibble over in McDonald's analysis. The description of sending arms to Ukraine as part of the 'soft power side of life' sounded odd. But what people seemed to object to most was the message that the world had changed and so had the UK's status in it.

It was telling how even the journalist who wrote the piece seemed taken aback. He had expected, for reasons he didn't elaborate, to find a man with 'a bullish view of our place in the world'. Instead, he saw in McDonald 'a man who could uncharitably be described as being resigned to British irrelevance'.

The reaction to McDonald shows that the urge for Britain to be a big international player is not simply a Conservative phenomenon. A case in point is that of the two aircraft carriers referenced by McDonald – the HMS *Queen Elizabeth* and the HMS *Prince of Wales*. They were commissioned under the Tories in the late 2010s, but the original contracts had been announced in 2007[9] under Labour. The programme went ahead despite significant questions at the time. In 2010, the government's strategic defence review said that only one of the carriers should be built. The construction of both went ahead anyway, since the cost of cancelling the building contract would have been higher than honouring it. The vessels went more than 50 per cent over their originally estimated £3.9bn cost. At first, the navy didn't have enough aircraft and had to borrow some from the US.

The Royal Navy webpage entry on the giant warships now drips with a thick coat of patriotic gloss.[10] They will 'fly the flag for Britain', 'protecting our nation's security and economic interests', it reads. The vessels are further tasked with 'extending the hand of friendship and building the relationships that are crucial to diplomatic affairs'. It is unclear whether the author of those words saw the irony that they sounded quite like the imperial-era strategy of gunboat diplomacy. 'The two ships are icons, standard bearers and symbols of a nation with a global role and global ambitions,' the blurb goes on.

The blend of aggression with proclaimed idealism is notable. The British Navy's biggest swords are simultaneously meant to be ploughshares. 'The Carrier Strike Group offers cutting-edge air, surface and underwater defence, but it is also a focal point for the worldwide democratic activity that is more powerful than any weaponry,' the website reads.

Elsewhere on the site, a strike warfare planner named Lieutenant Jeremy Vasquez is named alongside a perhaps inadvertently ominous quote. He says that 'diplomacy is always our preferred option', a phrase that seems to contain an undertow of menace. Relationships with foreign governments and partner forces are 'often key to preventing potential crises, from securing shipping routes to settling regional disputes,' he adds.

The most striking point here is that Lieutenant Vasquez is not a British officer but a US Navy pilot. It is a small sign of the effort the UK has had to make to equip, crew and accompany these two titanic ships. The website says the rest of each carrier strike group can be 'made up of submarines, warships and support vessels from other Navies'.

The *Queen Elizabeth* was deployed to the Pacific in 2021[11] as part of a seven-month trip that involved 'diplomatic engagement' with more than 40 countries. Three Singapore navy ships accompanied it in the South China Sea. In May 2023, Prime Minister Rishi Sunak said a UK carrier strike group would return to the region in 2025.

While the *Queen Elizabeth* has been on global manoeuvres, it has not been plain sailing for her sister ship. The *Prince of Wales* has suffered mechanical problems since it was commissioned in 2019.[12] In October 2020, it was forced out of action for six months after the engine room flooded. In August 2022, the ship broke down[13] again just a day after leaving Portsmouth for training exercises with the US. It was scheduled to return to service at the end of 2023.

The UK aircraft carrier deployments in Asia carry a significant risk. Any military unit in the region today could be caught up in the modern great power battle between China and the US. Washington has dominated the region's seas since the Second World War, but Beijing is attempting to assert its authority. The South China Sea is key to this. China claims rights over almost all these waters, bringing it into territorial conflicts with many countries in the region.

A UN tribunal comprehensively rejected China's expansive claims in a 2016 ruling, but Beijing has continued to build and expand strategic artificial islands. In 2022, the US claimed China had fully militarised three islands[14] on the Spratly archipelago between Vietnam and the Philippines. Journalists who overflew the area in a US aircraft reported seeing more than 40 vessels anchored at Fiery Cross Reef. (China claims all its South China Sea island military deployments are purely defensive.)

Fiery Cross is a sign of changing nautical times. It was named for a British tea clipper that ran aground there in the 19th century. Now China has occupied the area since 1988.

These tensions are why increasing an Indo-Pacific presence has proved contentious even in Nato, the 31-member mostly Western military pact. In 2023, a proposal for the alliance to set up a one-person liaison office in Japan was delayed because it could not win internal agreement. France led opposition from countries uncomfortable that it would extend the group beyond the Euro-Atlantic sphere it was founded to protect. Concerns about increasing the alliance's presence in Asia included that it could be – or be presented as – a provocation to China. At the same time, it would further stretch European Nato members at a time when many have military commitments to support Ukraine.

The 'Indo-Pacific tilt' is a quandary even for a military alliance the size of Nato. The perils are multiplied for Britain acting alone in a region where China, Japan and other countries have been building up their militaries. It is hard to see how the UK's Asia strategy meets Harold Wilson's test that the country should focus on 'places where we were needed'.

Wilson's launch of the east of Suez policy happened just as the former UK envoy to Brunei Francis Cornish was starting his diplomatic career.

Cornish was to notch up an unusual distinction: he witnessed not one but two of Britain's late retreats from imperial conquest. After seeing in Brunei's independence in 1984, he was at the handover of Hong Kong back to China in 1997. Both events said much about the shifting nature of British military power.

Cornish is based in retirement in the West Country city of Bristol. He works from a room with photos of the Somerset farmhouse where he and his wife worked for a while rearing sheep. Nowadays, he is not doing much, he says, before listing various activities including 'ringing church bells' and the English-Speaking Union.

He volunteers some days as a guide on the SS *Great Britain*,[15] Isambard Kingdom Brunel's celebrated ship launched in 1843. It is a reminder of the era of British nautical might, less than 40 years after the Battle of Trafalgar. It was a landmark invention, fashioned from iron, with a novel screw propeller and the most powerful engine yet used at sea. It is a symbol of the power of the Victorian imperial age and was dubbed 'the greatest experiment since the creation'.

Cornish is a lively conversationalist with the droll presence of someone who has seen it all. He clearly enjoys talking about the old days and highlights absurdities of his many postings. He has an affection for this past, coupled with an awareness of how it is part of a world that no longer exists.

Cornish was born in 1942, just a few weeks after the Singaporean envoy Chan Heng Chee. He trained at Sandhurst and joined the military, serving in the early 1960s with an armoured regiment in Libya to protect the then King Idris's regime. The UK presence in the North African state was intended as a bulwark against Gamal Abdel Nasser's neighbouring Egypt. Nasser and heavy US pressure had forced the British to retreat from the Suez Canal in 1956, an event that became emblematic of the UK's ebbing international power.

Cornish switched to the Foreign Office in 1968, embarking on a career there that would last almost three and half decades. A good part of that time was spent in Asia, starting in Malaysia. He arrived in 1970, with a communist insurgency underway. That conflict had its roots in the long-running revolt by pro-independence fighters against British rule in what was then called Malaya. The British fought brutally until independence in 1957,[16] killing civilians, forcing villagers into internment camps and spraying land with a herbicide similar to the notorious Agent Orange.

After this, Cornish spent time in Indonesia and was dispatched to Brunei in 1983. His main job there was to prepare what was then still a British protectorate for independence from the UK. He is candid about how little the country figured on London's agenda.

'When I was sent there it was extremely difficult to find anybody in the Foreign Office who knew about the place,' he says. 'It was a protectorate and quite frankly, I don't think I knew or was told what the heck a protectorate was. For a while I have a feeling I was Brunei's foreign and defence minister – but nobody explained that to me and it didn't seem to have any duties.'

He arrived in Brunei Town to occupy the 'rather splendid' house allocated to the top British official in the territory. The hillside residence is an expansive cluster of wooden buildings[17] known as Bubungan Dua Belas, or House of Twelve Roofs. The yellow, white and red structures were restored to a museum opened by Queen Elizabeth II[18] when she visited in 1998. It has had to be restored several times since, in an unending battle with encroachment by the surrounding jungle.

The sultan provided these benefits – and, when the time came, he duly took them away. That time was Independence Day on 1 January 1984.

'He provided a house, he provided a car, he provided a whole pack of servants,' Cornish recalls. 'I didn't hand them over voluntarily – they just disappeared on the day. There wasn't any drama about it. All the trappings of the former status disappeared.'

Cornish sees the comedy in his sudden change in circumstances. He says it came as a great 'relief' to his children. They had been horrified by the stress Cornish's official car caused to other road users. 'They were sitting in an ancient Daimler with other cars more or less driving off the road when they saw us approaching,' he said. 'The place was pretty feudal. The royal family was really the only entity that mattered.'

The high commissioner found his standing reduced 'enormously' at official events, too. At functions such as banquets, he now sat with the other ambassadors – including the new US envoy. Previously he had been at the sultan's side. 'That was extremely useful because it's the only place in the world where I could actually really feel I was doing my job, because I could talk to him about things,' Cornish recalls. 'And all that disappeared.'

One crucial vestige of British rule that survived was the Gurkha battalion. Digby Willoughby and his men had saved the sultan in 1962 – and he never forgot that.

'Brunei blew the whistle,' Cornish says, describing the sultan's appeal to London when confronted with the challenge to his rule. 'Britain, responsible for Brunei's defence and foreign policy, responded. And the response was largely in the form of Gurkhas.'

The Gurkhas themselves are a legacy of imperial Britain's voracious militarism and its sometimes callous approach to the non-nationals who fought and died for it. Soldiers from countries occupied by the UK were for long shoved into the background of history. Even troops whose contributions received coverage at the time, such as Indian Sikhs on the First World War's Western front, were shoddily treated[19] afterwards.

In 2021, the Commonwealth War Graves Commission and Prime Minister Boris Johnson apologised over failures[20] to appropriately commemorate Black and Asian troops. A report by the commission blamed 'pervasive racism' for the neglect of at least 116,000 and perhaps as many as 350,000 First World War casualties. Most of those not properly honoured were of African, Indian or Egyptian origin, the commission said. Its tone was a striking contrast to its defensiveness just 18 months previously, when it sniped[21] at a television programme and article on the same subject by Labour MP David Lammy.

The National Army Museum now acknowledges the important contribution[22] of troops such as the Royal West Africa Frontier Force. The contingent, comprising troops from the Gambia, Gold Coast (now Ghana), Nigeria and Sierra Leone fought in the brutal Burma campaign against Japanese forces. They 'served with distinction in Burma, showing incredible resilience in the face of extreme heat, disease, monsoons and a formidable enemy', the museum website says. 'Soldiers from all corners of the Commonwealth contributed to the defeat of Japanese forces in one of the most gruelling theatres of the Second World War.'

The British army's Gurkha brigade has an even more extensive history of entwinement with imperial conquest. Its insignia is the crossed blades of two kukri, the multi-purpose curved knife used in the Nepalese communities from which the Gurkhas are drawn. Gurkhas fought British attempts to annex Nepal in the early 19th century, impressing their adversaries in the process. In 1816, the two sides signed a peace treaty which provided for Gurkhas to serve in the army of the East India Company – a main vehicle for British conquest and plunder in South Asia.

The Gurkha brigade's website lists the many wars it has fought on behalf of the British Empire and since. They helped the bloody suppression of the 1857–9 revolt by Indian soldiers and civilians against the East India Company. They were part of the UK forces that put down the Boxer Rebellion in China in 1900, and they served in Burma, Afghanistan, Malta and Cyprus. They fought communist nationalist insurgents throughout the 12 years of the so-called Malayan Emergency[23] between 1948 and 1960.

For most of their time in the British military, Gurkhas had no right to live in the country they risked their lives for. Only in 2004 did the UK government grant such permission. Even then, it only applied to those Gurkhas who retired after 1997 – the date the brigade quarters moved from Hong Kong to Britain.

In the 21st century, campaigners including the actor Joanna Lumley helped secure stronger rights for Gurkhas. In 2009, Lumley, whose father had served in the 6th Gurkha Rifles, extracted concessions[24] after confronting Home Office minister Phil Woolas on live TV. Later that year, the government agreed to extend the right to live in the UK to Gurkhas who retired before 1997.

The Gurkha brigade official history deals with the Brunei uprising briefly.[25] The battalion was alerted at 11pm on 7 December 1962 and by 9am the following day its first members had landed in Brunei more than 1,500km (900 miles) away. They and other British army units dealt with the threat to the sultan's rule, but insecurity took hold in the broader region. It was the start of four years of British conflict with the Indonesian army in Borneo.

Borneo today is an island of dense jungle shared by three modern states. It houses parts of Malaysia and Indonesia. In a northern coastal enclave sits the entirety of the sultanate of Brunei. It has been ruled by Hassanal Bolkiah since 1967, when his father Sultan Omar abdicated in his favour.

Once the Gurkha contingent was stationed here, the military ties with Britain 'expanded not for the benefit of Brunei, but for the benefit of us', Cornish says. The British Special Air Service (SAS) began to do tropical environment training in Brunei. 'It was the sort of thing that we took advantage of because of the good relationship – and because Brunei has got some proper jungle to do it in. So the Gurkhas were there – and the sultan paid the bill.'

Cornish maintains that Britain had 'two objectives' when he was in Brunei. One was to 'shake the place off, make it independent'. The other was to 'make darn sure the military relationship was maintained'.

'The ministry of defence were very, very clear: if Brunei stopped paying for that battalion of Gurkhas, it would cease to exist,' Cornish says. 'So that was terribly important to the old boy . . . the sultan's father – and it was every bit as important to the chiefs of staff back in London.'

Cornish never had a sense that the military deal with the UK would wither over time. Ex-Sultan Omar[26] talked often about the importance of the relationship, he recalls. Omar passed that message on to his son, who trained at Sandhurst and had his own British armed forces links. 'Probably one of the main things that he inherited is that you need the British, you need the Gurkhas, to make sure there's no trouble at the ranch,' Cornish says.

I note that the sultan still pays for the arrangement. 'To this day?' Cornish replies, with apparent surprise. 'Quite extraordinary, isn't it? But there we are.'

I say to Cornish that the arrangement seems to present significant jeopardy. No leader of an authoritarian state, even one as rich as Brunei, can rule out a revolt against their rule. Britain would be in a tough position if the sultan were to say that it was payback time and he needed the Gurkhas. The outsourcing of the Gurkha financing to the leader of a foreign state felt like a big hostage to fortune.

Cornish agrees with that assessment. But he points to the financial counterpoint that the sultan's money has helped offset the dwindling of Britain's military. 'The Ministry of Defence would argue that "we are really up against it and our defence budget is being slashed the whole time",' he says.

The Gurkha deployment faces other potential risks. Brunei has an offshore oil industry, in which Shell dominates. Some of the operations are in disputed waters. Should maritime tensions in the region flare, those resource-rich seas are a possible flashpoint.

None of these arguments went on during Cornish's time in Brunei, he says. Rather, there were 'huge sighs of relief' in London post-independence that the place was peaceful and the British–Brunei relationship 'seemed to be okay'.

I ask if there was a sense of embarrassment in London that Brunei didn't achieve independence until the 1980s. Cornish replies that Britain's special status there was 'awkward' and 'out of tune with the times'. 'Certainly we wanted shot of the place,' he adds, clarifying later that he is referring to the need to sever the constitutional links between the UK and Brunei. 'It's not that we thought that it was going to get us into trouble. It's much more that it was wholly undemocratic, nobody quite understood how it managed to chunter on without any real trouble year after year. And therefore, nobody quite trusted Brunei and what was going to happen there.'

The arrangement since had 'worked out pretty well' for Brunei, Cornish says. Its leaders came to accept that Britain would still be supportive, even if the imperial-era ties were cut. The sultan's father understood that his family's rule would be 'perfectly safe' post-independence. Britain would continue to be his ultimate guarantor 'because we would stand by him,' Cornish concludes.

The British government releases little information about the Gurkha battalion. I asked the MoD a series of questions about it for this book. These included requests for confirmation on its strength, funding and the status of the agreement to continue its mandate. I asked specifically whether the deal would be renewed on 29 September 2023, which available public information[27] suggested might be the case. I inquired about what the UK's response would be to a request from the sultan for the force's deployment on an external or internal security matter. I requested comment on whether the UK saw any ethical difficulties in allowing the head of a dictatorship to fund a British military unit.

I received a reply from Lieutenant-Colonel Dave Walker, an army spokesperson. He said that the 'level of detail and complexity' involved in my inquiry led him to recommend I submit a Freedom of Information (FoI) request instead. FoI applications are generally reserved for inquiries requiring research significantly above and beyond that needed for a normal media query.

I wrote back to Walker saying I was surprised at his suggestion, as many of my questions seemed straightforward queries about current policy and practice. I proposed a phone call to discuss his concerns and a possible way forward, but he did not respond. I followed up with another message seeking clarification on why the MoD wouldn't respond to points that seemed neither particularly detailed nor complex. I again received no reply.

Francis Cornish, who started his diplomacy in the shadow of east of Suez, says he is troubled by the direction of British policy in Asia today. He says the Pacific naval deployments looked 'ill-conceived', because they would tend to be infrequent, rather token and would potentially leave the UK exposed. 'In real life, we are a bit player,' he said. 'People are slowly getting used to the fact that we are not able to contribute in the way that 10, 20, 30 years ago we might have been. But by golly, Michael, it's so different from how we regarded ourselves not so long ago.'

Britain's attempts since leaving the EU to convince the world that it was 'frightfully important' look 'rather pathetic', he says. The problem is not just Brexit itself, but 'the fact that we were incapable of thinking about anything else for a hell of a long time . . . For several years . . . we were so fixated about getting out of Europe. That's the distraction point – but the real point is that here we are on our own, at a time when we would be much, much better off in the company of others.'

In addition, Brexit has removed Britain from a multilateral grouping with an important role in tackling big global problems such as the climate crisis, Cornish continues. Instead the UK is 'gibbering at the sidelines with an awful lot of resentment still there'. 'I'm extremely pleased I'm no longer in the foreign service,' he concludes, with a mordant laugh. 'Because it would be an uphill struggle to be regarded as important. The best you could do would be to be regarded as interesting.'

It is both remarkable and predictable that the UK is still calibrating its place in the world, decades after the collapse of colonialism. Leaving the EU has made this process of adjustment even harder, not just in practical terms but emotionally, too. Part of the project of the most devoted Brexiters is about denying there has been any decline, absolute or relative, in the UK's international sway.

Asia is a petri-dish for the UK's future international security policy. British imperialism died late there, in places such as Brunei and Hong Kong. Now it is where a large majority of the world's population lives and where political and economic power is growing fastest. The UK must engage with this, but in ways that are calibrated with its status as a medium-sized country half a world away. Britain will never be a Pacific power – not least because it is not in the Pacific.

In 1993, Cornish moved to Hong Kong and stayed through to the handover to China in 1997. The deal had been agreed by Margaret Thatcher's government in 1984, but the transition happened just a couple of months into Tony Blair's premiership. That coincidence, with a youthful new prime minister in place in Downing Street, felt attuned to the idea that UK foreign policy was finally modernising.

The handover had a big impact on Britain's scant remaining military presence in Asia. The British closed down their Hong Kong naval base known as HMS *Tamar*, so named after the ship that had arrived a century before to reinforce British control of the territory. The UK had taken Hong

Kong during the 'Opium Wars', during which its military forced China to accept imports of the highly addictive drug. *Tamar* itself served as the base until the Japanese occupation, when it was scuttled to stop it being used by the invaders.

The Hong Kong handover day images are famous in the UK for the emotion of Chris Patten, the last British governor-general, and his family. Prince Charles picked the family up in the royal yacht *Britannia*. The Pattens boarded as midnight approached, with two of the departing top imperial official's daughters in tears.

I ask Cornish about his own feelings that day. I wonder if he felt a sense of British retreat or loss. 'No, what was going around in my mind was that colonies are out of fashion,' he says. 'I didn't feel remotely sad.'

He recalls instead looking at the royal yacht and feeling that it was out of time. It was dwarfed by the sharp-edged Bank of China tower that rises more than 300m (1,000ft) on Hong Kong island. By contrast, *Britannia* was 'a bit like Britain. It was very small, it was very splendid. The brass was beautifully polished,' Cornish says, with a wistful laugh. 'But up against the skyscrapers and glories of Hong Kong, it just looked overshadowed.'

The modern UK is patently not the 'dread and envy' of the world portrayed in 'Rule Britannia'. Some of its more complacent citizens have learned that it has a lot more to be humble about than they may have previously believed. The sense of political chaos, crumbling services and profiteering companies has cut deep. The country seems to be in that bleak psychological phase when the scale of its problems has become apparent, but no obvious solution is at hand.

These anxieties have stoked an appetite for cold-eyed explanations of Britain's apparent descent. One of the most prominent chroniclers of what might be called the realist school of the modern UK's evolution is the historian David Edgerton. His 2018 book *The Rise and Fall of the British*

Nation: A Twentieth-Century History targets what he views as damaging romantic myths about the country's development and destiny.

Edgerton is unsparing towards what might be termed both the boosterish and the declinist tendencies in British public life. One maintains that Britain is great, the other that it has fallen from greatness but could restore itself. Both of these ideas are rooted in certain ideas about the nature of the country that Edgerton, who is a professor of modern British history at King's College London, argues are mistaken.

He speaks to me from the study of his home in the capital, wearing a pastel-blue polo shirt that stands out against the decor of throne-room purple. Next to him are piles of background reading for his next book, a history of production. He talks much as he writes, with verve and an alacrity to cut in good-naturedly with a crease-lined smile if he disagrees with something. Most of all, he gives the sense of a man impatient to understand better. When he learns I am based in Japan, he asks for advice on arranging to see a shipyard, steelworks or other industry for his book.

'One actually learns more than one thinks from just seeing stuff,' he says. 'It won't make a sentence, even, but it will pervade everything.'

Edgerton brings distinctive insights to his chronicles of today's UK. He was born to a British father and an Argentine mother in Uruguay, where he grew up speaking both Spanish and English. He lived in Montevideo before coming to the UK when he was 11 years old. I ask if this gives him an insider-outsider's view of Britain's modern history. He agrees this is 'inevitably so', but says he doesn't want to claim the 'only way of having such a perspective is to be born overseas'.

'Let me put it the other way around: I think a lot of British historical writing is written within very narrow parameters,' he says. 'There's something in that, I think: that people who've studied nothing but British history will tell you a rather clichéd story. But those of us with any number of different backgrounds may see it slightly differently.'

Edgerton came to the UK in November 1970 to receive an early introduction to that decade's turbulent industrial relations. Strikes would plague the government of both the Conservative Edward Heath, in power since June, and the Labour administration that followed.

'The day we arrived, there was a bin strike – a very big bin strike,' he says. 'So all around London, you could see these piles of bin liners full of rubbish. I'd never seen a bin liner.'

The other side of England that struck the young Edgerton on first look was more positive. More than 150 years after William Blake coined the phrase 'green and pleasant land', the newcomer to the country made a similar observation. Edgerton still marvels at receiving the full Jerusalem visual experience on arrival.

'Although Uruguay is a pretty green place, England was even greener,' he says. 'So the *sheer green* was quite something.'

The boy from Uruguay noticed many things he had not experienced before, even though the England of the 1970s did not have a reputation for modernity. Edgerton recalls his wonder at motorways and an ICI chemicals factory he visited while at school. (His father was an industrial chemist.) In other respects, the UK was still catching up with the times. A few months after Edgerton immigrated, Britain decimalised its currency, in a sign it was looking to the future. A pound would henceforth simply be worth 100 pence, rather than 20 shillings or 240 pence or 960 farthings. It was a significant simplification, as well as a revolutionary change for people who had used the previous system their whole lives. TV broadcasts to guide the population through the transition included one called 'Granny Gets the Point'. One of several public information songs included the lyrics: 'They've made it easy for every citizen / 'Cause all we have to do is count from one to ten!'

This came as a relief to Edgerton, who had just come from decimalised Uruguay into this place of baffling and unnecessary currency complexity.

'I'd just had to learn the pounds, shillings and pence, which is quite hard if you come from a decimal system, I think,' he says.

In 1982, Edgerton was struck by another big event that had a strong personal resonance. Britain went to war over Argentina's invasion of the Falkland Islands, a British overseas territory. The Thatcher government sent a task force, harking back to Britain's days of naval supremacy. The UK military retook the territory after ten weeks, several ship sinkings and almost a thousand British and Argentinian deaths. It helped revive Thatcher's political fortunes and buoy her to a landslide election win the following year. The Falklands – almost 13,000km (over 8,000 miles) from London – remain British ground to this day.[†]

I ask Edgerton if his Argentinian mother faced any hostility over the war. He surprises – and heartens – me by saying that she did not. His main observation about the conflict is that he immediately knew how significant it was, because of the politics of the two countries.

'I knew when I first heard about the invasion of South Georgia that this was serious,' he said. 'Most of my British friends thought it was all a joke, on both sides – this was ridiculous gunboat stuff. But I had a very strong sense of the power of Argentine nationalism – and also British nationalism.'

The war sparked Edgerton's historical interest. It was really about Britain 'finding its militarist heart' again, he argues. 'It's one of the things that certainly led me to strengthen my interest in British militarism – and the relationship of the left to it. And the left's lack of understanding of the British state, especially in relation to the military.'

It is a subject Edgerton has explored in depth since. After doing a degree in chemistry, he shifted into the history of science and technology – and conflict. He argues that there is insufficient focus on the role of militarism

---

†   In November 2023, a British minister flew to the Falkland Islands after Argentina's new hard-right president Javier Milei promised during his election campaign to 'get them back'.

in shaping the UK and too much on what he calls 'welfarism'. The story of Britain is often told through the welfare state's rise under Labour and erosion under Thatcherite Conservatives. He is particularly vexed by what he sees as the mythologising of the Second World War as a 'people's war'. In this telling, public sacrifice was rewarded by the National Health Service and aspects of social progress that duly followed. 'These things are deeply ingrained,' he says.

I wonder if Edgerton's scientific background has given him a sense of empiricism and suspicion of sentimental grand narratives. At its best, the scientific method can enforce a certain humility that might have been welcome in the politics of Brexit. If you falsify a result in a laboratory, you risk being found out and held accountable – unlike if you put a misleading figure on the side of a bus.

Edgerton grabs the question and squeezes it into a different framing. He deplores what he saw as the 'utterly unrealistic' claims made by Leave campaigners about the possibilities for UK science post-Brexit. He has said previously[28] that the idea Britain is going to be a world leader in innovation is absurd. It is simply not feasible for a country that accounts for a small percentage of global manufacturing and a similar proportion of research and development.

'A certain fantasy about national science was absolutely central to Brexit,' he said. 'All the stuff about "science superpower".'

Edgerton wrote his thesis on the history of the UK colour photographic industry. The study gave him a sensibility that infuses his work, about the importance of stripping fanciful goals from economic planning. It showed how British manufacturers, outmatched by foreign rivals, were forced to retreat to a niche in black and white film.

The main industrial lessons Edgerton learned were that companies needed to be large, with expertise in either inorganic chemistry or centralised processing, marketing and distribution. The UK companies lacked this and so lagged behind the likes of Kodak and Agfa.

'If you don't have the base to develop . . . and you are not prepared to put in the money that you need, don't try it,' he concludes.

His big point here is about the need to be pragmatic in your ambitions. Britain's resources and educational institutions have given it a prominent role in the history of scientific and technological innovation. But that comparative advantage has been eroded by the rise first of the US and then of China, India and other modern-day powers. Bigger countries are better placed to provide the money and structures needed to turn ideas into national drivers of employment and wealth.

It is a phenomenon seen today in the way that successful parts of the British technology sector have been snapped up by overseas buyers. Arm Holdings, the chip designer, was bought[29] by the Japanese conglomerate SoftBank in 2016. In 2023, SoftBank listed Arm in the US – despite heavy lobbying by the UK government to list in London, too.

Edgerton contrasts today's British political bombast about innovation with the greater realism of Harold Wilson, Labour prime minister during the 1960s and 1970s. In 1963, the year before Wilson took the top job, he famously predicted[30] that Britain's future would be 'forged in the white heat' of the 'scientific revolution'.†

Edgerton's main takeaway from Wilson's sentiments concerns the need to be practical. The prime minister-to-be wanted to make sure that disputes between employers and trade unions didn't compromise Britain's ability to harness wider technological developments. He warned there would be 'no place for restrictive practices or outdated methods on either side of industry'.

Wilson understood the need to concentrate on getting full value from inventions from elsewhere, rather than obsessing only about British innovation. He was preoccupied with the 'need to redirect the R&D effort

---

†   It is widely known as the 'white heat of technology' speech, even though – as with Sherlock Holmes and 'Elementary, my dear Watson' – Wilson never uttered those words.

away from the military and away from prestige projects', Edgerton says. 'So it absolutely isn't this fantasy of unleashing British inventive potential.'

The Covid-19 pandemic has been a brutal reminder to countries including the UK that too little focus on the unglamorous businesses of processes and logistics can be dangerous. World supply chains seized up not due to technological breakdowns or limitations, but because components were being shipped much more slowly – or not at all. Deliveries of household goods from cars to dishwashers went from near-instant to months-long delays.

Suddenly the advantages of a country producing goods on its own soil became brutally clear. I reported from Brussels on the bitter dispute between the EU and Britain over the supply of Covid vaccines made by AstraZeneca. The irony was that the best vaccine in Europe had been developed by researchers at the German company BioNTech. The UK had been quicker to buy it than the EU, which failed to show sufficient confidence in its home-grown drug. The EU and the UK both restricted jabs exports, drawing criticism that rich nations were hoarding the drugs at the expense of poor ones.

An even more powerful allegory of global interdependence and its attendant vulnerabilities was the March 2021 container ship grounding[31] in the Suez Canal. The channel is one of the world's main international trade gateways. For almost a week, the vessel *Ever Given* became the 'Ever Taken Away' as it blocked hundreds of ships from passing. Estimates of the value of the goods delayed ran into billions of dollars.

Edgerton describes these developments as a kind of 'return of the real' to which politicians and societies need to adapt, not least in Britain. Perched on Edgerton's bookshelf is Ed Conway's 2023 book *Material World*. It explains how the availability of mundane materials such as sand and salt is essential to modern life.

'We've long had a problem of understanding, as it were, the material basis of our lives,' he explains. 'Economics has not been good at that, sociology has not been good at that, history has not been good at that. From the 1980s onwards, we all went shopping and ceased caring about where the stuff came from.'

Edgerton's point is part of a wider argument that UK politics needs to adapt better to the world as it is, rather than living in a fantasy version. He thinks the phenomenon of 'declinism' that he finds such a bugbear is an example of a failure to deal with actualities. In his opinion, a key weakness of this worldview is that it ignores how much of Britain's relative diminishment is due to forces beyond its control. A main one of these is the rise of other countries. Once nations across Asia, Latin America and Africa shook off imperialism and managed their own internal tensions, it was inevitable they would grow more powerful.

Edgerton finds intolerable the mindset that sees Britain as having some kind of innate superiority. He deplores it whether it comes from 'revivalist' Brexiters boasting about UK pre-eminence or Remainers lamenting lost global prestige. As he has written:[32]

> Both declinism and revivalism are symptoms of a nation unable to come to grips with its place in the world. Both are stuck in nationalist insularity: one claims the nation is reborn, the other that it can be reborn, to take its proper high place in world affairs. But understanding that real place, and the real nature of capitalism in the UK, and crucially in the world as a whole, is central to any possibility of transformative politics, and that requires England in particular to be modest about a nation that has much to be modest about.

The last sentence, about Britain having an inflated image of itself, is still political dynamite. It is true that UK politicians haven't boasted quite as reflexively as their US counterparts of being from 'the greatest country on earth'. But there is a quiet presumptuousness across British public life about the country's rightful place in the world.

A revealing habit is the way politicians use 'Great Britain' as if it were a term of aggrandisement rather than a geographical descriptor. British diplomatic missions around the world have for years produced publicity displays for the country with the word 'Great' written in very large letters. Again, it is not just Conservatives who do it: Labour leader Keir Starmer has proposed a new publicly owned power-generation company called Great British Energy.[33]

The clash between the narrative of Great British strategic achievement and the malfunctions of the country today has become increasingly glaring. A friend described the chaos of landing at Manchester Airport in August 2023. It was under renovation and each flight's baggage was spread across multiple carousels. She compared it, part tongue-in-cheek but part seriously, to some of the less organized small provincial terminals in poor countries in South-East Asia. 'It was like turning up at one of those little airports in Cambodia and Myanmar where there are bags laid out everywhere and nobody knows what's going on,' she said. (Manchester Airport didn't respond to a request for comment.)

I tell Edgerton that the lamentations on the state of Britain remind me of living in Lagos some two decades ago. There, you were constantly reliant on fixes and fixers for public services that didn't work well. You needed a generator for when the electricity went down and a tanker to truck in the water supply. When I returned to the UK in 2005, I observed how people often took for granted that basic life would work. The angst in Britain almost 20 years on feels like my epiphany in Nigeria's biggest city.

Edgerton says he sees the parallels, at a time of ballooning National Health Service waiting lists and breakdowns in other state functions.

'It's very marked,' he says. 'Once upon a time, it absolutely was the case that in the UK, the accessing of bureaucracy, of health services, all the rest of it, was – if not informal – then easy and quick. And now, it isn't.'

He also sees a growing disconnect between the severity of the problems and the smallness of the solutions floated by many mainstream politicians. It is the product of an 'increasing divergence in living standards and an increasing indifference to the lives of the poor', he argues. 'There's been a very powerful sort of media-political bubble, which has become very, very important and it's seemingly forced bits of the Labour Party at least to talk the same language. But I don't think anyone really believes it. Young people don't believe it. It's just not real.'

Britain's two main parties are trapped in the old ways of thinking because they are both implicated in it, Edgerton argues. The changes introduced by the Thatcher government became consensus once Labour broadly kept them in place during its 13 years in power. Even if the old system is collapsing, any attack on it therefore becomes an act of self-criticism.

'It's really striking that somebody like [Shadow Chancellor] Rachel Reeves will say something about "This is the result of globalisation", or of a focus too much on some sectors of the economy and not the whole economy. But then the analysis isn't fully followed through [with reforms]. So you can't fully articulate a serious kind of political-economic critique of where we are, from the Labour perspective. And the Tory side, they can't do that either.'

This helps explain why politics has become increasingly about gestures rather than concrete changes, Edgerton suggests. Conservative commitments to 'level up' poorer communities, promote economic growth and invest in the green transition have yielded little.†

'We all sign up to pledges and put things into legislation, but there is no willing of the means,' Edgerton says. 'It's just very, very striking.'

Edgerton's prescription is for the UK to embrace a 'politics of modesty'.[34] He makes it sound simple enough: 'getting things done' and – perhaps even more importantly – 'coming up with realistic ways to get things done'.

---

† After Edgerton and I spoke, Rishi Sunak watered down some environmental policies.

Edgerton cites the climate crisis as an example of an important subject to which the politics of modesty should be applied. He sees too much emphasis at present on investing in great technological leaps as a solution. Such calls for innovation are often 'ways of avoiding doing anything', he says.

'We need to solve the problem with the techniques we currently have,' he argues. 'So it's a kind of modesty of ambition, but also modesty of the means. But the import is that with modest means and modest ambitions, we'll actually achieve something. With immodesty, we'll achieve nothing.'

He notes that Labour has been trying to do this to some extent, but within extraordinarily tight limits. Spending commitments such as on the green transition have been made less expansive. Shadow ministers emphasise the pressure on government finances and the need to be fiscally prudent.

The danger in this approach is that too much negativity extinguishes hope. It risks feeding the strand of politics that might be termed the 'poor country fallacy'. This thinking is a cousin of declinism and holds that Britain's fall in the world means it should no longer be considered a rich nation.

Again, the sentiment is expressed across the political spectrum, often by people who don't seem to have much experience of the world's truly deprived nations. Whatever the relative declines in Britain's wealth compared with its European neighbours and the wider world, the rhetoric seems extreme. Britain has many poor people and inequality is a big problem – but that is not the same as being a poor country.

The political consensus is to exaggerate the limitations of state financial capacity in order to justify tight limits on public spending, Edgerton argues. Labour has taken this course because it wants to be seen as the party of 'sound money', as the Conservatives used to be.

'Labour wants to out-Tory the Tories,' he says. 'You combine that with a deeply entrenched view that the electorate you're after does not want to see higher taxes or any form of redistribution. You say there's no money left, when what you mean is you don't want to increase taxes.'

I observe that he is making the future sound rather forbidding.

'Well, yes,' he replies. 'But I am optimistic [because] the younger generation are elsewhere [in their thinking] – and the point will come where this younger generation will have to be reflected in politics.'

Edgerton's fear is that both the Conservatives and Labour offer shades of bleakness and are failing to propose the systemic reforms needed. If supposedly respectable parties aren't offering solutions, then extreme ones like the Brexit Party and its predecessor the UK Independence Party will fill the gap.

'We have a kind of UKIPisation, a Brexitisation of British politics,' Edgerton says. 'And of course that utterly transformed the Tory Party – but it's in the process of transforming the Labour Party as well.'

It has long been a proudly proclaimed truism in the UK that hard right parties haven't made the same inroads as in other European countries. They have reached government or are coming closer to it in states including France and Italy. Their numbers in parliaments are swelling in a much larger number of nations, including Germany. Edgerton argues it is misleading to suggest that Britain is bucking this trend. Brexit and the bonfire of national illusions that followed it have turned the Conservatives into a hard right party, he believes. Moderates have left or been expelled, while policies towards welfare recipients and asylum seekers have never been harsher.

'In the UK, there is insufficient understanding that Brexit is a hard right programme,' he says. 'What it has achieved in the UK is the transformation of one of the two great parties into a hard right party. And that is an extraordinary change.'

Edgerton was speaking before the October 2023 Conservative Party Conference brought many radical right messages to the fore. The then home secretary Suella Braverman summoned the textbook populist antagonism, as described by Dutch political scientist Cas Mudde, between the 'pure people' and the 'corrupt elite'.[35] She poured scorn on what she termed a 'luxury beliefs brigade' of 'politically correct critics' with 'status . . . and loud voices'. They told 'ordinary people' they were 'morally deficient' because they were 'upset about the impact of illegal migration, net zero or habitual criminals', she claimed.[36]

Braverman was sacked in November 2023, but her style has spread far within her party. In December, 10 Downing Street posted on X that Britain was a 'reasonable country' but its patience had 'run out'. It was an attempt to justify new emergency legislation to overcome the Supreme Court block on sending asylum seekers to Rwanda. The message had an unmistakably authoritarian edge, casting the government as the champion of a popular will stifled by judicial meddling.

Edgerton has chronicled previous eras in which far-right politicians have tried and failed to break through. Oswald Mosley's prospects imploded because of the Second World War. Enoch Powell was sacked as shadow defence secretary after his 1968 speech warning that immigration would cause violence and 'rivers of blood' in the UK.

I ask Edgerton if he thinks people are sufficiently focused on the danger of British politics slipping into a very dark place. He doubts it – and warns that the risks of not paying attention are big.

'This is one of those places that there is still a kind of British exceptionalism,' he says. 'That's why it's so important to say, "Look, the Tory Party has been transformed." Of course, it isn't fascism and all that, but it is something new – and it's very dangerous.'

Epilogue

Renewal

The night of the 1997 UK general election seems like a fever dream just over a quarter of a century later. It was the first time I had been able to vote in a national poll. People of my generation had only known Conservative rule, which had lasted 18 years. The idea that Labour would win in a landslide, rather than eking out a narrow victory at best, felt impossible to believe.

The scale of the triumph claimed senior Conservatives who had seemed immovable fixtures. One was Michael Portillo, the young defence secretary, who had been tipped as a future leader and prime minister. His defeat in the apparently impregnable Tory seat of Enfield Southgate became emblematic of a political earthquake. His nemesis, Labour's Stephen Twigg, seemed as shocked as everyone else as his win became clear shortly after 3am. The events even spawned the title of a book about the election: *Were You Still Up for Portillo?*

I was, because I was at the Picketts Lock Leisure Centre[1] in Enfield to see the result. My presence testified to the extraordinariness of the occasion. I was a trainee reporter for the *Financial Times*, having started working there just a few months before. I had volunteered to attend a count, but I was last in the queue for the biggest likely shocks. I accidentally landed the individual story of the night, thanks to the *FT* news editor's indulgence of my eagerness to be involved.

As Portillo's defeat was announced and he and the other candidates gave speeches, I prepared to try to get a few words with him. I stationed myself in a side room I knew he would pass through after leaving the stage. A few minutes later, he appeared and I introduced myself. 'Very nice to see you,' he said, politely if unconvincingly, without breaking his stride towards escape.

Portillo declined to speculate further about his future or his party's. Perhaps he already had a lurking sense that he was better off out of the Tory wilderness years to come. He instead reinvented himself as a personable presenter of television programmes about railway journeys across Britain and mainland Europe. It was all a world away from the harsh speeches he had once delivered at Conservative Party conferences.

After Portillo left, I took a cab home listening in astonishment as once-safe Tory seats continued to tumble to Labour. Shortly afterwards, a victorious Tony Blair appeared at the Royal Festival Hall on the River Thames's South Bank. He spoke, by accident or design, as the sun was rising on the morning of the last day before the May Day long weekend. He started with a sense of destiny – and a fondness for the rhetorical question – that would come to define his time in power. 'A new dawn has broken, has it not?' he declared. [2]

Those words look like hubris now, the product of a 1990s belief in the perpetual growth of economic output and Western power. Four years later, in 2001, in the contrasting atmosphere of the weeks after the September 11 terrorist attacks, Blair spoke with similar conviction. [3] 'This is a moment to seize,' he told the Labour Party's annual conference. 'The kaleidoscope has been shaken. The pieces are in flux. Soon they will settle again. Before they do, let us reorder this world around us.'

No British leader would dare talk like that today – and for good reason. The positive Blair-era legacy, such as the minimum wage, constitutional reform and investment in health and education, became shrouded in the Iraq War disaster. The 2008 financial crisis sealed Labour's fate, opening the way to an age of deep Conservative spending cuts and the chaos of post-Brexit politics.

The contrast between Blair's overpromise and the pinched mood of the 2020s feels stark. Today, the country is full of hardships and resentments with few signs of either being addressed. A long-governing Conservative Party is again deeply unpopular, but this time the Labour opposition provokes scant enthusiasm – and makes few substantial commitments.

The nation's apparent lack of confidence in its future is alarming. By July 2023, almost two-thirds of Britons thought the country was headed in the wrong direction,[4] according to an Ipsos poll. Just 13 per cent thought the opposite, suggesting the disillusionment was felt across a wide cross-section of society.

Even more troublingly, there was little evidence of belief that either main party would reverse the trend. A full 57 per cent of people thought the Conservatives couldn't run the country competently, against just 23 per cent who felt they could. Labour fared slightly better – but still, 45 per cent viewed their management negatively versus just 35 per cent who were positive.

A sense of rot seemed to be almost everywhere in British life. The normally sober Institute for Government think tank described public services as being in a 'doom loop'.[5] Hospital waiting times ballooned, court backlogs grew and school roofs decayed. In October 2023, the government said it would allow prisoners to be released up to 18 days early to reduce pressure on an overcrowded jail system.[6] More local councils across the country teetered towards bankruptcy.

The extraordinary financial scandal of pandemic official procurement rumbled on with scant accountability. In 2022, a House of Commons Public Accounts committee report had laid out the scale of the problem.[7] It said the Department for Health & Social Care lost 75 per cent of the £12bn it spent on personal protective equipment during the pandemic's first year. This was due to inflated prices and kit that didn't meet requirements.

Some of the useless gear was scheduled to be burned, a symbolic bonfire of Britain's pretensions to world-class institutional management.

The scandal over the Post Office's Horizon computer software is a telling companion to the pandemic purchasing fiasco. False flags from Horizon suggesting money was missing led to more than 900 local post office branch managers being convicted of crimes including theft. In the Covid equipment outrage, powerful people have escaped responsibility; in the Post Office debacle, powerless people were unjustly punished.

I had cause and time to ponder another aspect of the country's dilapidated public realm on train journeys to and from Exeter. Engineering works, strikes and floods delivered a carousel of disruption. Claiming compensation for delayed and cancelled trains soon turned into a remunerative side hustle.

The part-cancellation of the HS2 rail link between London and the north-west of England summed up the sense of mass-transit fiasco. The news that the project would no longer extend to Manchester emerged as the Conservatives held their annual conference in the city in October 2023. Social media filled with unflattering comparisons with other countries' high-speed ventures, Japan's bullet train inevitably prominent among them. An *FT* colleague summed up the increasingly farcical nature of it all, comparing the situation to the scathing television political satire *The Thick of It*. Even in that programme 'they didn't host a party conference in Manchester while scrapping a major public transport connection to Manchester', he noted.[8]

Political life in general increasingly felt like *The Thick of It*'s catalogue of skulduggery and blunders, superintended by sweary spin doctor Malcolm Tucker. In one episode, Tucker describes the crisis of the moment as resembling the prison-break film *The Shawshank Redemption*, 'but with more tunnelling through shit and no fucking redemption'. As the Conservatives' poll ratings lay marooned well below 30 per cent, their chances of escape did seem increasingly remote.

*

A problem with British politics that seems glaring from the outside is the way parties often infantilise voters. Brexit is symptomatic of a wider failure to be honest with the electorate about trade-offs and drawbacks. By September 2023, the view that leaving the EU had not worked well was quite widely shared across society. Yet no mainstream politician would fully articulate it. The referendum result has been fully honoured and it is time to move to an honest debate about Britain's relations within its region. The public seems to understand this better than the main parties are prepared to admit.

The other great damage done by Brexit is the opportunity cost of arguing over it and dealing with it for more than seven years. I have lived in four different countries since the 2016 referendum that committed the UK to leaving the EU. During that time, many other troubles facing the country have been sidelined. For all but the most zealous Leavers – and perhaps not even for many of them – Brexit has been a colossal waste of time, money and attention.

The UK's dangerous political stasis was inadvertently highlighted in a July 2023 article by Labour leader Keir Starmer.[9] It was published days before three byelections, including one in Selby in Yorkshire. It opens with an anecdote from there about a young family whose dream to buy a house has been thwarted by rising mortgage rates. That segues into a critique of how the country 'no longer seems to work' – and then moves on to the key argument that Labour won't spend recklessly.

'Pointing at problems and promising vast sums of money to fix them has too often been the comfort zone of Labour oppositions – and, inevitably, their final resting place,' Starmer writes.

The reluctance to make big spending pledges and set up hostages to fortune may be understandable, but the piece goes further. It contains an almost masochistic declaration of how constricted Labour will be.

'If we are to turn things around, then economic stability must come first,' continues Starmer. 'That will mean making tough choices, and having iron-clad fiscal rules. The supposed alternative – huge, unfunded spending increases at a time when the Tories have left nothing in the coffers – is a recipe for more of the chaos of recent years and more misery for working people.'

As election slogans go, 'tough choices and iron-clad fiscal rules' doesn't seem likely to set people's hearts racing on campaign doorsteps. The even bigger flaw is that, for all the piece's emphasis on the need for institutional reforms, it ignores many structural questions. It brushes past policies to help the 'working people' who have become a patronising trope in British politics and are cited approvingly in Starmer's piece. It doesn't highlight the increasing disparity between the asset-rich retired class and younger people who struggle to buy a property. It doesn't touch on a tax system that is skewed towards the wealthy and has too many loopholes the super-rich can exploit. It doesn't mention the urgent need for action to reduce post-Brexit import costs that are hurting small businesses and driving up the cost of food.

Both parties have surprisingly little to say about some of the biggest questions facing Britain. Labour seems almost as reluctant as its Tory rivals to acknowledge that many needed improvements will have to be funded through some kind of taxation, with the richest paying most. This is the price of services that are efficient and offer dignity both to their users and to those who provide them.

The debate over immigration is another depressing microcosm of how narrow British political debate has become. After official figures showed that net migration to the UK rose to 745,000 in 2022,[10] Labour focused on attacking the Conservatives for incompetent management of the system. Much of the rise was due to arrivals of international students and workers in health and social care. Neither party made much effort to explain how exactly they would lower the number without damaging universities or essential services. Nor did they seem very interested in making the positive case for the skills, cultural enrichment and revenues that new entrants bring to an aging UK.[†]

My refamiliarisation with my country has come after prolonged reflection on how it looks from abroad. The results have not always been encouraging, but they have been instructive. Many of the UK's problems are deeply ingrained, but there are still plenty of its citizens who want to do better and speak up about it. There are a surprising number of people outside the country who wish it well, too.

What everyone who has followed Britain from outside knows is that the country is in crisis. That is true both in the common modern meaning of 'crisis' and in its original sense of being a decision point. The nation seems politically paralysed, unable to plan to meet big long-term needs in areas such as housing, infrastructure and healthcare.

The UK can do so much better. I hope the chapters in this book have given a sense of some ways it might start to grapple with its troubles. A first step is to understand what exactly is going wrong – and why.

Britain feels in need of not so much a revolution as a reboot. It demands practical reforms to reduce inequality, halt the decline of public services and set a reasonable international policy. We need an overhaul of the institutions and individuals that govern us – and a rejection of those who have a track record of bad decisions.

The country needs to understand itself more deeply – and recognise that its internal disagreements may be less than some political and media narratives might suggest. You can see the energy-sucking pointlessness of social media culture wars particularly clearly when you are in another country. Tune out the provocateurs and you often find a lot of thought and

---

† Nor, conversely, did anyone prominently address the moral point of whether Britain should be taking care workers from poor countries with deprived health systems.

consensus, whether the subject is Brussels's traffic or Japan's gender politics. The same is true of debates in the UK, once the fury and posturing are stripped away.

Britain still presents a good face to the world on a grand occasion, but the decaying underlay is increasingly hard to hide. The monarchy is in many ways a metaphor for wider contradictions in society. The royals are excused taxes, can lobby politically in secret, and skirt questions about how they acquired their wealth. These are all things with which we must surely deal.

The UK still has much more to do to reckon with its past – and to use that process as a springboard to redress contemporary injustices. It should address the legacy of empire in a more serious way, beyond the initiatives taken by some institutions and individuals. We need to develop a fuller understanding of how colonialism's impact continues to be felt in systems of wealth and power that endure today.

Britain's political set-up is in urgent need of reform, both in the systems that run it and the people they throw up as our rulers. We need to think about our island vulnerabilities in which energy, metal and food supplies are prone to disruption and competed for ever more intensely. We should honestly appraise whether we can better harness the resources we have – and what we need to learn about doing so from other countries.

We need to recognise the ways the world has moved on. The rise of other international powers, some unleashed by the end of empire, has inevitably made the UK less important proportionately. The era of Western dominance is over – and this development is not widely mourned outside the sphere of US allies.

The ambivalence of many countries about the Ukraine War and the rise of China is a sign of this. They are more likely to fear than admire Vladimir Putin or Xi Jinping. But they must live with this new reality – and they recognise that China and Russia are not the first nations to grab land or dominate seas.

This shift gives the UK a pragmatic reason to show some humility in its international dealings. It should be very careful about being militarily active in places where there are strong forces and volatile situations over which it has little control. On the commercial side, Britain needs to ask itself if marginal trade growth is worth the price of appearing to indulge political oppression.

The UK should take a realistic view of the rest of Europe that is neither romanticised nor hostile. It must recognise that any country is damaged if it doesn't have access to or influences on initiatives its regional peers are cooking up. Whether you like your neighbours or not, it is in your interests to have a functional relationship with them.

Above all, the UK needs to reimagine what it is. There are groups out there campaigning passionately, sometimes radically, on subjects from the climate crisis to financial literacy. But the country lacks mainstream political figures who can pull together the threads and weave a coherent narrative of what an updated Britain might look like.

One lesson I have learned from my time abroad is that seismic social shifts often seem hard to contemplate almost until the very moment they occur. The UK is not Egypt, Libya or Syria, on the verge of revolt against a dictator. But I sense some of the same frustrated energy, with few avenues for release. We need more politicians who can channel that into the compelling stories needed to enthuse the public.

Pressure groups such as Republic and Just Stop Oil struggle to capture mass support – and sometimes draw heavy criticism. Republic's efforts to abolish the monarchy remain a minority pursuit. Just Stop Oil provokes jeers from crowds at sports events it disrupts, and angry reactions from some drivers on roads it blocks.

But they are on to something, as are other pressure groups. Polls suggest declining support for the monarchy and an appetite to reform it. Surveys – and heatwaves – show increasing public acceptance of the existence of a climate crisis and the need for strong measures to deal with it. In September 2023, the naturalist Chris Packham even presented a programme[11] asking if it was acceptable to break the law to protest against government climate policies.

The suffragettes who burned down Tunbridge Wells cricket pavilion in 1913 provoked outrage. Within five years, women were allowed to be elected to Parliament; in another ten they had the same voting rights as men. It took too long, but the goals of the direct action eventually became the law.

The tale Britain tells about itself has swung wildly in the years I have been abroad. Less than a year before I left, David Cameron spoke outside Downing Street[12] just after being sworn in as prime minister. He foreshadowed his infamous tweet five years later, in which he contrasted his 'stability and strong Government' with the prospect of 'chaos' under Labour leader Ed Miliband. 'I believe together we can provide that strong and stable government that our country needs based on those values – rebuilding family, rebuilding community, above all, rebuilding responsibility in our country,' he said.

The received wisdom now could hardly be further from those visions. The public discourse is of political malevolence, incompetence and putrefaction. At its extreme, it has stoked the idea that Britain is in some kind of national death spiral.

This is a dangerous attitude. It provides those who would dismantle the public realm even further with an excuse to do so. If no social services work anyway, why have them at all?

The pessimistic attitude that all is lost and we can never improve is another form of self-indulgence, when espoused by those living in comfort. How much we spend, and on what, is shaped by political decisions, as it always has been. Those can be altered.

Perhaps most importantly, we must remember that the UK still has a lot going for it – and much to be thankful for. After years spent reporting from states where political rights are severely curbed, I value more than ever the ability to speak and write with relative freedom. We must use and preserve this – and be consistent in applying those protections to views we don't like as well as those we do.

The goodwill Britain still enjoys around the world is remarkable, given much of what I've recounted in this book. In 2021, the UK was rated the most attractive country in the G20 in a survey of young people[13] by Ipsos for the British Council. We should make the most of this – and the continuing interest in the English language and UK higher education.

Britain is a much more socially progressive[14] and less bigoted place than it was a few decades back, for all its huge faults. Perhaps the best argument for Brexit was that racial prejudice seems stronger in many EU countries than it is in the UK. European institutional Brussels remains a very white place, the more so after the departure of Britain's MEPs.

As I was finalising this epilogue, I went to my new gym to work out. The facility had just revamped its leaky showers, but there was a fresh problem. The replacements lacked directional nozzles, so you unavoidably faced an initial full blast of the water at whatever temperature the previous user had set. One of my fellow exercisers grumbled that he'd heard the apparatus would have to be reconfigured again next week. 'They keep changing their minds – a bit like the government,' he growled.

When a discussion about showerheads turns into an attack on the country's rulers, it probably signals political change is in the offing. An election looms at a critical moment for the country. By the time this book is published, it might even have taken place.

It is an unsettling time to come home – but an exciting one. The hope that the Covid-19 pandemic would lead to greater equality in Britain and positive changes in how it is governed has been dashed. That is unsurprising:

it is a lesson as old as history that established systems of power and wealth don't change unless forced to do so.

The pressure for a far-reaching revival of the UK feels as though it is building. It seems inevitable that it will burst through the rigid showerhead of mainstream politics, whether the parties are ready or not. That impetus could be exploited by extremists for destructive purposes. Or it could be harnessed to offer people security and dignity – and propel Britain into a constructive role in a turbulent wider world.

In 2026, I will have to apply for the dark blue British passport introduced after Brexit. The document, made by a French company,[15] will be a reminder of the struggles in Britain that I have followed increasingly anxiously from overseas. It will be a bittersweet moment, but at least my embossed lion and unicorn will be restored. I hope with all my heart that the UK has begun to experience a similar sense of renewal by then. We can work together to make that happen.

ENDNOTES

All websites were accessed on 8 November 2023.

INTRODUCTION: RETURN

1. Weaver, M, ' "The UK seems to have imploded": how world's press sees Truss's Britain', *Guardian*, 30 September 2022, https://www.theguardian.com/politics/2022/sep/30/liz-truss-how-world-press-sees-uk

2. 'Liz Truss, la breve', https://www.elcolombiano.com/opinion/editoriales/liz-truss-la-breve-FH18867266

3. Woods, J, 'Britain is in a godawful mess – if we were French, we'd have a revolution', *Telegraph*, 16 March 2023, https://www.telegraph.co.uk/columnists/2023/03/16/britain-godawful-mess-french-have-revolution

4. Ford, J and Hughes, L, 'UK-China relations: from "golden era" to the deep freeze', *Financial Times*, 14 July 2020, https://www.ft.com/content/804175d0-8b47-4427-9853-2aded76f48e4

5. 'London protests at "attack" on Iran exiles at Iraq camp', BBC News, 9 January 2011, https://www.bbc.co.uk/news/uk-12144782

6. Hopkins, N, 'UK's eight-year military presence in Iraq to end on Sunday', *Guardian*, 18 May 2011, https://www.theguardian.com/world/2011/may/18/british-militarys-8-years-in-iraq-ends#:~:text=In%20all%2C%20178%20UK%20service,forces%20to%20train%201%2C800%20Iraqis

7. 'Rishi Sunak: golden era of UK–China relations is over', BBC News, 29 November 2022, https://www.bbc.co.uk/news/uk-politics-63787877

8. 'Blair's speech: full text', *Guardian*, 10 May 2007, https://www.theguardian.com/politics/2007/may/10/labourleadership.labour2

9. Chadwick, N, 'Tunbridge Wells Hospital (Pembury Hospital)', *Geograph*, 29 February 2012, https://www.geograph.org.uk/snippet/6370#:~:text=The%20site%20was%20first%20developed,by%20The%20Tunbridge%20Wells%20Hospital

10. 'Tunbridge Wells – landscape and visual impact assessment of proposed allocation sites within the High Weald AONB', Landscape Architecture Masterplanning Ecology, https://tunbridgewells.gov.uk/__data/assets/pdf_file/0007/385378/Landscape-and-Visual-Impact-Assessment_Section-6.3-RTW-sites.pdf

11. 'Local Coronation souvenir donated to Tunbridge Wells Museum and Art Gallery', Tunbridge Wells Borough Council, 28 March 2006, https://archive. md/20070308233941/http:/www.tunbridgewells.gov.uk/section.asp?catid= 796&docid=1834

12. 'Royal Tunbridge Wells', Wikipedia, https://en.wikipedia.org/wiki/Royal_ Tunbridge_Wells

13. https://www.britannica.com/place/Tunbridge-Wells-England

14. Burnton, S, 'How suffragette pavilion fire outraged Tunbridge Wells . . . and Conan Doyle', *Guardian*, 10 November 2020, https://www.theguardian.com/ sport/2020/nov/10/how-suffragette-pavilion-fire-outraged-tunbridge-wells- and-conan-doyle-cricket

15. Smith, C, '10 of Torbay's biggest mistakes over the years', Devon Live, 1 January 2021, https://www.devonlive.com/news/devon-news/10-torbays-biggest-mistakes- over-4866441

16. 'History of Smithfield Market', City of London, 18 May 2022, https://www. cityoflondon.gov.uk/supporting-businesses/business-support-and-advice/ wholesale-markets/smithfield-market/history-of-the-market

17. McCormack, B, 'Smithfield and Billingsgate markets are leaving central London for Dagenham', *Standard*, 22 November 2022, https://www.standard.co.uk/going-out/ foodanddrink/smithfield-billingsgate-market-markets-dagenham-dock-barking- and-dagenham-city-of-london-corporation-b1041659.html

18. Ibid.

1: BRITAIN'S TRICK MIRROR

1. 'About us', More in Common, https://www.moreincommon.org.uk/about-us/

2. Juan-Torres, M, Dixon, T and Kimaram, A, 'Britain's choice: common ground and division in 2020s Britain', More in Common, October 2020, https://www. britainschoice.uk/media/ecrevsbt/0917-mic-uk-britain-s-choice_report_ dec01.pdf

3. 'Is the UK a country? The union explained . . .', Evan Evans, https://evanevanstours. com/travel-guide/london-guide/is-the-uk-a-country-the-union-explained/

4. Jones, L, 'Britain vs England: what are the differences?', Lingoda, 7 November 2022, https://blog.lingoda.com/en/britain-vs-england-differences/

5. 'The difference between UK, Great Britain and the British Isles', Ordnance Survey, 3 August 2011, https://www.ordnancesurvey.co.uk/blog/whats-the-difference-between-uk-britain-and-british-isles

6. 'Is there a difference between Great Britain and the United Kingdom?', Babbel, https://www.youtube.com/watch?v=Nzp3Qrs7eqw

7. The Editors of Encyclopaedia Britannica, 'St George', *Britannica*, 20 July 1998, https://www.britannica.com/biography/Saint-George

8. 'Why is it called "Yorkshire Tea"?', Taylors of Harrogate Yorkshire Tea, 23 January 2017, https://www.yorkshiretea.co.uk/brew-news/why-is-it-called-yorkshire-tea

9. https://tregothnan.co.uk/

10. Culligan, K, Dubber, J and Lotten, M, 'As Others See Us', British Council, 2014, https://www.britishcouncil.org/sites/default/files/as-others-see-us-report.pdf

11. White, M, 'Promote British values to stop terror says Howard', *Guardian*, 17 August 2005, https://www.theguardian.com/uk/2005/aug/17/conservatives.july7

12. Walker, C, 'Blair defines "British values"', BBC News, 28 March 2000, http://news.bbc.co.uk/1/hik_politics/693591.stm

13. 'School Inspection Handbook' Ofsted, 6 October 2023, https://www.gov.uk/government/publications/school-inspection-handbook-eif/school-inspection-handbook-for-september-2023

14. 'How has inequality changed?', The Equality Trust, https://equalitytrust.org.uk/how-has-inequality-changed

15. 'GHE: life expectancy and healthy life expectancy', World Health Organization, https://www.who.int/data/gho/data/themes/mortality-and-global-health-estimates/ghe-life-expectancy-and-healthy-life-expectancy

16. Marshall, L, Finch, D, Cairncross, L, and Bibby, J, 'Mortality and life expectancy trends in the UK', The Health Foundation, November 2019, https://www.health.org.uk/publications/reports/mortality-and-life-expectancy-trends-in-the-uk

17. 'New threats to human security in the Anthropocene', United Nations Development Programme, 2022, https://www.un-ilibrary.org/content/books/9789210014007/read

18. Mishra, P, 'Fiction in a post-truth age', *London Review of Books*, 16 February 2022, https://www.lrb.co.uk/blog/2022/february/fiction-in-a-post-truth-age

19. The perils of perception, Ipsos, https://www.ipsos.com/en/perils

20. Ibid.

21. Ibid.

22. Professor Bobby Duffy, Kings College London, https://www.kcl.ac.uk/people/bobby-duffy

23. Vice-chancellor – Professor Wendy Thomson CBE, University of London, https://www.london.ac.uk/about-us/our-people/vice-chancellor#:~:text=Born%20in%20Montreal%20Canada%2C%20Professor,in%20the%20academy%20and%20government

24. The perils of perception – data archive, Ipsos, 16 December 2021, https://www.ipsos.com/en/perils/perils-perception-data-archive

25. 'Perceptions are not reality: what the world gets wrong', Ipsos, 14 December 2016, https://www.ipsos.com/en-uk/perceptions-are-not-reality-what-world-gets-wrong

26. 'The perils of perception and the EU', UK in a changing Europe, 9 June 2016, https://ukandeu.ac.uk/the-perils-of-perception-and-the-eu/

27. Carvel J, 'Opposition to immigrants hardens under Blair', *Guardian*, 7 December 2004, https://www.theguardian.com/uk/2004/dec/07/immigration.immigrationandpublicservices

28. Perraudin, F, 'Diane Abbott: Labour's "controls on immigration" mugs are shameful', *Guardian*, 29 March 2015, https://www.theguardian.com/politics/2015/mar/29/diane-abbott-labour-immigration-controls-mugs-shameful

29. Owen, J., 'The Windrush scandal was a failure of law, policy, politics and bureaucracy', Institute for Government, 20 March 2020, https://www.instituteforgovernment.org.uk/article/comment/windrush-scandal-was-failure-law-policy-politics-and-bureaucracy

30. 'What is the UK's plan to send asylum seekers to Rwanda?', BBC News, 13 December 2023, https://www.bbc.co.uk/news/explainers-61782866

31. Johnson, D and McNamee, M, 'Inside Bibby Stockholm: on board barge housing asylum seekers', BBC News, 7 August 2023, https://www.bbc.co.uk/news/uk-66270811

32. Peel, M and Smyth, J, 'Australia's policy of sending refugees to Cambodia draws ridicule', *Financial Times*, 23 April 2015, https://www.ft.com/content/bca15114-e99e-11e4-a687-00144feab7de

33. Lowy Institute Poll 2023, https://poll.lowyinstitute.org/charts/attitudes-to-immigration/

34. Smyth, J and Peel, M, 'Australia's flagship refugee resettlement policy adrift', *Financial Times*, 7 September 2015, https://www.ft.com/content/541d6c82-5545-11e5-9497-c74c95a1a7b1

35. 'Human development index', countryeconomy.com, https://countryeconomy.com/hdi?year=2015

36. Smyth, J and Peel, M, 'Australia's flagship refugee resettlement policy adrift', *Financial Times*, 7 September 2015, https://www.ft.com/content/541d6c82-5545-11e5-9497-c74c95a1a7b1

37. Boyle, D and Reaksmey, H, 'Australia's Cambodia refugee deal is dead', VOA News, 1 November 2018, https://www.voanews.com/a/australia-s-cambodia-refugee-deal-is-dead/4638263.html

38. Melhem, Y and Davidson, H, 'From Nauru to limbo: the anguish of Australia's last asylum seeker in Cambodia', *Guardian*, 28 December 2019, https://www.theguardian.com/australia-news/2019/dec/29/from-nauru-to-limbo-the-anguish-of-australias-last-asylum-seeker-in-cambodia

39. DiGirolamo, R, '"Lost" Aussie asylum seeker finds SA lifeline', *The Advertiser*, 27 September 2020, https://www.adelaidenow.com.au/subscribe/news/1/?sourceCode=AAWEB_WRE170_a_GGL&dest=https%3A%2F%2Fwww.adelaidenow.com.au%2Fnews%2Fsouth-australia%2Flast-australian-asylum-seekers-in-cambodia-thank-sa-group-for-desperately-needed-help%2Fnews-story%2Fe88fb54e00e79cbb1ac1ce0a0577ffb2&memtype=anonymous&mode=premium&v21=dynamic-groupa-test-noscore&V21spcbehaviour=append

40. Kettle, M, 'The Rwanda plan is dead in the real world, but will live on in the fantasyland of Tory politics', *Guardian*, 15 November 2023, https://www.theguardian.com/commentisfree/2023/nov/15/rwanda-plan-dead-real-world-live-on-fantasyland-tory-politics

41. 'Human development insights', United Nations Human Development Reports, https://hdr.undp.org/data-center/country-insights#/ranks

42. Braverman, S, 'Migration and Economic Development', *Hansard*, Volume 275, 19 December 2022, https://hansard.parliament.uk/commons/2022-12-19/debates/B5009C67-E69A-4248-8F16-77439DE48472/MigrationAndEconomicDevelopment

43. Silver, L, 'Boris Johnson wrote an article supporting staying in the EU two days before backing Brexit', *BuzzFeed News*, 16 October 2016, https://www.buzzfeed.com/laurasilver/it-was-always-about-cake

44. Swales, K, 'Understanding the Leave vote', NatCen Social Research, https://whatukthinks.org/eu/wp-content/uploads/2016/12/NatCen_Brexplanations-report-FINAL-WEB2.pdf

45. 'Mayor confirms world's first ultra low emission zone', Mayor of London Press Release, 26 March 2015, https://www.london.gov.uk/press-releases/mayoral/ultra-low-emission-zone

46. Tyers, R and Smith, L, 'Clean air zones, low emission zones and the London ULEZ', House of Commons Library, 11 August 2023, https://commonslibrary.parliament.uk/research-briefings/cbp-9816/

47. British Election Study, 27 January 2021, https://www.britishelectionstudy.com/bes-findings/age-and-voting-behaviour-at-the-2019-general-election/

48. Butler, P, 'Britain is much more liberal-minded than it was 40 years ago, study finds', *Guardian*, 21 September 2023, https://www.theguardian.com/society/2023/sep/21/britain-is-much-more-liberal-minded-than-is-was-40-years-ago-study-finds

49. Helm, T, 'Young adults have dramatic loss of faith in UK democracy, survey reveals', *Guardian*, 10 April 2022, https://www.theguardian.com/politics/2022/apr/10/young-adults-loss-of-faith-in-uk-democracy-survey

2: THE NOSTALGIA TRAP

1. Keynote address to the American Enterprise Institute, 26 September 2023, https://www.aei.org/wp-content/uploads/2023/09/230926-Keynote-Address-by-UK-Home-Secretary-Suella-Braverman-Transcript.pdf?x91208

2. Ian Howorth, Setanta Book Store, https://www.setantabooks.com/collections/ian-howorth#:~:text=Ian%20Howorth%20is%20a%20photographer,at%20the%20age%20of%2016

3. Faratin, P, 'Trapped in time? Britain and nostalgia – in pictures', *Guardian*, 2 May 2023, https://www.theguardian.com/artanddesign/gallery/2023/may/02/trapped-in-time-britain-and-nostalgia-in-pictures

4. https://twitter.com/DavidGHFrost/status/1684628986796658689

5. 'The golliwog caricature', Jim Crow Museum, https://jimcrowmuseum.ferris.edu/golliwog/homepage.htm

6. 'Essex pub that had golliwog dolls seized by police shuts its doors', Sky News, 3 May 2023, https://news.sky.com/story/essex-pub-that-had-golliwog-dolls-seized-by-police-shuts-its-doors-12872315

7. https://www.youtube.com/watch?v=1nL67W8zjXk

8. Phillips, J, 'Has Lilt been cancelled? Coca-Cola rebrands the "totally tropical taste" drink to "Fanta" after adverts were accused of "cultural appropriation"', *Mail Online*, 14 February 2023, https://www.dailymail.co.uk/news/

article-11748811/Has-Lilt-cancelled-Coca-cola-rebrands-totally-tropical-tasted-drink-Fanta-amid-concerns.html

9. Montgomery, S, 'Woke "sensitivity readers" overhaul *The Beano* as British comic given modern make-over', GB News, 26 July 2023, https://www.gbnews.com/news/beano-birthday-woke-modern-sensitivity

10. Nimmo, J, 'Yikes! Politically correct Dennis loses his Menace: The catapult's gone, Gnasher's teeth are fixed and Walter (or is it Jacob Rees-Mogg?) isn't even a softie in the remake of *Beano* classic', *Mail on Sunday*, 8 October 2017, https://www.dailymail.co.uk/news/article-4959398/Yikes-Politically-correct-Dennis-loses-Menace.html

11. Horne, M, 'The Beano's transformed itself – with help from the Roald Dahl sensitivity readers', *The Times*, 22 July 2023, https://www.thetimes.co.uk/article/the-beanos-transformed-itself-with-help-from-the-roald-dahl-sensitivity-readers-6smc7396q

12. Johnson, T, '"Monkey" is still magic but a little bit problematic', *Blunt Magazine*, 12 July 2021, https://www.bluntmag.com.au/film/monkey-is-still-magic-but-a-little-bit-problematic

13. Brogan, B, 'It's time to celebrate the Empire, says Brown', *Daily Mail*, 15 January 2005, https://www.dailymail.co.uk/news/article-334208/Its-time-celebrate-Empire-says-Brown.html

14. 'Work-related fatal injuries in Great Britain, 2023', Health and Safety Executive Annual Report, 6 July 2023, https://www.hse.gov.uk/statistics/pdf/fatalinjuries.pdf

15. Duncan Smith, Sir I, 'In the 1940s they kept coming to the office – even when Hitler's bombs were raining down', *Mail Online*, 9 October 2021, https://www.dailymail.co.uk/debate/article-10076329/SIR-IAIN-DUNCAN-SMITH-1940s-kept-coming-office-bombs-came-down.html

16. Overy, R., 'Why the cruel myth of the "blitz spirit" is no model for how to fight coronavirus', *Guardian*, 19 March 2020, https://www.theguardian.com/commentisfree/2020/mar/19/myth-blitz-spirit-model-coronavirus

17. Ratchliffe, R, 'Philippines presidency frontrunner praises "genius" dictator father', *Guardian*, 27 April 2022, https://www.theguardian.com/world/2022/apr/27/philippines-presidency-frontrunner-ferdinand-marcos-jr-praises-genius-dictator-father

18. Morella, C and Agence France-Presse, 'Martial law torture victim Etta Rosales relives horror as dictator's son rises', Agence France-Presse, *Philstar Global*, 23 February 2022, https://www.philstar.com/headlines/2022/02/23/2162837/martial-law-torture-victim-etta-rosales-relives-horror-dictators-son-rises

19. Gaw, Fatima, 'About me', https://www.fatimagaw.com/about-7

20. Purnell, K, 'The Philippines has highest average screen time on phones – study', Philstar Global, 21 May 2023, https://www.philstar.com/lifestyle/gadgets/2023/05/21/2267517/philippines-has-highest-average-screen-time-phones-study

21. Venzon, C, 'The Marcos revival: How late Philippine dictator's son went from exile to election favorite', Nikkei Asia, 27 April 2022, https://asia.nikkei.com/Spotlight/The-Big-Story/The-Marcos-revival-How-late-Philippine-dictator-s-son-went-from-exile-to-election-favorite

22. 'Senator Ferdinand "Bongbong" R Marcos, Jr, Senate of the Philippines', https://legacy.senate.gov.ph/senators/sen_bio/bmarcos_bio.asp

23. 'Ferdinand R Marcos Jr', President, Republic of the Philippines, https://pbbm.com.ph/president-bongbong-marcos/

24. Macasero, R, 'More Filipinos say quality of life got better, despite higher food cost – SWS survey', Rappler.com, 26 January 2023, https://www.rappler.com/nation/filipinos-quality-life-sws-survey-december-2022/

25. Fowler, C, 'Profile: "We must be careful not to unconsciously add to the toxicity" ', Museums Association, 14 November 2022, https://www.museumsassociation.org/museums-journal/people/2022/11/profile-we-must-be-careful-not-to-unconsciously-add-to-the-toxicity/

26. 'Charity Commission finds National Trust did not breach charity law', The Charity Commission, 11 March 2021, https://www.gov.uk/government/news/charity-commission-finds-national-trust-did-not-breach-charity-law

27. Jones, D, 'Becoming a Victorian', Spectator, 20 March 2010, https://www.spectator.co.uk/article/becoming-a-victorian/

28. Blake, R and Louis, W, Churchill, Clarendon Press, Oxford, 1993, https://books.google.co.uk/books?id=HQguDdnu8zgC&pg=PA464&lpg=PA464&dq=churchill+indians+beastliest+people&source=bl&ots=BIILx6rT7s&sig=ACfU3U3XdbLuJaqAy9_XNndCqKYS7VAokg&hl=en&sa=X&redir_esc=y#v=onepage&q=churchill%20indians%20beastliest%20people&f=false

29. Toye, R, 'Churchill's Empire', New York Times, 12 August 2010, https://www.nytimes.com/2010/08/15/books/review/excerpt-churchills-empire.html

30. Evans, R, London Review of Books, 2 December 2021, https://www.lrb.co.uk/the-paper/v43/n23/richard-j.-evans/short-cuts

31. Klaas, B, 'My "Life in the UK" test and a Great British travel guide', The Garden of Forking Paths, 8 September 2023, https://www.forkingpaths.co/p/my-life-in-the-uk-test-and-a-great

32. Trentmann, F, 'Britain First: The official history of the United Kingdom according to the Home Office – a critical review', History Journal, August 2020, https://historyjournalorguk.files.wordpress.com/2020/09/britain-first-frank-trentmann-september-2020.pdf

33. Connolly, K, '"Most are unaware": film highlights Germany's genocidal past in Namibia', *Guardian*, 22 March 2023, https://www.theguardian.com/world/2023/mar/22/most-are-unaware-film-highlights-germanys-genocidal-past-in-namibia

34. Baroness Hamwee, S, 'Letter to Kevin Foster, MP', House of Lords, 28 June 2022, https://committees.parliament.uk/publications/22850/documents/167769/default/

3: HEAVY REIGNS

1. Kottasova, I, ' "It's not a good look." As cost of living crisis bites, some Brits are questioning spending money on glitzy coronation', 2 May 2023, https://edition.cnn.com/2023/05/02/business/cost-of-living-doncaster-coronation-gbr-cmd-intl/index.html

2. Roy, L, 'Cost of Charles' Coronation: Brits are questioning spending money on glitzy coronation', *Firstpost*, 3 May 2023, https://www.firstpost.com/entertainment/cost-of-charles-iiis-coronation-why-some-brits-are-questioning-as-cost-of-living-bites-12538982.html

3. 'Almost six in ten Britons think the country is heading in the wrong direction', Kantar Public, 23 February 2023, https://www.kantarpublic.com/inspiration/thought-leadership/almost-six-in-ten-britons-think-the-country-is-heading-in-the-wrong-direction

4. Albert, E, 'Nothing in the UK works anymore', *Le Monde*, 27 September 2022, https://www.lemonde.fr/en/opinion/article/2022/09/27/nothing-in-the-uk-works-anymore_5998351_23.html

5. Midgley, D, 'The coronation of Queen Elizabeth II: How the *Daily Express* reported it 61 years ago', *Express*, 18 September 2014, https://www.express.co.uk/news/history/512126/Coronation-Queen-Elizabeth-II-Daily-Express-Archive-Everest

6. Wearden, G, 'Britons "need to accept" they're poorer, says Bank of England economist', *Guardian*, 25 April 2023, https://www.theguardian.com/business/2023/apr/25/britons-need-to-accept-theyre-poorer-says-bank-of-england-economist

7. https://twitter.com/Daily_Express/status/1654601659337654274?s=20

8. Malik, N, 'It's the "great noticing", as rightwingers accept that "Britain is broken". But their fixes won't make it any better', *Guardian*, 17 September 2023, https://www.theguardian.com/commentisfree/2023/sep/17/rightwing-britain-broken-tories-national-decline

9. https://www.theguardian.com/commentisfree/2023/jan/29/elitist-leadership-zahawi-schools-britain#comment-160976752

10. Calafati, L, Froud, J, Haslam, C, Johal, S and Williams, K, 'When nothing works: from cost of living to foundational liveability', Manchester University Press, June 2023, https://manchesteruniversitypress.co.uk/9781526173713/

11. Williams, K, 'Foundational liveability and the cost of living crisis', Sheffield Hallam University CRESR [Centre for Regional Economic and Social Research] Seminar Series 2022–3, 18 January 2023, https://www.shu.ac.uk/centre-regional-economic-social-research/events/2022-23-seminar-series#:~:text=The%20current%20%22cost%20of%20living,social%20infrastructure%2D%20are%20all%20crumbling

12. 'Child poverty facts and figures', Child Poverty Action Group, https://cpag.org.uk/child-poverty/child-poverty-facts-and-figures

13. Neate, R, 'Call for wealth tax as UK billionaire numbers up by 20% since pandemic', *Guardian*, 19 December 2022, https://www.theguardian.com/news/2022/dec/19/call-for-wealth-tax-as-uk-billionaire-numbers-up-by-20-since-pandemic

14. '"Real and rising risk" that Palace of Westminster will be destroyed by catastrophic event before it is restored, says PAC', *UK Parliament Committees*, 17 May 2023, https://committees.parliament.uk/work/7196/restoration-and-renewal-recall/news/195220/real-and-rising-risk-that-palace-of-westminster-will-be-destroyed-by-catastrophic-event-before-it-is-restored-says-pac/

15. 'Post-Brexit UK won't be like Mad Max, says David Davis', BBC News, 20 February 2018, https://www.bbc.co.uk/news/uk-politics-43120277

16. 'Number of "excellent" English bathing waters reaches record high', Water UK, 30 November 2022, https://www.water.org.uk/news-views-publications/news/number-excellent-english-bathing-waters-reaches-record-high

17. https://www.parliament.uk/globalassets/documents/mdr-main-10.09.19.pdf

18. 'Labour has maxed out Britain's credit card, says Cameron', Conservative Home, 9 November 2008, https://conservativehome.com/2008/11/09/labour-has-maxe/

19. 'One in six UK adults have no savings', Money & Pensions Service, 7 November 2022, https://maps.org.uk/en/media-centre/press-releases/2022/one-in-six-uk-adults-have-no-savings

20. 'Long-reigning British and Thai monarchs shared a bond', France 24, 9 September 2022, https://www.france24.com/en/live-news/20220909-long-reigning-british-and-thai-monarchs-shared-a-bond

21. Pegg, D, and Evans, R, 'Revealed: Queen lobbied for change in law to hide her private wealth', *Guardian*, 7 February 2021, https://www.theguardian.com/uk-news/2021/feb/07/revealed-queen-lobbied-for-change-in-law-to-hide-her-private-wealth

22. Dugan, E, 'King Charles greets Liz Truss with: "Back again? Dear, oh dear"', *Guardian*, 13 October 2022, https://www.theguardian.com/uk-news/2022/oct/13/king-charles-greets-liz-truss-dear-oh-dear-uk-prime-minister-weekly-audience

23. 'Prince Andrew loses military titles and use of HRH', BBC News, 13 January 2022, https://www.bbc.co.uk/news/uk-59987935

24. Newton, J and Smith, J, 'Controversial guests at King Charles' Coronation – former PM, Chinese deputy, wealthy sultan', *Mirror*, 2 May 2023, https://www.mirror.co.uk/news/royals/controversial-guests-king-charles-coronation-29829289

25. Connett, D, 'Prince Charles given €3m in cash in bags by Qatari politician, according to report', *Guardian*, 25 June 2022, https://www.theguardian.com/uk-news/2022/jun/25/prince-charles-is-said-to-have-been-given-3m-in-qatari-cash

26. The Royal Collection, https://www.royal.uk/the-royal-collection#:~:text=The%20Royal%20Collection%20is%20not,his%20successors%20and%20the%20nation

27. Regan, H and Olarn, K, 'Thailand's young voters spearhead "earth-shaking" calls for change in military dominated kingdom', CNN, 11 May 2023, https://edition.cnn.com/2023/05/11/asia/thailand-election-move-forward-youth-intl-hnk/index.html

28. Head, J, 'Thailand: Leading activist Arnon Nampa jailed over calls for royal reform', BBC News, 26 September 2023, https://www.bbc.co.uk/news/world-asia-66920855

29. Reuters staff, 'Thailand's king takes personal control of two key army units', Reuters, 1 October 2019, https://www.reuters.com/article/us-thailand-king-idUSKBN1WG4ED

30. Phaholtap, H and Streckfuss, D, 'The ten demands that shook Thailand', *New Mandala*, 2 September 2020, https://www.newmandala.org/

the-ten-demands-that-shook-thailand/#:~:text=On%20that%20date%2C%20
a%20representative,the%20king%2C%20reduce%20tax%20money

31. Seddon, S, 'Coronation: Met expresses "regret" over arresting six anti-monarchy
    protesters', BBC website, 9 May 2023, https://www.bbc.co.uk/news/uk-65527007

32. Gregory, J, 'King's Coronation: 21 people arrested face no further action, Met says',
    BBC website, 5 October 2023, https://www.bbc.co.uk/news/uk-67022199

33. Cooke, R, 'It was ludicrous but also magnificent: the coronation stirred every
    emotion', *Observer*, 6 May 2023, https://www.theguardian.com/uk-news/2023/
    may/06/it-was-ludicrous-but-also-magnificent-the-coronation-stirred-every-emotion

34. 'The Stone of Destiny', Edinburgh Castle, https://www.edinburghcastle.scot/see-
    and-do/highlights/the-stone-of-destiny

35. 'Rouge Dragon Pursuivant', College of Arms, https://www.college-of-arms.gov.uk/
    news-grants/news/item/162-rouge-dragon-pursuivant

36. Zsombor, P, 'Thailand bans book on King before publication', VOA News,
    6 August 2023, https://www.voanews.com/a/thailand-bans-book-on-king-before-
    publication/7213561.html

37. https://twitter.com/brokenbottleboy/status/1655448492821585920?s=20

38. Billington, M, 'The Coronation review – immaculately rehearsed, touching
    and Shakespearean', *Guardian,* 7 May 2023, https://www.theguardian.com/
    tv-and-radio/2023/may/07/the-coronation-review-immaculately-rehearsed-
    touching-and-shakespearean

39. Nickolls, L, 'Police powers: protests', House of Commons Library, 3 August 2023,
    https://commonslibrary.parliament.uk/research-briefings/sn05013/

40. 'Legislative scrutiny: Public Order Bill', House of Commons, House of Lords, Joint
    Committee on Human Rights, 8 June 2022, https://committees.parliament.uk/
    publications/22681/documents/166680/default/?utm_source=HOC+Library+-+
    Current+awareness+bulletins&utm_campaign=105721c92e-Current+Awareness+
    Home+Affairs+-17.06.2022.&utm_medium=email&utm_term=0_f325cdbfdc-
    105721c92e-104320940&mc_cid=105721c92e&mc_eid=bee607b1d0

4: FLAWED PROPHETS

1. 'Liz Truss's final speech as Prime Minister: 25 October 2022', gov.uk, 25 October
   2022, https://www.gov.uk/government/speeches/liz-trusss-final-speech-as-prime-
   minister-25-october-2022

2. Henley, J, '"Disgrace": world's press react to Truss resignation and UK political turmoil', *Guardian*, 21 October 2022, https://www.theguardian.com/politics/2022/oct/21/liz-truss-global-media-reaction-uk-political-turmoil

3. Hill, M, 'World's media assess Liz Truss's demise and UK political turmoil', *Independent*, 21 October 2022, https://www.independent.co.uk/news/uk/liz-truss-tories-world-washington-post-prime-minister-b2207464.html#lnh6hb04n1g1yj5ow2j

4. Politics.co.uk staff, '"We can make Britain grow again" – Liz Truss's Institute for Government speech in full', Politics.co.uk, 18 September 2023, https://www.politics.co.uk/news/2023/09/18/we-can-make-britain-grow-again-liz-truss-institute-for-government-speech-in-full/

5. Ibid.

6. Ferguson, D and agency, 'Liz Truss to "share lessons" of her time in government in new book', *Guardian*, 9 September 2023, https://www.theguardian.com/politics/2023/sep/09/liz-truss-to-share-lessons-of-her-time-in-government-in-new-book

7. 'Grange Hill – Series Nine, Episode Seven', Archive Television Musings, 19 September 2017, https://archivetvmusings.blog/2017/09/19/grange-hill-series-nine-episode-seven/

8. 'Bishops in the House of Lords', *Hansard,* 6 July 2023, https://hansard.parliament.uk/commons/2023-07-06/debates/E78C1ED3-2510-4BA1-A6C3-DC95B753B5D8/BishopsInTheHouseOfLords#:~:text=There%20are%20only%20two%20countries,the%20Islamic%20Republic%20of%20Iran

9. Williams, E, 'The UK: A Parable of Distrust', 19 January 2020, https://www.edelman.com/insights/uk-parable-distrust

10. McDermott, J, 'Britannia Unchained', *Financial Times,* 10 September 2012, https://www.ft.com/content/8109784a-f82c-11e1-bec8-00144feabdc0

11. Horton, H, 'Conservative party heading in "very dark direction", says former minister', *Guardian*, 10 November 2023, https://www.theguardian.com/politics/2023/nov/10/conservative-party-heading-in-very-dark-direction-says-former-minister-chris-skidmore

12. https://www.inc.in/leadership/past-party-presidents

13. Brunnstrom, D, 'US would welcome Modi as PM despite past visa ban', Reuters, 12 May 2014, https://www.reuters.com/article/modi-pm-usa-visa-idINKBN0DS1M120140512

14. Nasher, J, 'To seem more competent, be more confident', *Harvard Business Review,* 11 March 2019, https://hbr.org/2019/03/to-seem-more-competent-be-more-confident

15. Walters, J, '"George Clooney or Brad Pitt?!" BBC QT panellist compares Boris Johnson to Ocean's 11 star', *Express,* 4 February 2022, https://www.express.co.uk/news/politics/1560746/bbc-question-time-tim-stanley-boris-johnson-george-clooney-brad-pitt-latest-news-ont

16. McTague, T, 'It's Boris Johnson's Britain now', *The Atlantic,* 13 December 2019, https://www.theatlantic.com/international/archive/2019/12/boris-johnson-britain-uk-election/603466

17. 'Transcript: Eddie Mair grills Boris Johnson on the Andrew Marr show', *Independent,* 24 March 2013, https://www.independent.co.uk/voices/iv-drip/transcript-eddie-mair-grills-boris-johnson-on-the-andrew-marr-show-8547356.htm

18. 'Tourism summit looks at future of industry and global issues', *VietNam News,* 26 April 2017, https://vietnamnews.vn/world/375425/tourism-summit-looks-at-future-of-industry-and-global-issues.html

19. Cameron. D, 'David Cameron shares his experiences in leadership at an extraordinary and tumultuous time in global affairs', Washington Speakers Bureau, https://www.wsb.com/speakers/david-cameron/

20. Russell, M, 'How leadership rule changes have led to a fight for the very soul of the Labour party', *Observer,* 17 July 2016, https://www.theguardian.com/commentis free/2016/jul/17/labour-leadership-battle-jeremy-corbyn-party-organisation

21. Burton, M and Tunnicliffe, R, 'Membership of political parties in Great Britain', House of Commons Library, 31 August 2022, https://commonslibrary.parliament.uk/research-briefings/sn05125/

22. Ibid.

23. Forrest, A, ' "Concentrated power": 25% of Tory Party's individual donations come from just 10 people', *Independent,* 8 August 2021, https://www.independent.co.uk/news/uk/politics/boris-johnson-conservatives-rich-donors-b1898260.html

24. Walker, P, 'Ex-Mubarak minister Mohamed Mansour donates £5m to Tories', *Guardian,* 22 May 2023, https://www.theguardian.com/politics/2023/may/22/ex-mubarak-minister-mohamed-mansour-donates-5m-to-tories

25. Zayed, I and Hussein, S, '"Mohamed Mansour: A tarnished captain of industry', *ahramonline,* 10 March 2011, https://english.ahram.org.eg/NewsContent/3/0/6724/Business/Mohamed-Mansour-A-tarnished-captain-of-industry.aspx

26. Savage, M, 'Just one in 100 Tory MPs came from a working-class job, new study shows', *Observer*, 24 July 2022, https://www.theguardian.com/politics/2022/jul/24/just-one-in-100-tory-mps-came-from-a-working-class-job-new-study-shows

27. https://www.bbc.co.uk/news/special/politics97/background/pastelec/ge51.shtml

28. http://news.bbc.co.uk/1/shared/vote2005/html/scoreboard.stm

29. 'Election 2015 Results', BBC News, https://www.bbc.co.uk/news/election/2015/results

30. https://www.britannica.com/place/Myanmar/Government-and-society

31. Partridge, J, 'Tesco buys Paperchase brand but not shops, with 800 jobs at risk', *Guardian*, 31 January 2023, https://www.theguardian.com/business/2023/jan/31/tesco-buys-paperchase-brand-shops-jobs

32. 'Minister of State, The Earl of Minto', Gov.uk, https://www.gov.uk/government/people/earl-of-minto-the-earl-of-minto

33. Livingston, S, 'A Labour Peer is trying to abolish hereditary peers (again)', Electoral Reform Society, 7 December 2021, https://www.electoral-reform.org.uk/a-labour-peer-is-tying-to-abolish-hereditary-peers-again/

34. 'Life Peers', UK Parliament, https://www.parliament.uk/site-information/glossary/life-peers/

35. 'Boris Johnson was warned of Lebedev security concerns, says Cummings', BBC News, 16 March 2022, https://www.bbc.co.uk/news/uk-politics-60765665

36. Conn, D and Lewis, P, 'Revealed: the full inside story of the Michelle Mone PPE scandal', *Guardian*, 9 December 2022, https://www.theguardian.com/uk-news/2022/dec/09/revealed-the-full-inside-story-of-the-michelle-mone-ppe-scandal

37. Dodd, V, Aletha Adu, A and Conn, D, 'NCA questions Matt Hancock and Michael Gove in PPE Medpro inquiry', *Guardian*, 26 November 2023, https://www.theguardian.com/uk-news/2023/nov/26/matt-hancock-michael-gove-questioned-ppe-medpro-inquiry-national-crime-agency

38. 'Joseph Kagan, Baron Kagan', *Wikipedia*, https://en.wikipedia.org/wiki/Joseph_Kagan,_Baron_Kagan

39. 'Lord Jeffrey Archer', Visit Somerset, https://www.visitsomerset.co.uk/business/about-us/visit-somerset-ambassadors/jeffrey-archer

40. PA Media and Laversuch, C, 'Lord Ahmed: Disgraced peer fails in bid to overturn conviction', BBC News, 11 July 2023, https://www.bbc.co.uk/news/uk-england-south-yorkshire-66167468

41. Lord Ahmed's 'retirement', MPs and Lords website, https://members.parliament. uk/member/3470/career

42. Brader, C, 'Peerages: can they be removed?', House of Lords Library, 10 February 2022, https://lordslibrary.parliament.uk/peerages-can-they-be-removed/

43. McDonald, A, 'Nigel Farage: "Brexit has failed"', *Politico*, 16 May 2023, https:// www.politico.eu/article/nigel-farage-uk-eu-brexit-has-failed/

44. Taylor, R, 'Cameron refuses to apologise to Ukip', *Guardian*, 4 April 2006, https://www.theguardian.com/politics/2006/apr/04/conservatives.uk

45. *Daily Mail* reporter, 'Daniel Hannan MEP: Watch the tirade against Gordon Brown that's become a huge hit on YouTube', *Daily Mail*, 27 March 2009, https:// www.dailymail.co.uk/debate/article-1165007/DANIEL-HANNAN-MEP-Watch-tirade-Gordon-Brown-thats-huge-hit-YouTube.html

46. Sparrow, A, 'Cameron faces calls to disown Hannan NHS "mistake" criticism', *Guardian*, 5 April 2009, https://www.theguardian.com/politics/2009/apr/05/ cameron-hannan-nhs-prescott

47. Berman, S, 'Tory Brexiteer and new government adviser claims NHS "not nearly as good as" US healthcare in resurface video', *Indy100*, 6 September 2020, https://www.indy100.com/news/daniel-hannan-trade-adviser-healthcare-nhs-interview-9706921

48. Elledge, J, 'Remember when Daniel Hannan kept appearing on Fox News to attack NHS?', *New Statesman,* 15 May 2017, https://www.newstatesman.com/ world/2017/05/remember-when-daniel-hannan-kept-appearing-fox-news-attack-nhs

49. Euractiv, 'British MEP thrown out of Parliament group over Nazi slur', 1 February 2008, https://www.euractiv.com/section/eu-priorities-2020/news/ british-mep-thrown-out-of-parliament-group-over-nazi-slur/

50. Hannan, D, 'What Britain looks like after Brexit', *Reaction,* 21 June 2016, https://reaction.life/britain-looks-like-brexit/

51. Kuper, S, '"A nursery of the Commons"; how the Oxford Union created today's ruling political class', *Guardian,* 19 April 2022, https://www.theguardian.com/news/2022/ apr/19/oxford-union-created-ruling-political-class-boris-johnson-michael-gove-theresa-may-rees-mogg

52. Vine, S, '"Gosh, I suppose I better get up!" Sarah Vine (aka Mrs Gove) reveals what her husband said when he learned Leave had won the referendum . . . and how PM's resignation was "absolutely" not intended', *Daily Mail,* 29 June 2016,

https://www.dailymail.co.uk/debate/article-3665146/SARAH-VINE-Victory-vitriol-craziest-days-life.html

53. Crace, J, 'Over to you, says puffy-eyed Cameron as the Brexit vultures circle', *Guardian*, 24 June 2016, https://www.theguardian.com/politics/2016/jun/24/over-to-you-says-puffy-eyed-cameron-as-brexit-vultures-circle

54. Ross, A, '"Well, that didn't go to plan": Cameron's spin doctor on the Brexit vote', *Guardian*, 25 September 2016, https://www.theguardian.com/politics/2016/sep/25/that-didnt-go-to-plan-cameron-spin-doctor-brexit-vote-craig-oliver

55. Shakespeare, W, 'The St. Crispin's Day speech from *Henry V*', The Poetry Society, https://poetrysociety.org.uk/poems/the-st-crispins-day-speech-from-henry-v/

56. Knight, S, 'The man who brought you Brexit', *Guardian*, 29 September 2016, https://www.theguardian.com/politics/2016/sep/29/daniel-hannan-the-man-who-brought-you-brexit

57. Jack, I, 'Now to stride into the sunlight', *London Review of Books*, vol 39, no 12, 15 June 2017, https://www.lrb.co.uk/the-paper/v39/n12/ian-jack/now-to-stride-into-the-sunlight

58. https://twitter.com/DanielJHannan/status/705375753303683072

59. https://www.youtube.com/watch?v=vkof9CVerrQ

60. Hannan, D, 'Daniel Hannan: Let this be the last Conservative leadership contest fought under these destructive rules', *Conservative Home*, 20 July 2022, https://conservativehome.com/2022/07/20/daniel-hannan-let-this-be-the-last-tory-leadership-contest-fought-under-these-awful-rules/

61. Henley, J and Roberts, D, '11 Brexit promises the government quietly dropped', *Guardian*, 28 March 2018, https://www.theguardian.com/politics/ng-interactive/2018/mar/28/11-brexit-promises-leavers-quietly-dropped

62. MacAskill, A and Miles, T, 'Britain's Fox says UK-EU trade deal "easiest in human history", sterling falls', *Reuters*, 20 July 2017, https://www.reuters.com/article/us-britain-eu-trade-idUSKBN1A50QC

63. Hannan, D, 'Magna Carta: Eight centuries of liberty', *Wall Street Journal*, 29 May 2015, https://www.wsj.com/articles/magna-carta-eight-centuries-of-liberty-1432912022

64. Adoyo, 'The Kingsclere bed bug', *Atlas obscura*, 31 July 2020, https://www.atlasobscura.com/places/the-kingsclere-bed-bug

5: REVERSAL OF FORTUNE

1. Osborne, J, SNAC cooperative, https://snaccooperative.org/ark:/99166/w6bc6mpd

2. Sparrow, A, *Guardian*, 8 November 2018, https://www.theguardian.com/politics/2018/nov/08/dominic-raab-dover-calais-brexit-uk-france

3. Behr, R, 'Has nobody told Dominic Raab that Britain is an island?', *Guardian,* 8 November 2018, https://www.theguardian.com/commentisfree/2018/nov/08/dominic-raab-britain-island-ignorance-brexit-secretary

4. Bawden, A, 'Two in three state secondary schools in England teach just one foreign language', *Guardian,* 29 June 2023, https://www.theguardian.com/education/2023/jun/29/two-in-three-state-secondary-schools-in-england-teach-just-one-foreign-language

5. Keystone/Hulton Archive/Getty Images, 'Benn releases North Sea oil', *Getty Images*, 18 June 1975, https://www.gettyimages.ca/detail/news-photo/british-labour-secretary-of-state-for-energy-tony-benn-news-photo/469684655

6. 'Full text of "Financial Times, 1975, UK, English"', https://archive.org/stream/FinancialTimes1975UKEnglish/Jun%2019%201975%2C%20Financial%20Times%2C%20%2326696%2C%20UK%20%28en%29_djvu.txt

7. 'Business: priming the pump', *Time*, 30 June 1975, https://content.time.com/time/subscriber/article/0,33009,917597,00.html

8. Harvie, C, 'Fool's Gold: The story of North Sea oil', *Penguin Books*, 2 November 1995, https://warwick.ac.uk/fac/arts/english/currentstudents/postgraduate/masters/modules/resourcefictions/oil09/harvie.pdf

9. Hope, B, 'Alleged 1MDB co-conspirators sentenced to prison', *Wall Street Journal*, 16 June 2019, https://www.wsj.com/articles/alleged-1mdb-co-conspirators-sentenced-to-prison-11560677550

10. Ibid.

11. Fraser, I, 'Where did all the oil money go?', *Shredded*, 1 June 2008, http://www.ianfraser.org/where-did-all-the-oil-money-go/

12. Chakrabortty, A, 'Dude, where's my North Sea oil money?', *Guardian*, 13 January 2014, https://www.theguardian.com/commentisfree/2014/jan/13/north-sea-oil-money-uk-norwegians-fund

13. McDermott, J, 'There will be North Sea oil', *Financial Times,* 25 February 2014, https://www.ft.com/content/1b3ed177-be4a-33bb-9dac-2098b3e989f4

14. Dyck, J, 'Why the UK lost its oil wealth (and why Norway didn't)', *Medium*, 8 October 2019, https://medium.com/bc-digest/why-the-uk-lost-its-oil-wealth-and-why-norway-didnt-b4c96199288d.

15. Smith, N, 'North Sea oil: A tale of two countries', *Engineering and Technology*, 20 January 2021, https://eandt.theiet.org/content/articles/2021/01/north-sea-oil-a-tale-of-two-countries/

16. Manley, D and Myers, K, 'Did the UK miss out on £400 billion worth of oil revenue?', Natural Resource Governance Institute, 5 October 2015, https://resourcegovernance.org/articles/did-uk-miss-out-ps400-billion-worth-oil-revenue

17. Barnett, A, 'Thatcher and the words no one mentions: North Sea oil', Open Democracy, 8 April 2013, https://www.opendemocracy.net/en/opendemocracyuk/thatcher-and-words-no-one-mentions-north-sea-oil/

18. 'Thatcherism. Tony Blair', *London Review of Books*, vol. 9, no. 19, 29 October 1987, https://www.lrb.co.uk/the-paper/v09/n19/tony-blair/diary

19. 'The evolution of North Sea oil and gas receipts', Office for Budget Responsibility, March 2023, https://obr.uk/box/the-evolution-of-north-sea-oil-and-gas-receipts/

20. Powell, A, 'Gross Domestic Product (GDP): Key economic indicators', House of Commons Library, 19 October 2023, https://commonslibrary.parliament.uk/research-briefings/sn02783/

21. Gallagher, P, 'New hospitals could be delayed by economic turmoil, NHS leaders warn', *i News*, 30 September 2022, https://inews.co.uk/news/health/nhs-leaders-economic-turmoil-costs-new-hospital-projects-1885707

22. 'Charge and basic rate of income tax for 1988–89', *Hansard*, 3 May 1988, https://hansard.parliament.uk/commons/1988-05-03/debates/81d27363-36e4-40d3-a85f-84a0ba933f7d/ChargeAndBasicRateOfIncomeTaxFor1988–89#754

23. John Hawksworth, Linkedin, https://www.linkedin.com/in/john-hawksworth-9aa4931a0/

24. Blas, J, 'Protecting Nigeria oil SWF is no easy task', *Financial Times*, 10 October 2013, https://www.ft.com/content/69325c28-2440-11e3-a8f7-00144feab7de#axzz2qJ6YUFpy

25. 'Kuwait celebrates 62nd national day, 32nd liberation anniversary', *Asharq Al-Awsat*, 25 February 2023, https://english.aawsat.com/home/article/4178696/kuwait-celebrates-62nd-national-day-32nd-liberation-anniversary

26. 'Global SWF data platform', Sovereign Wealth Funds, https://globalswf.com

27. 'Abu Dhabi Investment Authority', ADIA, https://www.adia.ae

28. 'Right to buy extension to make home ownership possible for millions more people', Gov.uk, 9 June 2022, https://www.gov.uk/government/news/right-to-buy-extension-to-make-home-ownership-possible-for-millions-more-people

29. Eardley, F, 'Right to buy: past, present and future', House of Lords Library, 17 June 2022, https://lordslibrary.parliament.uk/right-to-buy-past-present-and-future/#heading-7

30. '£6 billion in Right to Buy discounts threaten future of scheme', Local Government Association, 1 August 2022, https://www.local.gov.uk/about/news/ps6-billion-right-buy-discounts-threaten-future-scheme#:~:text=Almost%20%C2%A36%20billion%20has,the%20Local%20Government%20Association%20reveals

31. Hanley, L, 'From Thatcher to Johnson: how right to buy has fuelled a 40-year housing crisis', *Guardian*, 29 June 2022, https://www.theguardian.com/society/2022/jun/29/how-right-to-buy-ruined-british-housing

32. Solsvik, T, 'Norway sovereign wealth fund to divest oil explorers, keep refiners', Reuters, 1 October 2019, https://www.reuters.com/article/us-norway-swf-oil-idUSKBN1WG4R9

33. 'Crude oil prices – 70 year historical chart', Macrotrends, https://www.macrotrends.net/1369/crude-oil-price-history-chart

34. 'UK Inflation rate 1960–2023', Macrotrends, https://www.macrotrends.net/countries/GBR/united-kingdom/inflation-rate-cpi

35. 'Hundreds of new North Sea oil and gas licences to boost British energy independence and grow the economy', Gov.uk, 31 July 2023, https://www.gov.uk/government/news/hundreds-of-new-north-sea-oil-and-gas-licences-to-boost-british-energy-independence-and-grow-the-economy-31-july-2023

36. Pickard, J, Parker, G, Mooney, A and Millard, R, 'Grant Shapps vows to "max out" UK's North Sea oil and gas reserves', *Financial Times*, 23 July 2023, https://www.ft.com/content/407b834e-a503-4de9-acab-fcf88d76dbb3

37. https://www.britannica.com/place/Russia/Leaders-of-Russia-from-1276

38. Roach, S, 'Would new North Sea oil and gas make Britain more energy independent?', *Channel 4 News*, 1 August 2023, https://www.channel4.com/news/factcheck/would-new-north-sea-oil-and-gas-make-britain-more-energy-independent

39. 'Energy trends. UK, April to June 2023', Department for Energy Security & Net Zero, 28 September 2023, https://assets.publishing.service.gov.uk/government/uploads/system/uploads/attachment_data/file/1187528/Energy_Trends_September_2023.pdf

40. 'British energy security strategy', Gov.uk, 7 April 2022, https://www.gov.uk/government/publications/british-energy-security-strategy/british-energy-security-strategy

41. Mawhood, B, Bolton, P and Hinson, S, 'British energy security strategy', *House of Commons Library*, 4 July 2022, https://commonslibrary.parliament.uk/research-briefings/cdp-2022-0128/

42. Lusty, P, Shaw, R, Gunn, A and Idoine, N, 'UK criticality assessment of technology critical minerals and metals', British Geological Survey CR/21/120, https://nora.nerc.ac.uk/id/eprint/535664/1/CR21120N.pdf

43. Webber, E and Whale, S, 'Sunak and Biden reach for critical minerals deal in show of unity', *Politico*, 8 June 2023, https://www.politico.eu/article/rishi-sunak-and-joe-biden-us-uk-washington-reach-for-critical-minerals-deal-in-show-of-unity/

44. 'EU moves forward with Critical Minerals Agreement negotiations with the US', *European Commission*, 14 June 2023, https://ec.europa.eu/commission/presscorner/detail/en/IP_23_3214

45. 'Resilience for the future: the UK's critical minerals strategy', Gov.uk, 13 March 2023, https://www.gov.uk/government/publications/uk-critical-mineral-strategy/resilience-for-the-future-the-uks-critical-minerals-strategy

46. Jozepa, I, 'Trade: key economic indicators', *House of Commons Library*, 12 October 2023, https://commonslibrary.parliament.uk/research-briefings/sn02815/

47. 'United Kingdom', European Commission, https://policy.trade.ec.europa.eu/eu-trade-relationships-country-and-region/countries-and-regions/united-kingdom_en

48. 'United Kingdom food security report 2021: introduction', Gov.uk, 5 October 2023, https://www.gov.uk/government/statistics/united-kingdom-food-security-report-2021/united-kingdom-food-security-report-2021-introduction

49. BGS blogs, 'Six changing coastlines and how climate change could affect them', British Geological Survey, 12 April 2022, https://www.bgs.ac.uk/news/six-changing-coastlines-and-how-climate-change-could-affect-them/

50. 'Imagine the Universe!' National Aeronautics and Space Administration, https://imagine.gsfc.nasa.gov/features/cosmic/earth_info.html

51. 'United Kingdom food security report 2021: introduction', Gov.uk, 5 October 2023, https://www.gov.uk/government/statistics/united-kingdom-food-security-report-2021/united-kingdom-food-security-report-2021-introduction

52. Simpson, N, 'Why don't the British eat seafood?', *Medium,* 18 July 2021, https://nicholashsimpson.medium.com/why-dont-the-brits-eat-seafood-88e0cbec4163

53. Blog, 'The Great British seafood dilemma', Seafood Cornwall, 9 May 2022, https://www.seafoodcornwall.org.uk/the-great-british-seafood-dilemma/

54. Ibid.

6: THE EMPIRE STRIKES BACK

1. 'Shell sued in UK for "decades of oil spills" in Nigeria', Aljazeera, 22 November 2016, https://www.aljazeera.com/news/2016/11/22/shell-sued-in-uk-for-decades-of-oil-spills-in-nigeria

2. Statement to Parliament on settlement of Mau Mau claims, government website, 6 June 2013, https://www.gov.uk/government/news/statement-to-parliament-on-settlement-of-mau-mau-claims

3. Cameron-Chileshe, J, 'Human Rights Watch demands full reparations from UK and US for Chagos Islanders', *Financial Times*, 15 February 2023, https://www.ft.com/content/19d5d97d-59b9-409f-87d1-39547fd3834a

4. Cox QC, B, 'Letter: Reparation and apology is price UK must pay for colonial sins', *Financial Times*, 4 May 2022, https://www.ft.com/content/11d60e3d-4d87-4ed9-8f19-0f076e7b1233

5. Anson, M and Bennett, M, 'Research paper: the collection of slavery compensation, 1835–43', Bank of England Museum, 25 November 2022, https://www.bankofengland.co.uk/museum/whats-on/slavery-and-the-bank/research-paper-the-collection-of-slavery-compensation-1835-1843

6. Ibid.

7. Mohdin, A, 'David Harewood says portrait stands for "resilience of my people" after Leeds unveiling', *Guardian*, 5 September 2023, https://www.theguardian.com/culture/2023/sep/05/engagement-is-the-way-forward-david-harewood-on-his-link-to-leeds-country-house

8. Nevett, J, 'Richard Drax: Jamaica eyes slavery reparations from Tory MP', *BBC News*, 30 November 2022, https://www.bbc.co.uk/news/uk-politics-63799222

9. Renton, A, 'Antoinette Sandbach's relatives owned slaves – and so did mine. We have to atone for that as best we can', *Guardian*, 1 September 2023, https://www.theguardian.com/commentisfree/2023/sep/01/antoinette-sandbach-relatives-slaves-ancestors

10. ABC News, 'Britain celebrates 200-year anniversary of the abolition of the slave trade', ABC News, 26 March 2007, https://abcnews.go.com/International/story?id=2981677&page=1

11. Conn, D, Mohdin, A, and Wolfe-Robinson, M, 'King Charles signals first explicit support for research into monarchy's slavery ties', *Guardian*, 6 April 2023, https://www.theguardian.com/world/2023/apr/06/king-charles-signals-first-explicit-support-for-research-into-monarchys-slavery-ties

12. Olusoga, D, 'The toppling of Edward Coulson's statue is not an attack on history. It is history', *Guardian*, 8 June 2020, https://www.theguardian.com/commentisfree/2020/jun/08/edward-colston-statue-history-slave-trader-bristol-protest

13. Cork, T, 'Second Colston statue plaque not axed and will still happen but mayor steps in to order a re-write', *Bristol Post*, 25 March 2019, https://www.bristolpost.co.uk/news/bristol-news/second-colston-statue-plaque-not-2682813

14. Walker, P, 'Abuse has led Sathnam Sanghera to "more or less stop" doing book events in UK', *Guardian*, 9 June 2023, https://www.theguardian.com/books/https://www.express.co.uk/comment/columnists 2023/jun/09/abuse-has-led-sathnam-sanghera-to-more-or-less-stop-doing-book-events-in-uk

15. O'Brien, H, 'Orwell's Burma: the trail that opened up for visitors', The Orwell Society, 25 February 2012, https://orwellsociety.com/orwells-burma-the-trail-that-opened-up/

16. Davison, P, 'Orwell goes East', The Orwell Society, 26 December 2012, https://orwellsociety.com/orwell-goes-east-by-peter-davison/

17. Hervé, G, 'My country right or wrong', *Ulan Press*, 31 August 2012, https://www.amazon.co.jp/-/en/1871-1944/dp/B00B4I3R66

18. McNeill, D and Hornyak, T, 'My country, right or wrong', The Foreign Correspondents' Club of Japan, December 2022, https://www.fccj.or.jp/index.php/number-1-shimbun-article/my-country-right-or-wrong

19. Forsyth, F, 'RIP the British stiff upper lip – today it trembles at every opportunity', *Express*, 6 August 2021

20. 'The history of Shell in Nigeria', Shell plc, https://www.shell.com.ng/about-us/shell-nigeria-history.html

21. Lobban, M, 'Removing rulers in the Niger Delta, 1887–1897, *Cambridge University Press*, 20 August 2021, https://www.cambridge.org/core/books/imperial-incarceration/removing-rulers-in-the-niger-delta-18871897/A98E79E85212C0EB9C06C961C4E9BA12

22. 'Shell from 1833 to 1945', Shell plc, https://www.shell.com/about-us/our-heritage/our-company-history.html

23. 'Frequently asked questions on the UNEP environmental assessment of Ogoniland', Shell plc, https://www.shell.com.ng/sustainability/environment/unep-environmental-assessmen-of-ogoniland/unep-faq.html

24. Jackson, P, 'Biography: Lewis Harcourt', *Journal of Liberal History*, 4 (Autumn 2003), pp.14–17, https://liberalhistory.org.uk/wp-content/uploads/2015/05/40-Jackson-Lewis-Harcourt-biography.pdf

25. Parris, M, 'Scandals in the House', *Independent*, 29 October 1995, https://www.independent.co.uk/arts-entertainment/scandals-in-the-house-1579987.html

26. Aigbogun, F, Associated Press, Lagos, 'It took five tries to hang Saro-Wiwa', *Independent*, 13 November 1995, https://www.independent.co.uk/news/world/it-took-five-tries-to-hang-sarowiwa-1581703.html

27. Arrowsmith, K, 'Bush Paths', *The British Empire*, https://www.britishempire.co.uk/article/bushpaths.htm

28. Pilkington, E, 'Shell pays out $15.5m over Saro-Wiwa killing', *Guardian*, 9 June 2009, https://www.theguardian.com/world/2009/jun/08/nigeria-usa

29. Holligan, A, 'Ogoni nine: Nigerian widows lose case against oil giant Shell', BBC News, 23 March 2022, https://www.bbc.co.uk/news/world-europe-60851111

30. 'Shell to pay 15 mln euros in settlement over Nigerian oil spills', Reuters, 23 December 2022, https://www.reuters.com/business/energy/shell-pay-15-mln-euros-settlement-over-nigerian-oil-spills-2022-12-23

31. Wilson, T, 'Shell profits more than double to record $40bn', *Financial Times*, 2 February 2023, https://www.ft.com/content/b929ba6f-9e89-44f1-8f82-a12660bbc2ba

32. 'Contributing to Nigeria's economy', Shell plc, https://reports.shell.com/sustainability-report/2022/powering-lives/contributing-to-communities/contributing-to-nigeria-s-economy.html

33. Rice, X, 'Pipeline leaks mar delta village', *Financial Times*, 20 March 2012, https://www.ft.com/content/96aee036-728f-11e1-9be9-00144feab49a

34. Adams, C and Wallis, W, 'Royal Dutch Shell agrees £55m Nigeria oil spill settlement', *Financial Times*, 7 January 2015, https://www.ft.com/content/06463b86-95c1-11e4-a390-00144feabdc0

35. https://www.britannica.com/topic/list-of-the-total-areas-of-the-worlds-countries-dependencies-and-territories-2130540

36. Shirbon, E, 'Shell wins UK Supreme Court case on 2011 oil spill off Nigerian coast', Reuters, 10 May 2023, https://www.reuters.com/business/energy/shell-wins-uk-supreme-court-case-2011-oil-spill-off-nigerian-coast-2023-05-10/

7: TINDER BRITAIN

1. Truss, L, 'Keynote Speech: The Network of Liberty', Conservatives.com, 3 October 2021, https://www.conservatives.com/news/2021/the-network-of-liberty

2. Cleverly, J, 'British foreign policy and diplomacy', Gov.uk, 12 December 2022, https://www.gov.uk/government/speeches/foreign-secretarys-speech-12-december-2022

3. Wintour, P, 'James Cleverly scales back plan for Global Britain's network of liberty', *Guardian,* 12 December 2023, https://www.theguardian.com/politics/2022/dec/12/james-cleverly-scales-back-plan-for-global-britains-network-of-liberty

4. 'EU population increases again after two years decrease', *Eurostat,* 11 July 2023, https://ec.europa.eu/eurostat/web/products-eurostat-news/w/edn-20230711-1

5. Robbins, S, 'Boris Johnson told former Thai leader he would run for prime minister a year ago', Sky News, 26 July 2019, https://news.sky.com/story/boris-johnson-told-former-thai-leader-he-would-run-for-prime-minister-a-year-ago-11770712

6. Truss, L, 'Britain is free and our exciting future lies far beyond Europe', *Express,* 7 November 2021, https://www.express.co.uk/comment/expresscomment/1517498/brexit-britain-liz-truss-asia-malaysia-thailand-indonesia

7. Department for Business and Trade and Nigel Huddleston MP press release, 18 August 2023, https://www.gov.uk/government/news/uk-trade-minister-in-indonesia-and-vietnam-to-turbocharge-trade-with-southeast-asia

8. Parker, G and Wright, R, 'UK strikes agreement to join Asia-Pacific trade bloc', *Financial Times,* 31 March 2023, https://www.ft.com/content/7b503583-b1d6-4763-a519-df46bdb3d924

9. 'Brexit analysis', Office for Budget Responsibility, March 2023, https://obr.uk/forecasts-in-depth/the-economy-forecast/brexit-analysis/#assumptions

10. Helm, T, 'UK's flagship post-Brexit trade deal worth even less than previously thought, OBR says', *Observer,* 25 November 2023, https://www.theguardian.com/politics/2023/nov/25/uks-flagship-post-brexit-trade-deal-worth-even-less-than-previously-thought-obr-says

11. 'Trade and Investment Factsheet: Belgium', Department for Business & Trade, 1 November 2023, https://assets.publishing.service.gov.uk/media/653f991e6de3b90012a7a5b1/belgium-trade-and-investment-factsheet-2023-11-01.pdf

12. 'Trade and Investment Factsheet: Vietnam', Department for Business & Trade, 1 November 2023, https://assets.publishing.service.gov.uk/media/653fcf886de3b9000da7a643/vietnam-trade-and-investment-factsheet-2023-11-01.pdf

13. Nigel Huddleston MP, https://twitter.com/HuddlestonNigel

14. https://twitter.com/DominicRaab/status/1407502225144913922

15. 'Release of Mu Sochua', Vital Voices Global Partnership, 23 July 2014, https://www.
    vitalvoices.org/release-of-mu-sochua/

16. Baliga, A and Dara, M, 'Breaking: CNRP's Mu Sochua flees country following
    "warning" of arrest', *Phnom Penh Post,* 3 October 2017, https://www.phnompenh
    post.com/national/breaking-cnrps-mu-sochua-flees-country-following-
    warning-arrest

17. 'Trade and Investment Factsheet: Cambodia', Department for Business & Trade,
    1 November 2023, https://assets.publishing.service.gov.uk/media/653fb3d2465
    32b001467f514/cambodia-trade-and-investment-factsheet-2023-11-01.pdf

18. Head, J, 'Cambodia election: This was more of a coronation than an election',
    BBC website, 23 July 203, https://www.bbc.co.uk/news/world-asia-66283745

19. Foreign, Commonwealth and Development Office press release, 24 July 2023,
    https://www.gov.uk/government/news/fcdo-statement-on-cambodian-elections

20. Turton, S, 'Hun Manet pledges "peace, stability" as new Cambodian PM', *Nikkei
    Asia,* 22 August 2023, https://asia.nikkei.com/Politics/Cambodia-s-new-leadership/
    Hun-Manet-pledges-peace-stability-as-new-Cambodian-PM

21. Seavmey, M, 'British navy ship renews old maritime friendship', *Cambodianess,*
    16 February 2023, https://cambodianess.com/article/british-navy-ship-renews-
    old-maritime-friendship

22. UK in Cambodia, https://twitter.com/ukincambodia/status/1641694168631357442

23. Raksa, S, 'Manet praises UK defence cooperation', *Phnom Penh Post,* 31 March
    2023, https://www.phnompenhpost.com/national-politics/manet-praises-uk-
    defence-cooperation

24. Sevastopulo, D, 'Chinese base in Cambodia nears completion in challenge to
    US naval power', *Financial Times,* 24 July 2023, https://www.ft.com/content/
    cec4bbb9-8e92-4fc1-85fb-ded826a735c5

25. Kuper, S, 'Can Southeast Asia save Brexit?', *Financial Times,* 12 October 2017,
    https://www.ft.com/content/ff258af2-ae0c-11e7-beba-5521c713abf4

26. 'Defence', *Hansard,* 27 July 1967, https://api.parliament.uk/historic-hansard/
    commons/1967/jul/27/defence

27. 'History of the European Union 1960–69', European Union, https://european-
    union.europa.eu/principles-countries-history/history-eu/1960-69_en

28. Vatikiotis, M, 'ASEAN is quietly coming apart at the seams', *Nikkei Asia,* 28 August
    2023, https://asia.nikkei.com/Opinion/ASEAN-is-quietly-coming-apart-at-
    the-seams

29. Robinson, G, 'Can ASEAN overcome the "Myanmar curse"?', *Nikkei Asia,* 1 November 2021, https://asia.nikkei.com/Spotlight/Comment/Can-ASEAN-overcome-the-Myanmar-curse

30. https://www.iwm.org.uk/collections/item/object/205210820

31. 'Statue of Stamford Raffles', *Singapore Infopedia,* https://www.nlb.gov.sg/main/article-detail?cmsuuid=fcd18cc9-d547-45c2-805d-7ce3f1e84c1c

32. 'GDP per capita, PPP (current international $)', The World Bank, https://data.worldbank.org/indicator/NY.GDP.PCAP.PP.CD

33. 'Purchasing power parities – frequently asked questions (FAQs)', OCDE.org, https://www.oecd.org/fr/sdd/prix-ppa/purchasingpowerparities-frequently askedquestionsfaqs.htm

34. 'GDP per capita (current US$)', The World Bank, https://data.worldbank.org/indicator/NY.GDP.PCAP.CD

35. 'Oral evidence: The FCO and the Integrated Review', Foreign Affairs Committee, House of Commons, 22 September 2020, https://committees.parliament.uk/oralevidence/894/html/

36. 'Singapore-on-Thames', *Wikipedia,* https://en.wikipedia.org/wiki/Singapore-on-Thames

37. Yeo, G. 'Britain should renew ties with old friends in Asia', *The Economist,* 27 October 2022, https://www.economist.com/by-invitation/2022/10/27/britain-should-renew-ties-with-old-friends-in-asia-advises-george-yeo

38. Davies, J, 'In London, Cambodian elites tread in the Kremlin's footsteps', *Radio Free Asia,* 10 August 2020, https://www.rfa.org/english/news/special/hunsen-family/russia.html

39. Willemyns, A, 'Hun Manet tells UN Cambodia's elections were fair', *Radio Free Asia,* 22 September 2022, https://www.rfa.org/english/news/cambodia/hun-manet-un-09222023150854.html

8: THE WIZARD BEHIND THE CURTAIN

1. 'Sandhurst Trust', Facebook, https://www.facebook.com/sandhursttrust/posts/the-son-of-an-indian-army-officer-digby-jeremie-willoughby-was-born-in-india-on-/2635038159857826/?locale=ms_MY

2. Harry, K, 'The Brunei rebellion of 1962', 2015, https://ris.cdu.edu.au/ws/portalfiles/portal/22703258/Thesis_CDU_55418_Harry_K.pdf

3. 'Integrated Review Refresh 2023: Responding to a more contested and volatile world', HM Government, 13 March 2023, https://assets.publishing.service.gov.uk/media/6 41d72f45155a2000c6ad5d5/11857435_NS_IR_Refresh_2023_Supply_AllPages_ Revision_7_WEB_PDF.pdf

4. Jacob, J, ' "Brexit 1967": Britain's retreat from empire and Cold War Southeast Asia', *LSE,* 13 December 2017, https://blogs.lse.ac.uk/lseih/2017/12/13/brexit-1967-britains-retreat-from-empire-and-cold-war-southeast-asia/

5. James, W, 'There and back again: the fall and rise of Britain's "East of Suez" basing strategy', *War on the Rocks,* 18 February 2021, https://warontherocks.com/2021/02/there-and-back-again-the-fall-and-rise-of-britains-east-of-suez-basing-strategy/

6. Lambert, H, 'Simon McDonald: "It's the end of the game for Britain" ', *New Statesman,* 13 May 2023, https://www.newstatesman.com/the-weekend-interview/2023/05/simon-mcdonald-interview-end-game-britain

7. Brown, F, 'Tory MP Chris Pincher to resign after suspension from Commons over groping allegations', Sky News website, 7 September 2023, https://news.sky.com/story/tory-mp-chris-pincher-resigns-after-suspension-from-commons-over-groping-allegations-12956582

8. Ulrike Franke, https://twitter.com/RikeFranke/status/1657694469288865793?s=20

9. Polmar, N, 'British Sign Carrier Contract', Military.com, 7 August 2007, https://www.military.com/defensetech/2007/08/07/british-sign-carrier-contract/amp

10. 'The Carrier Strike Group: our nation's spearhead', Royal Navy, https://www.royalnavy.mod.uk/news-and-latest-activity/features/carrier-strike

11. Vavasseur, X, 'UK aircraft carrier to return to the Indo-Pacific in 2025', *Naval News,* 23 May 2023, https://www.navalnews.com/naval-news/2023/05/uk-aircraft-carrier-to-return-to-the-indo-pacific-in-2025/

12. Wilcock, D, 'HMS Prince of Fails: Ministers reveal problem-plagued £3.2 billion Royal Navy aircraft carrier will spend a YEAR in port as it undergoes £25million repairs after breaking down last summer', *Daily Mail*, 20 April 2023, https://www.dailymail.co.uk/news/article-11985783/HMS-Prince-Fails-Problem-plagued-3-2-billion-aircraft-carrier-spend-YEAR-port.html

13. Martin, T, 'UK Royal Navy "confident" a starboard propeller problem on aircraft carrier not a class-wide issue', *Breaking Defense,* 1 February 2023, https://breakingdefense.com/2023/02/uk-royal-navy-confident-a-starboard-propeller-problem-on-aircraft-carrier-not-a-class-wide-issue/

14. Associated Press, 'China has fully militarized three islands in South China Sea, US Admiral says', *Guardian,* 21 March 2023, https://www.theguardian.com/world/2022/mar/21/china-has-fully-militarized-three-islands-in-south-china-sea-us-admiral-says

15. 'Our story', Brunel's *SS Great Britain*, https://www.ssgreatbritain.org/our-story/

16. https://www.britannica.com/event/Malayan-Emergency

17. https://bruneiresources.blogspot.com/2008/09/twelve-roofs-mansion.html

18. 'The twelve roofs mansion', *Daily Brunei Resources,* 11 September 2008, http://bruneiresources.blogspot.com/2008/09/twelve-roofs-mansion.html

19. BBC Teach, 'History KS3/KS4: What was the contribution of Indian Sikhs in World War One?', BBC, https://www.bbc.co.uk/teach/class-clips-video/history-ks3-ks4-what-was-the-contribution-of-indian-sikhs-in-world-war-one/zhkdhbk#:~:text=Indian%20Sikhs%20played%20a%20key,their%20involvement%20in%20the%20war

20. 'Commonwealth war graves: PM "deeply troubled" over racism', BBC News, 22 April 2021, https://www.bbc.co.uk/news/uk-56840131

21. 'CWGC statement in relation to the unremembered documentary', Commonwealth War Graves, 4 November 2019, https://www.cwgc.org/our-work/news/cwgc-statement-in-relation-to-the-unremembered-documentary/

22. 'Troops of the Royal West African Frontier Force in the Arakan, Burma, 1944', National Army Museum, https://www.nam.ac.uk/explore/royal-west-african-frontier-force-burma-1944

23. 'A short guide to the Malayan Emergency', IWM, https://www.iwm.org.uk/history/a-short-guide-to-the-malayan-emergency

24. Wintour, P, 'Joanna Lumley confronts Phil Woolas over Gurkhas', *Guardian,* 7 May 2009, https://www.theguardian.com/uk/2009/may/07/gurkhas-joanna-lumley-phil-woolas

25. 'A brief history of the Brunei Revolt and the Indonesian Confrontation', IWM, https://www.iwm.org.uk/history/a-brief-history-of-the-brunei-revolt-and-the-indonesian-confrontation

26. https://www.britannica.com/biography/Omar-Ali-Saifuddin

27. 'Gurkhas (Brunei)', *Hansard,* 12 July 1995, https://hansard.parliament.uk/commons/1995-07-12/debates/cedee13b-a478-4049-82ba-24a151ead70c/Gurkhas(Brunei)

28. Eaton, G, 'David Edgerton: "The UK needs a politics of modesty" ', *New Statesman,* 12 July 2023, https://www.newstatesman.com/encounter/2023/07/david-edgerton-uk-needs-politics-of-modesty?utm_source=substack&utm_medium=email

29. Gross, A and Lewis, L, 'Arm loses 40% of UK staff gained in SoftBank years', *Financial Times,* 4 October 2022, https://www.ft.com/content/932c6422-f7c8-4f61-a1ad-51cea238e2fb

30. ' "Labour and the Scientific Revolution", a policy statement made to the Annual Conference of the Labour party, Scarborough, 1963 by the leader, Mr Harold Wilson', 1963, https://web-archives.univ-pau.fr/english/TD2doc2.pdf

31. 'Egypt's Suez Canal blocked by huge container ship', BBC News, 24 March 2021, https://www.bbc.co.uk/news/world-middle-east-56505413

32. Edgerton, D, 'Yes, we're in a bad way. But to wallow in myths of British "declinism" won't help us thrive', *Guardian,* 12 June 2022, https://amp.theguardian.com/commentisfree/2022/jun/12/yes-were-in-a-bad-way-but-to-wallow-in-myths-of-british-declinism-wont-help-us-thrive

33. Elgot, J and Lawson, A, 'Great British Energy: what is it, what would it do and how would it be funded?', *Guardian,* 27 September 2022, https://www.theguardian.com/politics/2022/sep/27/great-british-energy-what-is-it-what-would-it-do-and-how-would-it-be-funded

34. Eaton, G, 'David Edgerton: "The UK needs a politics of modesty" ', *New Statesman,* 12 July 2023, https://www.newstatesman.com/encounter/2023/07/david-edgerton-uk-needs-politics-of-modesty?utm_source=substack&utm_medium=email

35. Mudde, C, 'The Popular Zeitgeist', *Government and Opposition* (vol. 39, no. 4, autumn 2004), https://www.jstor.org/stable/44483088

36. Suella Braverman speech, 3 October 2023, https://www.ukpol.co.uk/suella-braverman-2023-speech-to-conservative-party-conference/

EPILOGUE: RENEWAL

1. 'Nation rejoices as Portillo loses seat', *Observer,* 12 September 1999, https://www.theguardian.com/politics/1999/sep/12/conservatives.uk

2. Lawson, N, 'Twenty-five years on, it's clearer than ever that New Labour failed', *Prospect,* 28 April 2022, https://www.prospectmagazine.co.uk/politics/38588/twenty-five-years-on-its-clearer-than-ever-that-new-labour-failed

3. 'Full text: Tony Blair's speech (part two)', *Guardian,* 2 October 2021, https://www.theguardian.com/politics/2001/oct/02/labourconference.labour7

4. 'Most do not think the Conservative Party can run the country competently, and 4 in 10 dislike their policies', *Ipsos,* 13 July 2023, https://www.ipsos.com/en-uk/

most-do-not-think-conservative-party-can-run-country-competently-and-4-
10-dislike-their-policies

5. Harford, T, 'The data confirms we're stuck in a "doom loop"', *Financial Times*,
9 November 2023, https://www.ft.com/content/962c3194-4ac4-468d-bf1a-
7c62abc8a401

6. House of Commons Library, 'What is the government doing to reduce pressure
on prison capacity?', 19 October 2023, https://commonslibrary.parliament.uk/
what-is-the-government-doing-to-reduce-pressure-on-prison-capacity/

7. UK Parliament Public Accounts Committee, '£4 billion of unusable PPE bought
in first year of pandemic will be burnt "to generate power"', 10 June 2022, https://
committees.parliament.uk/committee/127/public-accounts-committee/news/
171306/4-billion-of-unusable-ppe-bought-in-first-year-of-pandemic-will-be-burnt-
to-generate-power/

8. Henry Mance on X, 2 October 2023, https://twitter.com/henrymance/status/
1708828384875126949?s=51&t=-DsSz

9. Starmer, K, 'Labour will rebuild broken Britain with big reforms, not big spending.
That's a promise', *Observer*, 15 July 2023, https://www.theguardian.com/
commentisfree/2023/jul/15/labour-approach-britain-failed-tory-rebuild

10. Gross, A, and Strauss, D, 'Sunak under pressure as net migration to UK hits record
745,000', *Financial Times*, 23 November 2023, https://www.ft.com/content/
9ac523da-1c15-43e8-9ccc-bbfdbce4b74a

11. 'Chris Packham: is it time to break the law?', Channel 4, 20 September 2023,
https://www.channel4.com/programmes/chris-packham-is-it-time-to-break-
the-law

12. 'David Cameron's speech outside 10 Downing Street as Prime Minister', Gov.uk,
12 May 2010, https://www.gov.uk/government/speeches/david-camerons-
speech-outside-10-downing-street-as-prime-minister

13. 'The view from the other side: perceptions of the UK abroad in 2021', Ipsos,
8 December 2021, https://www.ipsos.com/en-uk/view-other-side-perceptions-
uk-abroad-2021

14. Butler, P, 'Britain is much more liberal-minded than it was 40 years ago, study
finds', *Guardian*, 21 September 2023, https://www.theguardian.com/society/2023/
sep/21/britain-is-much-more-liberal-minded-than-is-was-40-years-ago-study-finds

15. 'A new era dawns for the British passport', Thales, https://www.thalesgroup.com/en/
markets/digital-identity-and-security/government/customer-cases/uk-passport

Acknowledgements

This book is a synthesis of years of experiences that mean I owe debts of gratitude to far more people than I can mention here. Family, friends and contacts in the six countries I have lived in during the last 20 years all helped make it possible. Writing a book is a fundamentally antisocial activity that places big burdens on those closest to the author – and a constellation of demands on many others. I am deeply grateful to all those who have supported me in various ways over my time researching and writing what you have just read.

I would like to thank all of those who made time to talk to me and help me with aspects of my research, including Ryn Jirenuwat, Cliff Venzon and Shaun Turton.

I am grateful to all those who read and suggested improvements to the text, in particular Robin Peel, Samantha Lister and Abbie Fielding-Smith. Toni Baum once again combined a sharp eye for detail with excellent insights on the bigger picture.

I would like to thank my agent Will Francis, editor Jake Lingwood, and Leanne Bryan and the rest of the team at Octopus. Thank you to Shona Abhyankar for smart publicity.

I am grateful to the *Financial Times* for permitting the use in this book of certain content related to previous *FT* articles. The *FT* has not seen, and does not endorse, the context in which such content has been published in the book.

I am very grateful to many colleagues at the *Financial Times* and Nikkei for their support in London, Tokyo and various places in between. Thank you to Roula Khalaf, Tobias Buck and the other *FT* people who have helped make my return to headquarters fascinating, congenial and fun. I would like to give a special shout out to my super science team-mates Hannah Kuchler, Clive Cookson, Sarah Neville and Ian Johnston.

Many others have generously helped ease my return to the UK, including FanMan Tsang, Tom Penn, Sarah Brown and Mike Davis.

Most importantly, I want to thank Mary, Robin, Sam, Lorin and Owen for all their love and all they have done for me.